Fire in the Heart

To Jill,

With best wishes

Mark

Recent Titles in
OXFORD STUDIES IN CULTURE & POLITICS
Clifford Bob and James M. Jasper, General Editors

Fire in the Heart: How White Activists
Embrace Racial Justice
Mark R. Warren

MARK R. WARREN

Fire in the Heart

How White Activists

Embrace Racial Justice

OXFORD
UNIVERSITY PRESS

2010

OXFORD

UNIVERSITY PRESS

Oxford University Press, Inc., publishes works that further
Oxford University's objective of excellence
in research, scholarship, and education.

Oxford   New York
Auckland   Cape Town   Dar es Salaam   Hong Kong   Karachi
Kuala Lumpur   Madrid   Melbourne   Mexico City   Nairobi
New Delhi   Shanghai   Taipei   Toronto

With offices in
Argentina   Austria   Brazil   Chile   Czech Republic   France   Greece
Guatemala   Hungary   Italy   Japan   Poland   Portugal   Singapore
South Korea   Switzerland   Thailand   Turkey   Ukraine   Vietnam

Copyright © 2010 by Mark R. Warren

Published by Oxford University Press, Inc.
198 Madison Avenue, New York, NY 10016

www.oup.com

Oxford is a registered trademark of Oxford University Press.

Library of Congress Cataloging-in-Publication Data
Warren, Mark R., 1955–
Fire in the heart : how white activists embrace racial justice / Mark R. Warren.
   p. cm.
Includes bibliographical references and index.
ISBN 978-0-19-975124-2; ISBN 978-0-19-975125-9 (pbk.)
   1. Unites States—Race relations.   2. Race discrimination—United States.
3. Racism—United States.   4. Whites—United States—Attitudes.
5. Social action—United States.
I. Title
E184.A1W256 2010
305.800973—dc22   2010009517

9 8 7 6 5 4 3 2 1

Printed in the United States of America
on acid-free paper

To my father, Russell,

To my partner in life, Roberta,

To our daughters, Sade and Imoh,

With love and hope for a better world

The problem of the twentieth century is the problem of the color line.

—W.E.B. Du Bois, *The Souls of Black Folk*

Lord, in the memory of all the saints who from their labors rest, and in the joy of a new beginning, we ask you to help us work for that day when black will not be asked to get back, when brown can stick around, when yellow will be mellow, when the red man can get ahead, man, and when white will embrace what is right.

—From the benediction delivered by Reverend Joseph Lowery
at the inauguration of Barack Obama as the first African American
president of the United States, January 20, 2009

CONTENTS

PREFACE: "EMBRACING WHAT IS RIGHT"

In the white community, the path to a more perfect union means acknowledging that what ails the African American community does not just exist in the minds of black people; that the legacy of discrimination and current incidents of discrimination, while less overt than in the past, are real and must be addressed. Not just with words, but with deeds—by investing in our schools and our communities; by enforcing our civil rights laws and ensuring fairness in our criminal justice system; by providing this generation with ladders of opportunity that were unavailable for previous generations. It requires all Americans to realize that your dreams do not have to come at the expense of my dreams; that investing in the health, welfare, and education of black and brown and white children will ultimately help all of America prosper.

—Barack Obama[1]

I STARTED THE WRITING of this book the week before the 2008 Iowa caucuses, where a majority of white Democrats cast their ballot for an African American man for president of the United States. I finished writing the book in the week before Barack Obama's historic inauguration. While Obama did not center his platform on racial justice, he spoke eloquently about healing America's racial wounds. His election was widely seen as a step forward for racial justice. Indeed, endorsing his candidacy represented support for racial justice as part of a larger vision Obama articulated for a better America. As such, Obama's campaign shows the possibilities for tens of thousands of white volunteers to take action for racial justice and for millions of white Americans to take positive steps to vote for a better future that includes greater justice.

Obama's white supporters "embraced what is right" at that historic moment. In other words, they did not work or vote for Obama because they felt that they *should*. Rather, they *wanted* to do so. They responded to Obama's call for a more perfect union and saw it in their own interests. I do not wish to exaggerate the meaning of Obama's election for racial justice. People likely had multiple reasons for voting for Obama, but in a very important way many white Americans embraced this step toward racial justice.

I started the research for this project several years before Obama declared his candidacy. I first heard Obama's name from Madeline Talbott, a Chicago community organizer I was interviewing for this project. She told me one reason she held hope for progress in racial justice lay in the white support she saw for Obama's effort at the time to win the Democratic nomination for Illinois senator. I returned home from the trip to the news of his success and began to follow his career more closely. Yet at the time few people would have believed that white Americans would vote for a black man in numbers sufficient for him to win the presidency.

Obama had barely finished giving his acceptance speech when some pundits began declaring that America had entered a postracial era. To them, Obama's election meant that racism was a thing of the past. Yet, a few days before finishing the book, on New Year's Day in 2009, a white Bay Area transit police officer shot an unarmed African American in the back and killed him. Thousands of young African Americans and others outraged by the shooting of Oscar Grant III demonstrated in the streets of Oakland. Many denounced the killing as part of a pattern of police violence against young black men. Some vented their anger by vandalizing hundreds of cars and businesses.[2]

While Obama's election represents a historic step forward, the struggle for racial justice continues. Certainly, people of color will continue to work against the systems that trap poor African American men like Oscar Grant. However, further progress also depends, as Obama's election did, on the active support of large numbers of white Americans. In Barack Obama we have a very powerful story of individual success. How might white Americans come to be engaged in efforts to deal systematically with the racial injustices experienced by Grant and millions of other people of color like him?

As Obama's presidency began to implement its agenda in health care reform and other areas, the headiness of his election victory was transformed into the day-to-day grind of pressure politics and compromise necessary to pass specific legislation. While it's important not to exaggerate the significance of white support for Obama's election, we should also not lose sight of the optimism and possibility that historic event offers. Indeed, we need to learn the lessons of that movement to understand the conditions under which white Americans can be moved to support racial justice efforts, a subject to which I return in the conclusion to this book.

I began this project with a puzzle in mind: How do people who are not themselves victims of discrimination come to develop a commitment to act for racial justice? I decided to seek some answers to that question by interviewing white people that had become activists for racial justice. In this book I present the findings of my interviews with fifty such activists from across the country.

While studies of white racism might fill a small library, the studies of white antiracism, if you will, could fit in a small bookcase. Perhaps this is as it should be in the sense that white racism has outweighed antiracism throughout history. Yet if we are interested in the possibilities of social change, we need to understand both the processes that perpetuate racism and those that lead in the direction of racial justice. This is a book about the possible.[3]

It turns out that, throughout U.S. history, many white Americans have been activists for racial justice. They participated in large numbers in the abolition movement against slavery and in the civil rights movement of the fifties and sixties, among other efforts, yet their stories are not well known. I hope this is changing. Yet when I asked white students at Fordham College, where I used to teach, to name white people who inspired them by their commitment to racial justice, they could not list a single person. So I have continued to ask students who expressed concerns about racism the same question. Occasionally someone names John or Robert Kennedy and once in a while Morris Dees from the Southern Poverty Law Center, but that's about it.[4]

In fact, it might be fair to say that white racial justice activists are held in some suspicion both by white Americans and people of color. John Brown represents a potent symbol of this suspicion, at least by whites. Brown was a militant white abolitionist who led the armed assault on Harper's Ferry, which helped precipitate the Civil War and the eventual end to slavery. Yet what was the scholarly consensus about Brown for the next hundred years? White scholars declared Brown mentally deranged. They pointed to his fiery evangelical rhetoric. However, even to this day we are not short of religious firebrands, whose mental capacities have remained unquestioned. Neither are we short of black Americans who led violent slave revolts and whose rationality is respected. Yet it seems that something must be wrong with a white American who is militantly antiracist.[5] Meanwhile, many people of color can be suspicious of white activists. Black scholars like W.E.B. Du Bois, who wrote a biography of John Brown, held him in high regard, but other white abolitionists were often criticized for paternalism. Young whites came south to support the civil rights movement in the sixties, but controversy surrounded their role as well. Black activists in more militant groups like the Student Nonviolent Coordinating Committee (SNCC) worried about white domination of the movement and eventually asked whites to leave the organization. Some black friends of mine, when I told them I was writing a book on white racial justice activists, laughingly declared that it must be a short book.[6]

Actually, it's not a short book. In fact, I had no trouble finding many committed activists to interview for this study. Nonetheless, the jokes reveal something of the unease that continues to surround the white activist. Some may even worry about my intentions as a white person. Will I write a book that promotes the idea that white people are the saviors of people of color? I hope that this book contributes to a change in attitude and to a deeper understanding of and appreciation for the role that white people can play and are playing in efforts to promote racial justice—not as "saviors" but as serious collaborators with activists of color.

I felt the time had come for this kind of broad study, a comprehensive examination of white racial justice activists across the country. I have been inspired and stimulated by some earlier work. Becky Thompson interviewed white activists in order to paint a sensitive and nuanced history of racial justice movements from the sixties through the nineties. Eileen O'Brien's pioneering work examined white activists working primarily with two organizations, an anti-Klan group in the Midwest and trainers with the People's Institute for Survival and Beyond in New Orleans. Meanwhile, white authors like Tim Wise began writing accounts of their lives full of insight and advice for other whites concerned about racism.[7]

Indeed, I began to meet more and more white students alarmed about racism at Fordham and then later at the Harvard Graduate School of Education, where I now teach. These students struggled for ways to help advance the cause of racial justice. Yet I was troubled that most of the attention was being paid to questions of white privilege and white identity. Whiteness studies in the academy, in my view, focused too exclusively on what it meant to be white and on white identity development. These are important issues, but I worried that white people might spend all of their time in introspection and never actually do anything. I wanted to study people who were committed to taking action for racial justice.[8]

As a work of scholarship, this book contributes to our understanding of the processes that lead some whites to an awareness of racism and a commitment to combat it. In addition to my scholarly purposes, I also hope the book inspires and helps white students at places like Fordham and Harvard and people like the white volunteers in Obama's campaign to deepen their commitments to racial justice and activism. The road to commitment has not been an easy one for the activists I interviewed, as we will see. The work for racial justice continually challenges them, as does the struggle to build truly collaborative relationships with people of color. But participating in the struggle for a more just society has given white activists tremendously fulfilling lives and, like the Obama volunteers, a place in history.

ACKNOWLEDGMENTS

THE ORIGINS OF this book as a research project go back several years. However, I have been struggling with the ideas in this book ever since, as an emerging young adult, I realized I was different from the other white kids with whom I grew up. My father played a big role in that. I dedicate this book in part to my father because he was the first person who taught me that racism was wrong. A New Deal Democrat through and through, my father was a Teamster Union activist in his younger days and strongly supported the civil rights movement as it rose to national prominence in the sixties. Through the years we talked constantly about politics, and my father never lost his faith in the possibility of building a better world. I only regret he was not with us to celebrate Barack Obama's historic election.

During those years I became a political activist myself. For many years I worked mainly with other white activists as progressive circles seemed to mirror the segregation of the larger society. We were against racism for sure, but we did not have our feet planted very firmly on the ground. Eventually I was fortunate to find a multiracial group of talented and committed activists. I built close relationships with African American organizers who taught me about the black experience as we struggled to build a caring community dedicated to changing the world. I would like to thank all of the friends and activists with whom I worked during those years, many of whom are named here, for helping me start to understand what it takes to work hard for racial and social justice.

During those years I met and fell in love with Roberta, my partner in life. Her experience growing up as a black person in London gave her a determination and enduring passion to fight poverty and racism. Together we have raised two beautiful daughters. As we have built a family together, the struggle against racism has become a deeply personal matter to me. At the same time I have been inspired by the possibility for new kinds of relationships and the hope that children bring.

I hope that these brief comments will help readers set this book in the context of my own life journey. Eventually I became a scholar, and I undertook this project as a carefully designed piece of sociological research. I draw upon the data I collected, that is, the interviews I conducted with fifty activists, to make arguments and build theory. I wrote this book to contribute to knowledge and understanding. However, I also wrote it to help all Americans, including my family and my activist friends, who are struggling to find ways to cross over the color line that has so deeply divided us.

Many, many people contributed to the ideas that find their way into this book and gave me the practical support and encouragement I needed to write it. First of all, I would like to thank the activists I interviewed for this book. I am inspired by their commitment and learned tremendously from their thoughtful reflections about the workings of race in American society. Some of them also discussed the ideas in the book or commented on parts of the manuscript. For their thoughtful comments, I would like to thank Perry Perkins, Susan Sandler, Madeline Talbott, Chester Hartman, John Heinemeier, Christine Clark, and Tony Fleo.

I discussed the ideas in this book with many friends and colleagues. For their insight and assistance, I would like to thank Lory (Tomni) Dance, Karen Mapp, Phil Thompson, Dayna Cunningham, James Bernard, Marshall Ganz, Xavier de Souza Briggs, John Diamond, Mica Pollock, Larry Bobo, Lani Guinier, Helen Haste, William Julius Wilson, Robert Putnam, Theda Skocpol, Charles Payne, Margaret Weir, Sara Lawrence-Lightfoot, Mil Duncan, and Jose Calderon. In addition, a number of people read and made helpful comments on drafts of the manuscript. I greatly appreciate their effort to make this work stronger and better. I would like to thank Roberta Udoh, Chris Winship, Michele Lamont, Rick Weissbourd, John Rogers, Abby Ferber, Tommie Shelby, Jane Mansbridge, Omar McRoberts, Malia Villegas, Jim Jasper, and one anonymous reviewer for the press. I talked about this project early on with Tomni Dance, and her enthusiasm and support have been wonderful to me.

I presented parts of this work at the following venues and received helpful comments from participants: the W.E.B. Du Bois Institute for African and African American Research at Harvard University, MIT's Department of Urban Studies and Planning, the Civic Engagement Workshop at Tufts University, the Donald Bouma Lecture Series at Calvin College, the Institute for the Study of Social Change at the University of California–Berkeley, the Carsey Institute at the University of New Hampshire, the Everyday Antiracism working group at Harvard, and sessions at annual meetings of the American Sociological Association and the American Education Research Association.

I was fortunate to have many wonderful students help me as research assistants. I would like to thank them not only for their terrific work but also for their excitement about the project and their contribution to the ideas contained in this book. This group includes Soo Hong, Malia Villegas, Cynthia Gordon, Jennifer Mott-Smith, Justin Draft, and Margaret Richardson. I am indebted to Soo, in particular, for helping me through so many stages of the project, during which she became a valued friend.

Many others helped with practical and technical matters. I would like to thank Ray Maietta and Cheri Minton for help with the data analysis software. For efficient and cheerful assistance I would like to thank the research librarians at Gutman Library: Kathleen Donovan, Carla Lillvik, Marcela Flaherty, and Leila Kocen. My staff assistant, Melita Garrett, has helped me in so many ways, big and small. Faith Harvey and Pat Varasso helped with financial accounting. Finally, I'd like to offer a special thanks to librarian Bob Rogers for his support, encouragement, and inspiration.

Institutional assistance has come from many sources. I would like to thank Henry Louis Gates and the W.E.B. Du Bois Institute for African and African American Research at Harvard University for offering me a fellowship that enabled me to design this project. The Russell Sage Foundation financially supported my research, as did the Mark DeWolfe Howe Fund at Harvard Law School. The Graduate School of Education at Harvard University also supported the project by providing both research funds and leave time. More generally, I would like to thank the graduate school for offering me a supportive environment in which to conduct this project. Dean Kathy McCartney and Associate Dean Daphne Layton helped me with concrete assistance at various points, which I truly appreciate.

Meanwhile, I have been fortunate to work with Karen Mapp and a group of doctoral students in the Community Organizing and School Reform research project at Harvard's Graduate School of Education. I have received warm support and great encouragement from this community, and our work together has taught me many things that have informed this book. Thanks go to Mara Tieken, Kenneth Russell, Carolyn Leung, Thomas Nikundiwe, Meredith Mira, Anita Wadhwa, Ann Ishimaru, Cynthia Gordon, Paul Kuttner, Mandy Taylor, Helen Westmoreland, Connie K. Chung, Keith Catone, Soojin Oh, Soo Hong, Roy Cervantes, Zenub Kakli, Phitsamay Sychitkokhong, Sarah

Dryden-Peterson, Tiffany Cheng, Kerry Venegas, Sky Marietta, and Dulari Tahbildar.

Rick Weissbourd and Avery Rimer opened up their Vermont home to me for concentrated periods of writing. I don't know whether I could have completed the project without those getaways. Rick, as my office mate and friend, provided steadfast support and enthusiasm for this project all through its trials and tribulations. I would also like to thank Rick's mother, Bernice Weissbourd, for her interest in and support of this project, in memory of her late husband and his social justice values. John and Kathy Campbell, Linda Tubach, and Bob McCloskey also opened their homes up to me for periods of writing as well, and I appreciate their generosity.

My editor, James Cook, shared my vision for this book from the moment he saw the manuscript. I have valued his enthusiasm, assistance, and support throughout the publishing process.

My friends and family have been a terrific source of support through the years of working on this project. I would like to thank my mom, Elena, my sisters and their families—Cindy, Michael, Nancy, Russ, and Jarrett—my late mum, Florence, and my brothers- and sister-in-law David, Adam, and Frances. My mum Florence was a special inspiration to me, a woman who reached out warmly across the color line when it was very hard and danger-ous to do so. I seem to have so many friends who have given me loving sup-port and encouragement. In addition to those mentioned earlier, I would like to thank Bernard and Nancy Duse, Barbara Wallen, Gary Paraboschi, Bob Halperin, Johanny and Melusi Hlatshwayo, James Bernard, Margarita Choy, Nancy Love, Marshall Moore, Ricardo Guthrie, Shawn Thomas, Ranjay and Anu Gulati, John, Julie, Becky, and the entire Wilson family, Tony and Col-leen Fleo, and Mabel Thompson among others. I would also like to thank my friends in England: Andy Harris, Venkat Nilakantan, Marie-Helen and Dun-can Kerr, Melanie Curtis, Vivian Stachin, Steve Desborough, and Al Martin.

Roberta Udoh has been my partner and soulmate throughout life. She has believed in me and supported this project wholeheartedly; without her help I would never have been able to write this book. I dedicate this book to her as well. As primary caregiver to our daughters, she has taught me how to raise a new generation of healthy young people who care deeply about social justice. Roberta more than anyone else has taught me this. Racial and social justice is not a cause "out there." It concerns how we live our lives on a daily basis, how we relate to people with dignity and respect, and how we work with others in big and small ways to fight oppression and build healthier human communities. Roberta personifies the passionate and caring life—the fire in the heart—and for that and everything else I thank her.

Our daughters, Sade and Imoh, have grown up with this book. In fact, I doubt they can remember a time when I wasn't working on it. To Imoh I owe thanks for suggesting the title. I dedicate this book to them and their future as well. For my part, I have enjoyed watching them grow into beautiful, young women who care about others and have minds of their own. They are also, like their mother, great dancers and a lot of fun.

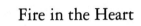

Fire in the Heart

CHAPTER ONE | # Introduction
From White Passivity to Racial Justice Activism

All that is necessary for the triumph of evil is that good men do nothing.

—Edmund Burke

THIS BOOK IS about how white people can move from passivity to action in response to racism in America. It is a book about the possible—and the necessary. Indeed, I believe that further progress in racial justice depends on many more white Americans coming to an understanding of racism and developing a commitment to take positive action.[1]

In my view, white passivity is the primary obstacle to further progress in achieving racial justice. Most whites do not want to keep people of color down; they do not work intentionally to do so. Rather, they remain passive—or apathetic, as Tyrone Forman has argued—in the face of continued racial inequality in the United States. In fact, most white Americans believe that racism is largely a thing of the past and therefore requires little action.[2]

Certainly important progress has occurred since the Jim Crow era. Legal segregation has ended, and opportunities have opened up for many African Americans. The black middle class has grown significantly since the sixties, with the proportion of black workers in white-collar jobs climbing from 11 percent in 1969 to 26 percent by the turn of the century. Meanwhile, the black poverty rate fell dramatically in the sixties and seventies, from nearly 60 percent to 30 percent. As I finished writing this book manuscript, Barack

Obama was elected to the nation's presidency, an inconceivable event forty years ago, perhaps even a few years ago.[3]

Yet racial inequality remains significant and in many ways quite persistent. African Americans earn, on average, about 57 percent of what whites earn and face twice the unemployment rate of whites at all levels of skill. The black poverty rate has remained mostly flat since the seventies; at nearly 30 percent, it is three times that of whites. Meanwhile, more than a third of all black children grow up in poverty in the United States, while 10 percent of white children live in poverty. If we consider low-income families to include those living on less than 150 percent of the poverty line, or $21,000 per year for a family of four, then more than half of all black children grow up poor or nearly poor—more than half.

Wealth disparities are particularly striking. Middle-income blacks have about 15 percent of the wealth of middle-class whites; in fact, the highest-income blacks control financial assets similar to those of the lowest-income whites. In addition, 61 percent of black households have no financial assets at all. About 47 percent of blacks own their own home, while nearly 75 percent of whites do so; although this represents an increase from the 40 percent of black homeowners in the sixties, the gap between blacks and whites has actually increased since that time.[4]

For low-income blacks and Latinos concentrated in our nation's cities, conditions are truly dire. Far greater proportions of African Americans and Latinos than whites live in high-poverty neighborhoods that suffer from multiple problems, from crime and violence to environmental degradation and blight. Residents of these neighborhoods lack access to good jobs, good housing, and good schools. The consequences for the young people growing up under these conditions can be extreme: Nearly half of all black and Latino youth fail to graduate from high school on time. At the same time fully 30 percent of black males in their twenties are in the criminal justice system—in prison, on probation, or on parole.[5]

I have stressed the particularly difficult circumstances of poor African Americans. Some have debated whether racism or economics has more to do with inequality today. Undoubtedly, class and race are profoundly interconnected. Indeed, racism has historically been so intertwined with economic exploitation that it has never made sense to dichotomize the two. Was slavery a system of racism or of economic exploitation? The choice is a false one. Racism remains centrally implicated in economic and other forms of inequality faced by African Americans today. Moreover, studies consistently show profound inequality between blacks and whites at similar income levels and demonstrate the persistence of racialized dynamics in housing, employment, the criminal justice system, and other areas.[6]

White Passivity in the Age of Institutional
and Color-Blind Racism

In the face of such clear evidence of racial injustice, why don't whites care? In part, many white people remain ignorant of the continued existence of racial inequality. Fully 81 percent of whites believe that blacks have as good a chance to get a job as whites, 79 percent think black children have as good a chance as white children to get a good education, and 86 percent say that they have the same chance as whites to get affordable housing. In a national survey sponsored by the Kaiser Family Foundation, 61 percent of whites said they believed African Americans had equal or better access to health care, half thought educational levels were the same or better for blacks, and nearly half thought the average African American had an income that was similar to or better than that of the average white person.[7]

This ignorance finds its roots in part in continued segregation. Despite some early gains in residential integration in the sixties and seventies, racial segregation has entrenched itself in American life. Many poor blacks are "hypersegregated" into urban neighborhoods that are almost entirely non-white. Furthermore, after some initial gains in the sixties and seventies, our schools are, in fact, more segregated today than in the late sixties. As a result, whites live in racial isolation from blacks, many living in virtually all-white communities. Only 15 percent of whites have even one close friend who is nonwhite. Whites may be less knowledgeable about racial inequities because they do not know people of color who experience them. They may occasionally hear statistics like those quoted earlier, but these statistics remain just that: numbers, not real people whom they know.[8]

Racial segregation also reinforces continued group identity by race. People of any group tend to care more about others whom they consider to be like them. We know that racial groups are not rooted in biology; rather, they are socially constructed. Yet these social inventions and group differences remain quite powerful when developed over hundreds of years of legal codes and social customs. As a result, even whites who recognize the existence of racial discrimination may feel that racism is not their immediate concern. Although some scholars have questioned how much of a white identity exists, most white Americans appear clear at least that they are not black. In a now well-publicized experiment, Professor Andrew Hacker asked his white college students how much money they would demand if they had to change from white to black. The students asked for fifty million dollars or one million dollars for every year they had to be black.[9]

White passivity may also be related to the nature of institutional racism today. Scholars have shown how contemporary patterns of racial inequality become perpetuated through institutional processes that do not require racist intent or overt prejudice on the part of individuals. For example, a key cause of educational injustice lies in the fact that low-income African American children attend school in aging buildings with fewer resources and lower proportions of qualified teachers than white children. Why do they do so when segregationist laws no longer exist? To summarize a complicated set of historical processes, a variety of racially discriminatory government housing policies, combined with white flight, worked to concentrate poor black families in inner-city neighborhoods. At the same time, financing schools through local property taxes ensures that inner-city school districts have fewer resources to provide for education than more affluent and whiter suburban communities. As a result, low-income black children receive an inferior education with highly unequal outcomes compared to most white children. Yet contemporary racial intent is not necessary to explain this inequality.[10]

Institutional racism is harder to recognize as racism. Recent research on "cumulative disadvantage" has showed how racial disadvantage builds up over time through the interactions of institutional processes like those briefly discussed. White Americans may not easily comprehend the historical and structural causes of inequality, but they can readily see its effects in crime, drug abuse, and broken homes. As Michael Brown and his associates have pointed out, "This phenomenon of selective perception is understandable in a sense, because the causes—the fundamental social processes that led to the symptoms—tend to be relatively invisible in the present, while the symptoms are all too visible." Blaming cultural deficits in communities of color becomes easier than taking positive action to change structures.[11]

Sometimes forms of prejudice operate within institutional racism and work to perpetuate it. For example, one reason low-income black families remain trapped in inner-city neighborhoods is that real estate agents continue to direct black families away from more affluent white communities. Meanwhile, studies have shown that police stereotyping of young black and Latino men contributes to their higher rates of arrest. Job discrimination falls particularly hard on less-skilled black men from inner-city communities, as employers' stereotypes make it more difficult for them to get decent-paying jobs. The individual and the institutional are related in complicated ways. After all, individuals act within institutions: Some can passively follow normal institutional practices; others can challenge them.[12]

However, racial prejudice today is more subtle and complex and in that sense is not always appreciated as racism. Many people understand racism only as intentional prejudicial actions perpetrated by individuals—overt racism if you will. This form of blatant racism, while more dominant before the civil rights movement, has now declined. Surveys of white attitudes document this dramatic shift. While 68 percent of white Americans supported segregated schools in 1942, only 7 percent did so in 1982. The percentage of white Americans who believe that whites should receive preference over blacks for jobs dropped from 55 percent in 1942 to 3 percent in 1972. In other words, whites broadly reject the ideas of legalized segregation and open discrimination, as well as the inherent inferiority of blacks to whites.[13]

Racial prejudice mainly takes a cultural form today by blaming black failure on a lack of effort or care rather than attributing it to biological inferiority. Consequently, whites can hold ambivalent views about people of color, sometimes expressing prejudice and other times egalitarian views. How whites act appears to depend on the situation and on a confluence of factors about the particular person of color in question. In some circumstances whites treat people of color with respect and as equals, voting for Barack Obama for president, for instance. At other times, they judge blacks on the basis of stereotypes, such as when they cross a dark city street when a group of young black men approaches them. Whites appear to judge low-income blacks in more stereotypical ways than middle-class African Americans, but even more affluent blacks face discrimination as well.[14]

This kind of racial prejudice fits well into the dominant color-blind ideology of our era. With the demise of legal segregation and the rise of legal protections for civil rights, people of color now, formally at least, have equal opportunity. Under this dominant ideology, whites can explain continued racial inequality by reference to the cultural deficits of African Americans. White Americans are also strong believers in the American dream—that in the United States anyone can achieve and that success depends on hard work and merit. Accepting the reality of racial inequality and discrimination runs counter to these deeply held beliefs and may be resisted for that reason as well. White Americans can find consistency in their beliefs in the American dream by locating the causes of racial inequities in the cultural deficits of people of color.[15]

Media portrayals continue to reinforce stereotypical images and cultural explanations for racial inequities. For example, television news programs focus on black crime and poverty far out of proportion to the reality of black lives. At the same time, primetime television shows overportray successful black professionals. On the one hand, that practice could be seen as racial progress, normalizing black success. However, studies show that, since these black characters typically exist in a largely white world, whites perceive them as unrepresentative of their race. Indeed, whites interpret these examples of individual success as proof that anyone can make it in the United States through hard work and merit, thereby reinforcing cultural explanations of black poverty. Meanwhile, since most whites live their lives segregated from people of color, particularly from poor blacks and Latinos, they have little direct experience with the operations of institutional racism.[16]

Because whites no longer view black inferiority as biological and turn to cultural explanations for patterns of racial inequality instead, many do not recognize some of their own attitudes as based upon prejudice. In other words, police officers may believe that young black men deserve special scrutiny because they are more likely to commit crimes. Teachers may believe that black kids work less hard at school because their parents do not value education or because they live in poverty. Most white Americans like these claim they are color blind and no longer discriminate. Indeed, white Americans often resist when confronted with evidence of their own racist thinking. Of course, from the point of view of persons of color who are being judged—and mistreated—because of the color of their skin, these actions are by definition racist.[17]

Whites may continue to be passive in the face of racism because it aligns with their structural position in American society. By that I mean that whites benefit, relatively speaking, from their position in the racial hierarchy. A long line of sociological research has demonstrated that people at the top of a social system are likely to adopt beliefs or accept an ideology that justifies their position in society. White Americans' views about race may be no different.[18]

There has been an outpouring of research and writing on the concept of white privilege. If people of color are disadvantaged by racism, then whites must be advantaged by the same system. In other words, racism indicates a relationship among racial groups, that is, a racial hierarchy with whites on top. These advantages can be quite material, for example, when whites have access to better-paying jobs and higher housing values. They can be powerful in perpetuating white advantage, for example, in the ability to send one's children to good schools. However, privilege can also lie at the more personal or status level, as in the ability to shop without being suspected by store staff. Some scholars have stressed that one of the primary privileges of being white is simply the ability to take whiteness for granted. White culture is "normal," while other so-called subcultures are judged against it.[19]

The concept of white privilege, however, is not without its problems. One might not think of these benefits as "privileges" but more as rights or forms of social provision that everyone should have. Moreover, the term masks important class differences among whites. In other words, not all whites are equally privileged. Poor and working-class whites lack many of the privileges that more affluent whites enjoy. Nevertheless, the poorest white person can still experience the psychic benefit of feeling superior to a person of color. Finally, whites may have a broader or longer-term interest in joining with people of color, which trumps any short-term advantage to white privilege. I discuss this particular issue in greater depth later in this book, but suffice it to say at this point that the concept of (relative) white privilege helps us understand why whites might remain passive and less likely to acknowledge the operations of racial discrimination or injustice.[20]

The Failure of Political Will

The concept of white privilege helps shift the burden of explaining racial inequality away from the cultural deficits of people of color and toward the practices of the dominant society. Long ago W.E.B. Du Bois critiqued American society for targeting African Americans as the "problem." Black Power advocates in the sixties, for their part, asserted that the "problem" lay in the morality of the dominant white society, which at worst sought to perpetuate racism and at best stood passively by, turning a blind eye to racial discrimination. From this standpoint, white Americans have a particular responsibility to address persistent racial inequity and injustice. The Kerner Commission issued a political and moral challenge to Americans in the wake of the riots of the sixties, calling for a "massive, compassionate, and sustained" assault on the crisis of the inner city. However, as the civil rights movement receded in the seventies and a new consensus settled in, Americans largely failed to address this challenge. We are now left with that legacy.[21]

Understanding the workings of institutional racism and the legacy of historic discrimination sheds a spotlight on the need for positive action to achieve racial justice. Unless positive action is taken, the so-called normal workings of the system will continue unabated. In other words, although positive intent to discriminate is not necessary to perpetuate racial inequities, positive intent to act is necessary to rectify racial injustice.

Action, of course, needs to come both from white people and from people of color. Certainly organized action by people of color themselves will continue to play a critical role in working to advance the cause of racial justice. However, since whites continue to dominate the positions of power in American institutions, progress toward racial justice will require moving whites from passivity to action against racism.

Yet, in the face of all of the factors reviewed here, it is perhaps not surprising that most whites remain passive in the face of continued racial inequality. Although scholars have done a good job of analyzing the persistence of racism, we have by contrast very little understanding of how to build a consensus for action. Consequently, we face the following pressing question: How can white Americans come to care enough about racism to take action against it?

A New Movement?

Certain factors may help in moving whites from passivity to action. Although I have described the force of color-blind ideology, which supports the persistence of racism, it would be wrong to see this ideology as monolithic. In fact, American racial ideology contains important contradictions and alternative currents. First of all, there is a strong consensus that racism is wrong and unacceptable. Few whites will defend discrimination on the basis of race.[22]

Second, many white Americans remain troubled by the persistence of racial inequality. They may be swayed by the tenets of color-blind ideology to look for cultural explanations, and they may not normally be alarmed enough to move beyond passivity. However, many remain concerned. White Americans, for example, were widely repulsed by the treatment of African Americans in New Orleans in the aftermath of Hurricane Katrina. Moreover, the fact that the phrase "driving while black" has entered the American vernacular indicates recognition of the continued reality of racial discrimination and a sense that it is wrong.[23]

Indeed, there is growing interest among many white Americans in addressing racism. The last ten years has witnessed a small but rapidly expanding literature by white activists and commentators specifically directed toward white people. These include *White like Me* by Tim Wise, *Uprooting Racism: How White People Can Work for Racial Justice* by Paul Kivel, and *Lifting the White Veil* by Jeff Hitchcock, among others. There are now conferences devoted to the subject, like the annual white privilege conference sponsored by the University of Colorado at Colorado Springs, which drew more than one thousand attendees at its 2008 meeting. A number of racial justice or antiracism training programs and manuals directed at white Americans have emerged as well and have helped build networks of white activists across the country.[24]

The tens of thousands of white volunteers for the Obama campaign suggest the new possibilities of our time. Yet it would be too much of an exaggeration to call this emerging phenomenon a movement. White racial justice activism remains fragmented into localized efforts. Moreover, it is little studied. We have limited understanding of how some white Americans come to be concerned about racism and develop a commitment to act for racial justice. The purpose of this study is precisely to advance that understanding.

Design of the Study

Much new scholarship on race concerns itself with what white people think or how they identify themselves. I take a different approach. I start with action. As we have seen, whites can state a belief in racial justice and yet remain passive in the face of continued inequities or participate perhaps unintentionally in the perpetuation of institutional racism. In this study I start with whites that are active in working for racial justice and work backward, so to speak, to identify the processes that shaped their commitment. I also explore the understandings they have developed through these processes and through their activism.[25]

I decided to examine these issues by conducting in-depth interviews with white activists. As discussed later, I reviewed a wide range of relevant literature to help guide the study. This review helped me shape the interviews by identifying some of the issues to explore with activists. However, I did not have specific hypotheses or propositions to investigate with my subjects. Rather, I saw this as an exploratory and largely inductive study. In other words, I expected that the themes and analysis would arise from exploring issues at length with activists and then carefully analyzing the interview material. In-depth interviews would bring rich new information about a largely unexplored field of human endeavor. I could then look across the interviews to identify patterns and themes that would help us understand how some white Americans develop an understanding of racism and a commitment to act for racial justice.

Each interview lasted about three hours. I asked the activists to tell me about their lives. How did they initially become concerned about racism? How did they become active in working for racial justice? I sought to find out how their understanding of racism and their commitment changed over the course of their activism. I asked a series of questions intended to identify and explore the sources of their beliefs, the influence of their experiences and relationships, and the kinds of historical events and social settings through which their activism developed.

While the first part of the interviews focused on constructing this kind of life narrative, the second part of the interviews explored the activists' contemporary understanding of their work. Do they try to influence the beliefs and behaviors of other whites? How do they try to build collaborative relationships with people of color? What kinds of challenges, dilemmas, and problems do they face in doing racial justice work and living lives committed to activism? In actual practice, the interview questions sometimes flowed back and forth across the past and the present, and I became interested in seeing how the various parts of the interviews related to each other.

I wanted the interviews to reveal each activist's own story and understanding, but I also wanted to be able to compare the interviews. Consequently, I chose a semistructured format. In other words, I made sure to ask the same questions to everyone, so that the interviews would be comparable. Nevertheless, as is common in semistructured interviews, I pursued interesting lines of discussion unique to each activist, asking each subject follow-up questions and probing for further details and explanations. This probing is particularly important because I wanted the subjects to discuss formative events and to focus on "choice points" when they made important decisions that have shaped the course of their lives. I also wanted to get the subjects to reflect deeply about their experiences.[26]

Because I wanted to explore these issues in depth, I decided to interview fifty activists. I thought this number was large enough to capture a variety of activists but small enough to enable me to explore each person's views in detail. As it turned out, fifty was plenty, providing me with a wealth of rich material to analyze.

I wanted to make sure I chose these activists carefully. I did not want all of them to work in one or two groups or to live in the same part of the country. Because I thought of the study as exploratory, I wanted to cover as wide a variety of white activists as possible. At the same time, it is beyond the bounds of a qualitative project like this to systematically cover activists who have been working to address all forms of racism, so I knew that I needed to limit the selection as well.

There is no list of white racial justice activists from which I could randomly choose names, so I conducted what social scientists call purposeful selection; that is, I developed specific criteria relevant to the purposes of the research project to help me select the participants. First, I decided to focus on activists whose work with regard to racism primarily involves African Americans and secondarily Latinos. I prioritized racism toward African Americans for several reasons. Antiblack racism represents perhaps the central dynamic in U.S. history and the sharpest racial dividing line. Even today, African Americans remain the most segregated group, and there is evidence that whites particularly resist integration with African Americans, whether in housing or in interracial relationships. Much evidence suggests that white employers prefer to hire immigrants of color rather than native-born blacks. In many ways, whites who cross over the black/white racial line may have made the greatest commitment to racial justice.[27]

However, I wanted to make sure to include some activists who focused on working for racial justice for Latinos, who have become the nation's largest minority group. There is some debate as to whether Latinos constitute a racial group and whether they experience racism per se rather than, let us say, a form of ethnic prejudice more similar to what southern Europeans faced in earlier periods of large-scale immigration. A diverse group, Latinos include Chicanos, who trace their roots to the American Southwest prior to the expansion of the United States, and Cubans who came to the country with a favored status due to anticommunism. Nevertheless, there is strong evidence of persistent segregation and discrimination against most Latino communities. Certainly, the activists in this study believe that Latinos face antibrown racism and consider racial justice for Latinos to be an increasingly important part of America's racial justice agenda. So do I.[28]

The pool of fifty activists was simply too small to include any significant number of activists who work with a full range of racial groups, including Asian Americans and Native Americans. I also could not capture the issues surrounding anti-Muslim discrimination; although such discrimination is religious in focus, it is bound up with American racism and is certainly an important feature of contemporary racial dynamics. It turned out, however, that activists in the study had rich histories. A number of these activists have worked against racism toward a variety of groups, so some of these experiences enter the study. In the end, however, this work is largely biracial in that it is mostly concerned with black/white relations. I would not want to deny the particular dynamics of race relations involving other groups. Nevertheless, I believe that the findings of this study of racial justice will be informative for our broader understanding of achieving racial justice in an increasingly multiracial and diverse America.

In order to help focus the study, I decided to select activists who work in three arenas that I consider to be central to advancing racial justice: education, criminal justice, and community organizing/development efforts to address urban poverty. These three arenas are arguably critical to the well-being and life chances of African Americans and Latinos. Within these arenas, however, I chose activists who have worked in quite a variety of ways. For example, in education, I included the founder of a charter school, a high school teacher who started a teacher-parent-student alliance for educational justice, a multicultural curriculum developer, and a district official who does racial equity work with public schools. In the urban/community arena I included community organizers, fair-housing advocates, and leaders of community development corporations, as well as the head of a homeless coalition and organizers of community-based programs to work with inner-city youth. In criminal justice, I included juvenile-justice advocates, lawyers addressing police violence and the death penalty, and legal advocates working to link civil-rights strategies to community-based efforts at justice reform.

I wanted to cover activism across the country but believed it would be useful to choose activists grouped in certain localities. I decided on seven localities: Los Angeles, the San Francisco Bay area, Dallas, Chicago, the Baltimore/Washington area, New Orleans, and Greensboro, North Carolina. To some extent, issues of race have a context and a character that are peculiar to any particular locality. Interviewing several people in one area helped me understand and consider contextual influences better than if I had interviewed fifty people in fifty different localities. In addition, by choosing activists grouped by locality, I was able to maximize my limited funds and travel time.

I decided to include a roughly equal number of men and women and activists of different ages. I expected that there might be important differences between younger and older activists and between men and women. I also wanted to make sure that I included activists who worked in faith-based groups and those that were more secular in orientation. When interviewing the activists, I collected data on their age, gender, socioeconomic status, level of education, religious affiliation, marital status, and place of birth/residence, and I report this information in the appendix.[29]

Finally, I had to define what I meant by a "white American" and by a "racial justice activist." I defined white Americans as American-born citizens of European heritage who identified themselves as white. Although there is some scholarly debate over the definition of who is white, I think this rather pragmatic definition is acceptable for the purposes of this study. I defined racial justice activism broadly as efforts to address issues of racial discrimination and racial inequities. I decided not to include work that is oriented solely toward helping individual people of color or providing services to them. Following my understanding of institutional racism discussed earlier, I wanted activists who have been working to change the policies and practices of institutions. Indeed, too much emphasis is typically placed on racism at the individual level without sufficient attention to the institutional processes that perpetuate racism. I decided to start with activists who work for institutional change and then ask them whether and how they try to address racism at the individual level.[30]

With my criteria in hand, I still had to identify and select specific activists to interview. I contacted groups and organizations active in racial justice issues, following the listings provided in a report by the Applied Research Center that compiled foundation grants for racial justice. I asked representatives of these groups to identify what they saw as important forms of racial justice work. I mapped these types of activities onto the three arenas identified earlier. I then sought to identify activists who would represent as much of this range of work as possible.[31]

To identify individual activists, I asked representatives of the contacted groups for referrals in my areas of interest. I then contacted potential subjects and asked them a series of questions to determine whether they met the criteria discussed earlier and would be willing to be interviewed. I wanted to make sure that all of the activists considered themselves to be committed to working for racial justice. Since I thought that many personally sensitive issues might arise in the interviews, I wanted to get a sense that the person would be open and honest with me. It turned out that these activists were very interested in being interviewed. They wanted to tell their story. Moreover, they appreciated the fact that I wanted to study and write about white activism for racial justice, something they felt had received too little attention. In other words, they wanted to help me.[32]

I continued to build the pool of potential interviewees by asking people I interviewed for other suggestions, a practice called "snowball sampling." I worked to balance the eventual group of activists to include roughly equal numbers across the three arenas of activism, the seven localities, between men and women, and across age groups.

When research criteria meet the real world, however, nothing is ever clean and simple. It turns out that some people active in one arena used to be active in another, or perhaps they had crossed the boundaries between the two. For example, a community organizer who worked for years on affordable housing now mobilizes people to work for educational reform. Moreover, people currently working in one locality might have had a long period of activism somewhere else.

As this is an exploratory study, these problems are not fatal. In the end, I feel confident that the pool of activists I interviewed fulfilled the purpose I established. I believe that it comprises a broad and fairly representative group of contemporary white racial activists. At the same time, we must always be careful about limitations and biases in the pool of interview subjects. For example, my selection process might have missed certain kinds of people or experiences. If anything, though, my pool of activists is strong on diversity.

I conducted all of the interviews myself and in person so that I could build the kind of rapport with the interviewees that would encourage them to speak openly. I think my own position as a white person concerned about racial justice likely helped them open up to me. However, although I was quite sympathetic to their stories and views, I did try to keep some distance so as to maintain an independent perspective. I recorded the interviews and had them professionally transcribed. I then analyzed the transcripts using Atlas.ti, a computer-based software analysis program.

I developed the analytic themes presented in the rest of this book by first "coding" the data in each interview, that is, sorting the information into analytical categories. I developed these categories in two ways, inductively (from what I heard people say in the interview) and theoretically (from propositions that come from relevant literature). Although I started with some codes from prior theory and research, in the end the analysis was largely inductively built. I analyzed the experiences and views expressed by each subject using these codes. I sought to understand a subject's development as a process that occurred in context, so that the relationships between various experiences and views could be specified. I also examined the coded material in all of the interviews in order to identify commonalities and differences. Few commonalities were shared 100 percent by all of the activists. In the rest of the book I report findings that reflect a majority experience and, in the footnotes, state the proportion of activists to which it applies.

In this book I use the activists' real names. I believe this practice increases the realism and authenticity of the work. I also speak about their work in the organizational positions they held at the time of the interview. Some of the activists have since changed affiliation. Finally, although I analyzed all of the interview transcripts to build the analysis, I was not able to include quotations or stories from all of the subjects in the book itself. The reader can find a full list of all of the activists interviewed (with their affiliations) at the back of this book.[33]

In the pages that follow I use the term *racial justice activist* rather than *antiracist activist* for two reasons. First, it stresses what activists are for rather than what they are against, and that turns out to be a key theme of the book, as we will see. Second, although some of the people in this study use the term *antiracist* to describe themselves, most do not. Several of them told me that they had never even heard the term *antiracist* before. Others felt it sounded too ideological. Nevertheless, I occasionally use the term *antiracism* when I would like to stress the idea of opposition to racism or when interviewees themselves use that term.

In interpreting the findings presented here, I think it is important to note that I studied only people who are committed racial justice activists. In this study I identify the processes that led them to their commitment to racial justice. However, I did not study white nonactivists. There may be white people who experienced some of the same things as these activists but did not respond in the same way. I cannot tell you why the people I studied—and not others—moved to racial justice activism. However, I do provide rich details that explain how those processes work to move whites toward racial justice. I argue that these experiences and mechanisms might be necessary, even if not sufficient, to help develop commitment. In the end, the analysis presented in this book needs to be examined in light of the experiences of many other white activists and in ways that allow for comparisons to nonactivists. Indeed, I hope that this work will inspire much more research on white racial justice activists, using the fullest array of methods.[34]

I have presented here a fairly detailed description of how I conducted this study because I believe it will help readers interpret and consider the merits of this analysis. However, social scientists, students, and others may want to know more. I present further details of my methods and a discussion of the methodological issues raised in this project in the appendix at the end of the book.

The people I interviewed placed their stories in my hands. In what follows in the chapters, I try to be fair and balanced and to treat these activists with dignity and respect. I seek to tell their stories in a way that is authentic to them. I often present lengthy quotations from the activists and descriptions of their experiences. However, in the end, I am weaving their stories and views together to present my analysis of white racial justice activism. I am the conductor of this symphony, but I have let many of the activists make solo performances.[35]

Beyond the Interest/Altruist Trap

I began this study with the sense that the interest-based accounts of racism that dominate the field of race relations were insufficient to enable one to understand how white Americans might come to support racial justice. From the interest-based point of view, racial conflict is about group-based competition between blacks and whites or between whites and people of color more broadly. In other words, whites act to defend their group interest against competing demands by people of color for limited resources like jobs, housing, and education. In terms of the white privilege discussion presented earlier, whites defend their structural position of privilege in the racial hierarchy. As Eduardo Bonilla-Silva says, reflecting a broadly shared view, "Since actors racialized as 'white'—or as members of the dominant race—receive material benefits from the racial order, they struggle (or passively receive the manifold wages of whiteness) to maintain their privileges."[36]

To be fair, these interest-based theories were developed to explain white racist actions, not white support for racial justice. They are certainly helpful in understanding the dominant patterns of racism today. In other words, racism is not primarily a matter of bad ideas in people's heads. Rather, it is rooted in material forces that generate inequalities in wealth and power in society—as it has been since its modern origins during the time of slavery. Nevertheless, the interest-based approach to race relations has framed the manner in which scholars have thought about the possibilities for white anti-racism in ways that I believe are quite limiting.

Within the interest-based race relations literature, there are two alternative ways to understand white opposition to racism. The first account, the coalitional model, focuses on larger, shared interests. Whites can come to support demands of people of color when they see their common rather than opposed interests. Some scholars use the term *cross-cutting cleavage* to denote this situation. For example, social class can cut across racial lines. In this case, whites who share the same class status with people of color can come to align themselves with them. The classic Marxist view asserts that white workers and black workers are both oppressed by the same capitalist system. White workers can unite with black workers when they come to see their shared interest in overthrowing that system. William Julius Wilson offers a somewhat different and more recent account, in which he argues that growing economic inequality means that the large majority of whites share common interests with people of color for progressive social policy. In all of these variations, recognition of a larger shared interest trumps the narrower advantages whites gain through racial privilege.[37]

These larger projects, like the passage of Social Security legislation and other forms of social provision, may be of great benefit to people of color. However, the problem remains that white support for racial justice per se never appears central to these coalitions. In other words, whites are not necessarily supporting racial justice; they are simply aligning themselves with people of color for common goals. Critics have pointed out that whites will often abandon black demands if they perceive them to subvert the larger project. In a classic example, President Franklin Roosevelt refused to support federal antilynching legislation because it threatened to subvert the coalition he needed to pass New Deal legislation.[38]

Derrick Bell has argued that, although rare, there are times when whites have supported racial justice demands by people of color. He offers an "interest convergence" theory to explain why they did so. Convergence arises when whites are compelled to support black demands in defense of their own interests or political projects. For example, the Kennedy administration and white Democratic legislators backed civil-rights legislation in the sixties because their larger ambitions on the world stage were being subverted by America's tarnished image at home. People around the world witnessed segregationist opposition and violence to black people's demands, making them more cautious in supporting America's foreign policy agenda and the country's broader claim to be the leader of the free world. Bell's focus, however, remains on white elites, that is, legislators who have the power to back legislation like the Civil Rights Act. Phillip Thompson takes a more grassroots approach to interest-based coalitions. He argues that in many cities progressive whites might support black demands when they appear as a requirement for a coalition that can advance a common cause. In a similar vein, William Julius Wilson argues that white support for affirmative action is necessary if whites want blacks to join the broad coalition whites need to confront the economic power of the elites.[39]

With interest conversion and these other coalitional variants, however, the problem remains that whites are not authentically in support of racial justice. They are only temporarily supporting an issue or a set of demands because it is necessary for something else that they want. In the negotiations of interests that drive the coalitional model, there is not much room for a deeper connection across the racial divide that could lead whites to embrace racial justice as their own cause.

The second account, the altruistic model, also accepts that whites' interests are normally in competition with those of people of color. According to this view, whites who support racial justice are acting against their own interests for altruistic reasons. They support racial justice because it represents the right thing to do, a purely moral cause. They do it *for* people of color and not for themselves or other whites. Critics, however, have argued that purely moral appeals have never carried the day to any great extent, as interests trump morality for most whites. Moreover, people of color regard altruistic white people—the do-gooders and helpers—with suspicion for their paternalism. The ally who is there *for* others might give up when the going gets tough.[40]

In a way, altruist accounts face the same problem as coalitional accounts. In neither approach can whites come to see a direct stake for themselves in racial justice. I call this the *interest/altruist trap*. In neither model can we conceive of whites truly caring about racism, and therefore they cannot be deeply committed to racial justice. In both cases, whites remain behind the lines of race, as it were.

The problem, in my view, is that both coalitional and altruist accounts rely upon interest-based understandings that are overly deterministic. We know that interests are not somehow objectively given. Rather, individuals and groups construct an understanding of their interests through dynamic social and political processes that tie closely to group identities. Yet long traditions in many fields of social science remain captive to the idea of computing the objective interests of groups. For example, Marxists and other social scientists have argued that workers have an objective interest in socialism. Scholars and activists have spent a great deal of time and energy trying to explain why socialism "didn't happen here" in the United States. They have sought to figure out why American workers do not appear to see their objective interests rather than questioning the idea of objective interests in the first place.[41]

In a way, the coalitional and the altruistic models can be seen as pragmatic responses to current realities. In other words, given all of the forces that reinforce racial division, and given the traditional alignment of social and political identities along race, the utilitarian coalition partner or the altruistic ally are the best we can hope for. Since both approaches leave group identities and boundaries intact, however, they do not seem to offer a strategy for whites to come to any deep appreciation of racism and strong support for racial justice.

Perhaps we can open up new possibilities by appreciating the fact that individuals and groups are capable of determining their interests in a variety of ways. The process may well be conditioned by structural relationships, but in the end a person or a group can decide for themselves what their interests are. If that is true, we can break free of the interest/altruist trap and ask what would be necessary for white Americans to refashion a sense of their identity and interests to align them with the cause of racial justice. That is the project of this book.

This is a study of the possible, the admittedly unusual case of white racial justice activists. I chose whites who have demonstrated a commitment to racial justice and then sought to examine how they came to do so. Are they, nevertheless, acting altruistically *for* people of color? Do they, in fact, offer a common-interest account of themselves? Or have they somehow refashioned their sense of group boundaries and identities and constructed a sense of self and group so that they can have a firmer commitment to racial justice? If so, how exactly did they come to do that?

The Skeleton of an Alternative Approach

There has been little study of these questions in the field of race relations. However, I can draw upon scholarship in related fields for clues to some of the answers we might find. Social movement scholars have sought to identify routes to activism. They have traditionally centered their analysis on identifiable social movements and asked how such movements recruit activists.[42]

Of course, we lack an identifiable racial justice movement in the contemporary United States. Many of the activists I interviewed are trying to build such a movement, but they are working mostly in fragmented efforts within their own networks. There is a bigger difference at hand, however. Social movement research has largely focused on the participation of members of an oppressed group, for example, African Americans in the civil rights movement. Here it can be taken for granted that those who are involved have personal and group experience that makes them aware of oppression, provides them with a compelling interest in justice, and fosters a shared identity with others in the movement. Members of the oppressed group still have to develop what has been called an "oppositional consciousness" capable of leading to activism, but personal and group experience and shared understanding already orient them in that direction. Of course, the situation is quite different for whites vis-à-vis racial justice.[43]

Newer scholarship has opened up some promising lines of inquiry in part because it sees traditional scholarship as too narrowly focused on rational, interest-based accounts of activism. These scholars argue that morality and emotions also play important roles in many contemporary movements. James Jasper, for example, suggests that people, whatever their social location, get involved in social movements when they experience a moral shock. They may see a particularly heinous example of injustice that violates their sense of right and wrong. These kinds of shocks make people angry or outraged at injustice, and the resulting emotions serve as powerful motivators for action.[44]

I also found that moral shocks play a key role in starting the white activists in my study down the road to racial justice. In chapter two I locate these shocks in what I call seminal experiences and describe the kind of anger and moral impulse to act that they inspire. However, moral shocks, as important as they are, cannot themselves rework a sense of common interests and identity. We are left at altruism if we stop at moral impulse.

Even if you are morally inclined to oppose racism, if you do not personally experience racial discrimination or oppression, how do you come to a deeper understanding of it and thereby a stronger sense of injustice? Part of the answer may lie in relationships. Sharon Nepstad has studied what she terms "oppositional consciousness among the privileged." In particular, she seeks to understand how Americans came to be active in the Central American solidarity movement of the 1980s. How could they come to reject the Reagan administration's rationale for U.S. foreign policy? Sitting in their comfortable living rooms, how could they learn about the reality of life in Central America? It turns out that solidarity movement leaders arranged to bring Central American freedom fighters to the United States to meet with American activists and tell their stories. They also organized visits by Americans to the conflict zones. Nepstad shows us the critical role these relationships played in fostering a deeper sense of the injustice of U.S. foreign policy and a commitment to the solidarity movement.[45]

We might think that overcoming America's dominant color-blind racial ideology will be significantly harder than rejecting a particular foreign policy position no matter how buttressed with Cold War ideology. If anything, relationships might be more important and need to be much deeper and more multifaceted than the kinds of connections made in brief visits. Indeed, in the few studies of white racial justice activists, the impact of relationships stands out. Eileen O'Brien has found that relationships with people of color gave the white activists she studied what she calls "approximating experiences" of racism—in other words a way to appreciate the experience of being a person of color. I also found that white activists' relationships with people of color became critical to their development of an understanding of racism. But I found more as well. I found that white activists came to care about racism, and not just understand it, through these relationships. Moreover, as whites worked together with people of color, they began to develop a sense of common identity and shared fate. In chapter three I examine closely how crossing the social line of race can lead to the development of a political commitment to racial justice.[46]

Meanwhile, studies of activism in other domains can also help us understand how people can deepen their personal stake in the cause of social justice. Nathan Teske, in his study of social justice, right-to-life, and environmental activists, helps us to get out of the interest/altruist trap by showing how activism offers a way for people to lead a fulfilling life following moral beliefs. Anne Colby and William Damon found that, for many social activists, activism does not represent a denial of self but rather a way to define the self as a moral actor.[47]

I also found that the white activists in my study developed a clear sense that they were in it for themselves. In chapter four I describe the kinds of meaning and fulfillment activists find in this work. However, I found something beyond the narrowly personal. Working together with other whites and people of color, white activists begin to develop a collective vision of a future society based upon racial justice. They develop a commitment to working for a better, more humane society for all, based upon justice principles. If they start off being *against* racism out of a moral impulse, they end up being *for* racial justice in pursuit of a moral and political vision. They come to understand white people's interest in racial justice as a central part of achieving a better society for all.

Martin Luther King Jr.'s vision of the "Beloved Community" inspired many civil rights activists. Yet scholars of social movements have typically concentrated on what people are *for* in the very immediate sense of movement demands; surprisingly little research has been conducted on activists' broader visions. Robin D. G. Kelley, however, has recently shown how African American activists have always been motivated by "freedom dreams," that is, by visions of a future society based upon justice. Dreams like these are built collectively, as Kelley reveals.[48]

In chapter four I explore in detail the kinds of visions that white activists construct. However, I found that these activists were not primarily visionaries. Rather, they worked in the present to create their future visions. In other words, they work to create a just society as they build multiracial communities, collaborate with people of color, engage with other whites, and work to establish racially just institutional policies and practices. I discuss these efforts in great detail in chapters five and six, looking at activists' experiences in engaging other whites and building multiracial relationships.[49]

These multiracial groups and networks become important venues for the development of a direct stake in racial justice for whites linked to the development of new political identities. Many social movement scholars have identified such "free spaces" as important institutional sites within which new identities can be formed. I found, though, that white racial justice activists face a difficult challenge in forging a new identity. Racial identification is so strong and the racial dividing lines are historically so powerful that white activists often feel stuck between the worlds of whites and of people of color. Social movement scholars have long argued that people can hold multiple identities, but they have rarely examined the friction between them. In chapter seven I examine the tensions and dilemmas activists face as they negotiate the divide between their social identity as white and their political identity as racial justice activists.[50]

I hope I have given enough of a skeleton of the story I tell in the rest of the book to guide the reader. The following chapters put flesh on these so far rather thin bones. I give the reader something of a picture of the whole book here because, as we will see, the process of development of commitment to activism occurs dynamically with and through activism. In other words, a simple model in which we find one motivational cause that leads to activism does not work. I trace the development of commitment and of new understandings and identities over time in people's lives both before they become activists and then through their activist experiences. In what follows I have charted these routes.[51]

| ## Starting Down the Road

Seminal Experiences and the Moral Impulse to Act

J IM CAPRARO GREW up in Marquette Park, Chicago, in the fifties and early sixties, a child of Italian Catholic immigrants. His neighbors, like his parents, were white working-class ethnics who had moved out of Chicago's inner city to this neighborhood of modest homes. Jim's family and the nuns and teachers at his Catholic high school taught him that the future was bright, that America was the land of opportunity, "the greatest country in the world." After all, Americans had recently elected their first Catholic president, and folks in Marquette Park could aspire to moving even further up and out to the Shangri-la of Chicago's more affluent suburbs. When Jim was sixteen, however, he experienced an incident that would profoundly alter his sense of the world. It was the summer of 1966, and Jim's parents had just given him permission to use the family car for the first time on a date. This was going to be a big day for Jim, but not for the reason he had in mind:

> This evening was going to be the biggest time in my life, you know, my first date with a girl in a car. It was a Chevy Bel Air, a '63 Chevy Bel Air. I was primping all day, just getting prepared for this date, and just way too full of nervous energy. I went out in the afternoon to take the car and get it gassed up or something, because I got to prepare, right?
>
> As I went out, a very strange sequence of experiences happened. First thing was, I couldn't take the car and gas it up because there were school buses double-parked on my block, blocking all the cars in. Nobody's going anywhere. Although they looked like school buses,

they were powder blue. I'd never seen that before. Then all of a sudden, policemen start piling off the school bus next door. They're right in front of me, forming up, military-like, shoulder to shoulder with batons in their hands. They had blue helmets on. I had never seen police riot gear before. That's what they had, riot helmets. They all started to double-time, quick-march south in this long formation. It looked like thousands. I don't know, maybe it was a few hundred. But it just was—wow! Something's going on. I wonder what.

I saw a huge crowd of white people, four or five deep, on the sidewalk going out into the street. There were policemen with batons holding them off away from the street. And I think it was the owners—somebody—were passing out beer bottles. It wasn't cans in those days. It was bottles. People were throwing the beer bottles, just hurling them, at something. Across the street there's some big hubbub, and I could see black people. I could also see clergy who were not black. They all had signs, and the signs said things like End Slums, Open Housing. It was a demonstration. And it was going past the Marquette Park monument. . . . People are jeering and yelling, "N-ggers go home," and it's terrible. It's ugly. And it was so strange because, literally twenty minutes before, I'm thinking, "Got to gas up the car. I'm going on a date!"

At the intersection, a black couple came up in a car. The police had kept the crowd pretty well off the street, but it was work for them, right? And a black couple just coming out on the street gets stopped at the stoplight. The crowd pushes past the police and surrounds this car. I remember this so vividly—it's a Corvair, which was a small car then, Chevy Corvair. Crowd totally surrounds the car. The people inside the car are really afraid. I mean, they're just terrified. People start rocking this car back and forth. The people inside are literally huddled. The light is red. They're stopped. There's a crowd all around them. The police are trying to peel the crowd away from the outside. A girl about my age jumps up on the hood, screaming and yelling and swearing at the people inside and kicking at the windshield in front of the driver. I remember thinking she would have mangled their faces if there wasn't this windshield.

The crowd starts to go that way. I get about two blocks down, and I see people with brown shirts and swastikas and bullhorns, trying to take this mob and rally it together. At which point in time, I said, "I'm getting out of here."

I don't know that I was there more than a half an hour, maybe forty minutes, but it was the longest half hour in my life. And it changed my life forever. Kind of an epiphany, I guess. When I went home, that night I couldn't sleep. I had this never-ending stream of thoughts. Everything I thought I had learned or was led to believe, I thought was a lie. We're not the greatest country in the world. I was always taught that we were the greatest. Six years ago, John Kennedy was elected president. What happened? How could we be the greatest country in the world? How the hell could that be? What just happened two blocks from my house? This can't be the best neighborhood. Look at what people do! Look at how they were behaving. How could that be? Anybody could grow up to be president—I believed this, right? Well, I didn't think the people who were marching in the park that day had any shot at ever being president.

I got pissed. Mad, I mean. How dare these people do this stuff? This is a democracy. People have a right to say things and march and think of themselves as being equal with everybody else and in fact be equal to everybody else.

Jim returned to Brother Rice High School that fall and began questioning many things he was taught. He grew his hair long and spoke out against the Vietnam War. After high school, he worked in the same Motorola plant as his parents while attending college at night, eventually becoming quite a student activist and an antiwar activist. He worked with black student activists and felt "It was all part of the same big thing. It was all part of the world that should be created." One day, he heard Black Power advocate Stokely Carmichael tell white activists that if they were serious about fighting racism, they should go home and make a difference in their own white communities. And that's exactly what Jim decided to do.

In the meantime, the Klan and the Nazi Party had moved into Marquette Park to organize white residents against racial integration. Black protesters countered with their own marches, and Marquette Park "became the racial battleground of America," according to Jim. He first took a job for the Southwest Community Congress to work against block busting and redlining, practices designed to keep blacks out of the neighborhood. He then helped build what became the Greater Southwest Development Corporation, which follows a twin strategy: to promote business and economic development to stabilize the neighborhood while working to stop discriminatory and predatory lending practices that prevent integration.

Jim's decision to return to his neighborhood was not an easy one, and it marked a significant change in his thinking. His initial reaction to Carmichael was "Shit, I can't go home because home is bad. It's wrong." However, the more he thought about Carmichael's challenge, the more he felt responsible for changing his community:

> *Newsweek* reporters in the eighties would come here and say, "Well, how could you work there? It's racist." And I'd say, "Well, that's why we work here." When I began to describe it, I said, think about it like Vietnam and the United States' battle against communism. We became the racial battleground, just like Vietnam was the political and ideological battleground.

In fact, coming home for Jim also meant reconnecting with the core values of his family and faith. In order to do this kind of work, Jim says this:

> You got to think for yourself. You got to ask, what makes sense to me? What's my logic about this stuff? And once you go there, you're not very far from, "What do I really believe? What's at the center of my values?" Even though my parents were afraid, they had very good values. And I had really good values, I think, because of them.

In Jim's eyes, the problem was not his neighbors' values; rather, the problem was the contradiction between those professed values and his community's practice in regard to racism:

> I was motivated by both the Catholic faith and my parents. In retrospect it was the true essence of Christian values that I was trying to follow. I'll never forget in fifth grade Sister Robert Marie teaching in religion class about Jesus and the law of love. That really stayed with me, that good Christian people are supposed to love people, and if you follow, Jesus you do that.
>
> Later, when I said, "It's all a lie," I think there was a schism in my brain. We're supposed to be the greatest country in the world, but how could we be the greatest country in the world? To be great you've got to reconcile with God, and you can't reconcile with God if it isn't about love. So there's a disconnect there. It wasn't about the church. It was about secular society and its inability to abide by what the church had taught.

For thirty-five years now, Jim has lived and worked in Marquette Park, advocating for stable integration and economic development in one of the country's foremost symbols of Northern racism. In fact, Jim now bristles at people who stereotype Marquette Park. White flight has largely ended, and the neighborhood is quite diverse, although Jim finds it a struggle to attract new white residents. Moreover, as whites and blacks have met in neighborhood institutions, Jim sees them begin to build relationships and thereby combat hatred and racial prejudice. In a way, Jim wants to re-create the community of his childhood but also ensure that it is open to and inclusive of all races. Growing up, his white neighbors feared the inner city to their backs and looked longingly toward the Shangri-la of the suburbs. Jim wants to create a multiracial Shangri-la right in Marquette Park.

Seminal Experiences and Anger at Injustice

I have told Jim's story at length because it powerfully captures themes I discovered in the interviews I conducted. Virtually all of the white activists I interviewed—forty-six out of fifty—could clearly recall at least one incident that dramatically altered their sense of race. I call these *seminal experiences*. Representing profound moral shocks, they are accompanied by powerful emotions, typically anger or outrage at injustice. These experiences make whites aware, for the first time, of the reality of racism. They lead to righteous anger for the very reason that racist practice violates the values of justice and equality with which these people had been brought up and in which they deeply believe.

For some of the interviewees, seminal experiences led directly to a commitment to racial justice activism. For example, Joshua Kern's seminal experience came while attending Georgetown Law School, when he taught as a volunteer at a failing and dysfunctional high school. Josh grew up in an affluent community in suburban New Jersey and attended a Jewish high school that promoted justice concerns, but after college Josh worked in business consulting for a number of years. Frustrated with the meaninglessness of this career, he entered Georgetown in the late nineties, hoping to find an alternative vocation. He volunteered for Georgetown's Street Law Program to teach at Ballou High School, considered by many one of the worst high schools in Washington, DC. He recounts this powerful experience:

> They had this PA system at the school that, no exaggeration, in a fifty-minute class, went off three or four times, for a minute at a time. So every ten minutes you were interrupted for a minute by an announcement. And the announcements were of no value for the most part. But the one that really got me was the time the administrative assistant of

the school got on the loud speaker and said, "Dr. Bridges, please call Dr. Johnson. Dr. Bridges, please call Dr. Johnson." It sounded just like a hospital. I said, "You are interrupting every class, thousands of students here. There's like a hundred classes going on right now. You are interrupting every class to get one person to call another person."

The message that that sends to the kids is we don't think you can learn. We don't value your education at all. We might have a teacher in front of here who's pretending to teach you something, but in every way that we interact with you, the student, we are sending you the message: we don't think you can be successful; we don't think you can learn. It just got me so fired up because it had no educational value. It had no value at all.

Josh later talks about the impact that traveling from the most to the least privileged place in the District of Columbia had on him:

It was being at the law center and learning about the law and how law is the means and justice is the end and then driving two miles away and seeing a place where there's really no justice and then just traveling back and forth from Ballou to Georgetown Law. It's like the most privileged place in the city to the least privileged place in the city. Had I not been at the law center and had that experience at Ballou, it might not have had the same impact on me. I think it was that dichotomy.

That spring semester Josh organized a group of Georgetown Law students to study urban education and eventually write a charter school proposal. The next fall they opened Thurgood Marshall Academy in Anacostia, the district's poorest neighborhood. The charter high school faced many challenges early on but eventually became quite successful. In 2007 every single one of the school's graduates went on to college. Josh talks about the anger at injustice that was ignited at Ballou and continues to burn in him and sustain his commitment today:

I care about the injustice. That's what I care about. I care that there's a question of fairness that I find deeply disturbing. It's the thing that made me angry at Ballou, and it's the thing that still motivates me. And that's it. At the most basic level, the most fundamental level, I feel like the fairness issue is what drives me. Justice. Coming from a law background, it's about law and justice. There's such a huge injustice here at every level that I can't escape it. It's in your face all day long, every day.

For most of the subjects in the study, however, their seminal experiences did not result in immediate action. Like Jim Capraro, these shocks began a process, a first step toward racial justice awareness and commitment. For example, Mark Soler grew up in middle-class Silver Spring, Maryland, and graduated from Yale in 1968. He received a draft deferment to teach elementary school in northeast Washington, DC, but he was completely unprepared for what he found there:

> The school system then was segregated like it is now, largely all African American kids. The school had been built two years after the end of the Civil War. It was an old, old school that was falling down. The heaters either didn't work or worked all the time. So it was either too hot in the room or it was too cold. The kids, my students, were bused from southeast Washington. They were all poor, and they would often come to school without heavy enough clothing and wet if it was raining.
>
> It got me how horrible the system was. And the education system was terrible. There was no black studies curriculum. The curriculum consisted of a list of famous black Americans, period. Nothing else other than that. These kids were dying to learn about successful black role models, and there was nothing about that. The physical conditions were terrible. Supplies were a mess. We didn't get textbooks for weeks after the school year started. I just thought, "This is just terrible." At that point I said, "I'm going to go to law school, and one thing I want to do in law school is I want to use that as a way to stop this thing from happening for other kids."

On Mark's last day teaching, an encounter he had with the principal sealed his commitment:

> I remember on the last day I taught, I told the kids I was going to leave, and I really was very emotional. I was going to miss them a lot. I didn't tell them 'til the end because I didn't want to have drawn-out good-byes. So I said good-bye to them. I think it was the end of the semester, and the principal said, "I want to see you before you leave."
>
> The principal was white, and she had not done any classroom teaching in thirty-five years. She was very tough. I thought she had essentially no connection with the kids. Zero. So I went in to see her, and I said, "This is a terrible school, and this is a terrible system, and can't you do more to make this better for these children who are going through it?" And she said, "Well, you shouldn't be critical like that."

I said, "Of course I should. I'm being an advocate for these children, and they're just being mistreated, and they're not getting educated here." She said, "You know, you're just as insolent as your students are." And I said, "You can say what you want to about me, but you can't talk about my students like that. I'm never going to be a public school teacher again. I'm going to go to law school and be a lawyer, but you can take this job, and you can shove it up your ass."

I turned, I walked out, and I was trembling. I was so angry with her I didn't know what to do. This was forty years ago, and I'm still remembering it very vividly. . . . It was a very, very powerful experience about the helplessness of some people in society and particularly how children are being mistreated. There just had to be a better way of doing some of these things.

Mark did go to law school and eventually became a juvenile justice lawyer. In that position he began touring juvenile detention centers. What he saw in those facilities stoked his feeling of anger at injustice, which had its beginning in that DC school:

I've probably gone through as many juvenile facilities as anybody else in the country because I've been so active in this area for so long. It is largely young African American men and Latinos. Mostly African American boys are in there, and they're getting the shit beat out of them. Morally and physically and spiritually they're just getting crushed in these situations, and there is not any respite from it. From South Dakota we actually have videotapes of the kids being chained to their beds and gassed and led around on a leash just like Abu Ghraib. That stuff is absolutely horrible.

Mark is now the president of the Youth Law Center. He has shut down many juvenile facilities but is also credited with being one of the initiators of the Building Blocks for Youth campaign. This initiative works to build coalitions at the local level to develop alternative approaches to address juvenile justice issues. For Mark, like many activists in this study, anger at injustice is a sustaining force in his commitment:

They are kids. They may have serious charges against them. They may put up a tough façade. But I go in there, and after all I'm a middle-aged white man. I'm going in and interviewing young African American boys who are thirteen, fourteen, fifteen years old. I couldn't come from a more different life than they do. And yet, after about five minutes, they open up and talk to you about what they're going through and what their lives are like. If they have a veneer, it's an inch thick. You can quickly get under that, and then they're babies. Just like my son was a baby and just like all kids are babies underneath. Some of them are older and bigger, and they look tough and everything. But they're just babies. And they're really being terribly, terribly mistreated by the state. That gets me angry all the time. It's one of the things that has kept me in the same job for twenty-five years.

Some of the activists in this study experienced their moral shocks after, rather than before, their activism began. A few serendipitously began work that has a racial justice component and had their seminal experience at that point. For example, when David Utter graduated from law school in the late eighties, he knew he wanted to do public interest law, but he was not particularly focused on issues of racism. He ended up in Atlanta, where he took a job with the Southern Center for Human Rights. The center's director, Steven Bright, inspired David with his commitment to racial justice. Bright assigned David to work on prison issues and capital crime cases. In 1990 David drove to the Louisiana State Penitentiary in Angola to represent prisoners with mental illnesses. He tells this story of his first visit:

You drive on this completely deserted dirt road for twenty miles, and you come to these massive, beautiful, green, rolling hills—a farm but one that has this huge gate and barbwire. On the right-hand side there's administrative buildings and death row. There are seven or eight different prisons within the prison. You have the main prison, and then you have Camp A, B, C, D, E, and F, and most of those camps are cell blocks, up to five hundred cells of concrete and steel, eight-by-ten cells. I went there in August, and the only places that are air-conditioned are the administrative buildings and places where the guards are. Everywhere else that the prisoners live day in and day out is un-air-conditioned in the middle of the Louisiana summer.

You routinely see white guards on horseback with shotguns in front. In back in rows two by two, shoulder to shoulder, forty or fifty inmates, all black, all in standard prison uniforms carrying hoes and manual tools. They walk five miles out into the fields and manually work the farm in the morning, walk back with these white guards on horseback, get fed, walk back. That was their day—literally. These mother f-ckers built a golf course on this plantation, on this prison, and they refused to use any machinery. The prisoners had to move mountains of dirt by hand so they could have rolling greens.

Of the 5,000 inmates I bet you 4,500 are black. Generations of prison guards have worked and lived on the prison, almost all white. There was not a whit of difference between a prison guard and the prisoner in terms of education and morals. The black guy in a fit of anger killed somebody or was a heroin addict and got caught with heroin. There are a handful of guys that are in some true sense bad guys. Most of them just had some very bad circumstances and made some very bad choices and are now being overseen by white guys who beat their wives, have no education but because they're prison guards they're overseeing them. If you don't see the racism and the parallels to slavery and the history of oppression when you go there, then you got to be pretty blind.

I just decided that I would pour all of that emotion, all of that anger, all of that frustration, all of that guilt into being the best lawyer I could for my clients. I was going to be a good lawyer for them for the first time that they'd ever, ever experienced. It's the same thing with my work with the kids today. I think that's where the emotion lives; it's in this work.

David moved on to juvenile justice work in New Orleans, where he cofounded the Juvenile Justice Project of Louisiana (JJPL). He helped lead several well-known efforts to close juvenile detention centers like the one in Tallulah. In 2005 he won a "Leadership for a Changing World" award from the Ford Foundation.

Moral Shocks and Value Conflict

These accounts illustrate how the activists' seminal experiences can lead to an awareness of the reality of racism and recognition that it is wrong. The events provoke anger and a shocked recognition of the violation of deeply held values. In other words, they take on a moral meaning for activists. Why should this be so?

In 1944 Swedish social scientist Gunnar Myrdal published *An American Dilemma*, a mammoth study of the African American experience in the United States. Myrdal argued that racism represented a contradiction between the "American Creed," that is, deeply held values of equality and freedom, and the reality of the treatment of black people in this country. Myrdal's study has been controversial from the beginning. Some critics point out that slavery and racism were not aberrations of American ideology but were fundamental to the system at its origins and that slavery was in fact enshrined in the U.S. Constitution.[1]

Nevertheless, I think Myrdal was indeed correct that Americans hold deeply to the values of equality and justice. Most white Americans are brought up to believe in these values and, generally speaking, to believe that America lives up to them. In fact, most of the activists I interviewed feel that in working for racial justice they are carrying out the values cherished by their family, community, church, and nation. Many of the interviewees said that their own parents were a bit more sympathetic to issues of race than the average person in their community. Fourteen of the fifty subjects indicated that their parents, although not radically different from other whites, either treated black people "better" than others or disagreed with more overt, yet common, forms of racism in their community. The witnessing of racist practice violates these deeply held values and creates a sense of shock and value conflict.[2]

This conflict with deeply held values leads to a feeling of anger at this injustice. William Gamson has identified the development of a sense of injustice as critical to social movement activism because it "focuses on the righteous anger that puts fire in the belly and iron in the soul." Gamson calls this a "hot cognition," not just an intellectual judgment. If you are committed to your values, the sense of injustice can lead to an obligation to act. The first step toward commitment, then, resides in what I call a moral impulse.[3]

The witnessing of racism through a direct experience appears important. Most whites continue to grow up in segregated communities where they seldom see instances of racism. None of the interviewed activists reported viewing racism on television, for example, as having the same kind of impact on them. Rather, a more profound effect appears to occur when whites have direct experiential evidence of the existence of racism in the form of an immediate, palpable event.

Seminal experiences represent abrupt events, a crystallization of awareness in time.[4] Activists speak of more gradual developments before and after such events. Jim Capraro, for example, talks of watching the civil rights movement on television at home while his mother made sympathetic comments. He also talks about beginning to see some contradictions around race in his community. He describes himself as confused at the time:

> I remember when we'd drive in a car, and we'd go through a black neighborhood, we'd be told, lock the doors and roll up the windows.... But I also remember my mom and dad both having black friends at work and feeling kind of confused about this whole race

thing from an early age because at work it was okay, but when we were in the car it wasn't okay, and in the neighborhood it didn't exist.

I think it makes sense that a powerful change in racial awareness would come abruptly. It's not the experience per se that causes the change. Instead, it is how the person interprets the experience and the meaning the person ascribes to it. Psychologists have studied what happens when people receive information that appears to contradict deeply held beliefs, a situation they capture in the concept of cognitive dissonance. It is difficult for people to hold two opposing beliefs at the same time. In other words, people cannot believe that their community is egalitarian and yet is acting in a racist way at the same time. For this reason many people will hold on to an explanation that might fit the experience without requiring them to reject the dominant ideology. For example, they might adopt the rationalization that black people pushed too far and caused the riot in Chicago or that black people don't care about education and so the conditions of DC schools are understandable and not the fault of institutional and individual racism.[5]

For a seminal experience to have an effect, the affected person has to make a real shift to begin to challenge the dominant ideology. Faced with direct experiential evidence of racist practice, the subjects in my study chose an alternative view, that is, they chose to become aware of the reality of racism. The design of this study does not allow us to identify the exact reason these subjects, rather than others, made that choice, but it does suggest that this kind of change is likely to crystallize in abrupt moments.

Pushing against Dominant Institutions

Scholars who study social justice activism have sometimes found that activists tell "conversion stories." Nathan Teske calls these involvement stories and describes them as "dramatic narrative accounts of the development of their political activism." The accounts given by racial justice activists share some similarities with these conversion stories. However, they are somewhat different as well. Social movement scholars tend to focus on the decision point to join a particular movement. I have been tracing the development of commitment over time in the lives of activists. I have not seen a one-time conversion; rather, I often see the process of commitment growing over time. Seminal experiences represent part of a series of events and factors that shape commitment and eventual activism.[6]

In addition to conversion, scholars have also identified a route into activism they call "compliance." Some activists grew up in activist families and inherited a commitment to activism from their parents. We might therefore suppose that activists who grew up in families committed to racial justice would not require a seminal experience. They would have been brought up to appreciate the reality of racism and to feel an obligation to work for racial justice. I found some support for this view. Eight of the activists in my study stated that they grew up in such families. Three of the four activists in the study with no reported seminal experience came from this group of eight. These three reported that they are directly carrying out a family tradition of activism.[7]

However, five of the eight activists who grew up in activist families reported having a seminal experience, which tells us something important about the workings of racism. Dominant institutions appear to continually push whites away from racial understanding and toward "a white world" despite their families' influence. For example, twenty-eight-year-old Rachel Breunlin developed a strong racial awareness at a young age. Rachel's mother was a fair housing activist, and her parents chose to raise their family in a racially mixed suburb outside of Chicago. Rachel's aunt adopted four black children, so Rachel grew up with black cousins. Rachel tells the story of hearing another child use the "N word," repeating it to her mother, and getting "the worst shaming of my life." She recounts an experience at a young age in which a white friend of hers moved to a different neighborhood; when the friend came back to visit, she said it wasn't safe in Rachel's part of town. Rachel felt betrayed and says the event "stuck with me, probably forever." Meanwhile, her brother liked basketball, and black kids would always be over at her house playing. So "housing and place have always seemed very important to me in terms of racial justice." Even as a teenager, if she heard racist remarks, she'd say, "You're talking about my family."

Nevertheless, when Rachel became a student at Tulane University, she felt she had landed in the middle of a mostly white, privileged "bubble" in the midst of mostly poor, black New Orleans. She found herself in an all-white friendship group, as the school was heavily segregated. Over time, she became increasingly uncomfortable with that situation. "I just felt like society was sort of channeling me in that kind of direction. . . . If you're a white person in America, and you just go through your patterns in your normal life and don't make much of an effort, then you'll stay in a fairly segregated field." As a result, Rachel decided to switch from the all-white anthropology department to African American studies and women's studies, which were "pretty feisty" and dealt with issues of race.

As she was leaving Tulane University, Rachel's discomfort with her white world came to a head, and she decided to make a bigger change. She enrolled in graduate school and studied for a master's degree in applied anthropology at the local public university, the University of New Orleans. She moved into a largely black neighborhood and conducted her master's research project at a jazz club while teaching in a program called Students at the Center, which placed writing teachers in public schools. She taught in the high school closest to her house and was shocked by what she found there:

> ...the lack of quality books, the physical condition of the building, and the reading and writing skills of many of the students. Some could not read at all and had just been passed through the system for years. Others were on a second- or third-grade level. Very few would have been able to go on to college without taking remedial classes.

Moreover, the school was terribly overcrowded:

> New Orleans had schools of last resort. And John Mac was one of those schools. They can't turn anyone away. So the enrollment just grew beyond capacity. Teachers weren't able to have their own space, so they didn't put anything in their rooms. There were no books, no posters or anything. Some teachers went out of their way to do it, but for the most part it was just graffiti all over the place. A very, very unattractive place to teach and to go to school.

During her second year at John Mac, there was a shooting at the school, which prompted a lockdown. Students and visitors had to enter through a side gate surrounded by barbed wire with metal detectors. Rachel lost her classroom and had to teach in the back of the library. She finally decided she needed to do something different to engage her students, so she began asking them to write stories about their community:

> After a few years of living in the Seventh Ward, just a few blocks away from the school, I started to get a much better sense of the culture and community that I was teaching in. I was tired of hearing what the kids couldn't do instead of what they could do. If you start learning more about working-class African American culture in New Orleans, it's one of the most incredible cultures I've ever been privileged to be a part of. Scholars from around the world come down to write about its place in the African diaspora and its unusual place in the history of the U.S. I wanted the students to see these connections and to write their own stories about them.

The Students at the Center program funded her class, which enabled the class size to be limited to fifteen students. With this group, Rachel started a writing project called "War outside My Window," where the young people wrote about the Gulf War and about violence in their own neighborhood. The project was a big success. When she graduated from her master's program, she started the Neighborhood Story Project (NSP) with fellow teacher and writer Abram Himelstein. Students interviewed community residents and wrote the stories they heard. NSP commercially published five books authored by the students, eventually to great local acclaim. The NSP is now supported by the University of New Orleans and has worked with a wide range of grassroots organizations on books about their neighborhoods.[8]

Several of the people from activist families I interviewed described experiences similar to Rachel's. The normal workings of the system continually pushed them toward a white world despite the influence of their families. Living in the dominant world, they ended up having seminal experiences that shocked them back toward a recognition of racism. For example, in the fifties, Laurie Olsen grew up in San Francisco in a multiracial community of activists where antiracism was an important and explicit value. In fact, Laurie was a red-diaper baby whose parents were communists, and this has given her a "very, very, very deep faith and credo and belief system about the world and about what we're doing here." Her friends at a young age were a multiracial group, and she had a particularly close friendship with an African American girl. But the school she attended was largely white. When desegregation came to San Francisco, black kids were bused to her middle school, and the school responded by hardening the racial lines:

> What the school did was create white homerooms and black homerooms. It was the white classes where the "good" students got put. So there was the systematic separating of us, which led to social dynamics where both African American and white kids really circled the wagons. I succumbed to that social pressure and just felt totally lost about why and how I was letting it happen. Then our friendship ended, and we had been best friends for all of elementary school.
>
> I had some very deep experiences personally in that time that were really, really painful and didn't mesh well with the ideology in our home. How was I letting all this happen? I was feeling so totally hopeless, and I was feeling all of the weight of the privilege of being moved into the classes with the white kids.

Laurie was ashamed of her behavior because it conflicted with her home culture and says she learned "the lessons of silence and passivity" at that time.

When her mother received a fellowship from Radcliffe College, Laurie ended up at an exclusive, all-white private school in New England. She went on to study anthropology in a largely white, private college and later worked with Margaret Mead in New York. Laurie became active in feminist issues without paying much attention to issues of race. Eventually she returned to California to take a job doing policy research on high school dropouts and had the following seminal experience:

> I went around the state interviewing students that were dropping out, and the race issues just hit me in the face. It was like I had somehow gotten away from it, and here it was that the kids who were dropping out were mostly African American and Latino kids . . . There were particular kids whose stories just deeply, deeply affected me. But it was more the pattern and just realizing, "Oh, my God, how could I have forgotten?" That is really the way I felt. How could I have left this behind? It was really from that point that I got back to race as a really key issue.

Laurie began working on issues of racial justice in education. Eventually she helped found and now directs California Tomorrow, an advocacy group that focuses on immigration issues and education.

Laurie talked about the continuing struggle to bring up her sons in a multiracial way. When they were young, they grew up in the multiracial friendship network that Laurie and her husband were part of. For personal reasons, though, the boys were sent to a private high school that was largely white. When they then went on to attend private colleges in New England, Laurie realized that their world was gradually becoming whiter and whiter. Reflecting on this experience, Laurie says:

> It requires constant intentionality to not be pulled into white enclaves. . . . It's been interesting with my eldest son now because he is living in San Francisco, and he's become very politically active. He is struggling to gain his own understanding of racial issues as an adult and gain his own comfort level in dealing with people of color. He's really struggled and is struggling. His values are there, which I think is a result of his upbringing. But he does not have the comfort, the set of skills, and the sense of self to really actualize it yet. I know that that's a result of the choices we made and the world we raised them in. We let them become part of white enclaves.

A number of activists in this study reported experiencing several seminal events in their lives. The stories we have just heard help us to understand why this may be the case. Even as white activists become committed to racial justice, the forces of dominant institutions continue to push them toward "a white world."

The Analytical and Cognitive Dimension

I have so far emphasized the emotional and moral components connected to seminal experiences. Activists speak of the moral outrage at injustice that they feel, but what do they say about the cognitive dimension? We might expect that whites would need some alternative frame in order to make sense of what they are seeing. If our dominant color-blind ideology says that the system is not racist, what kinds of knowledge and frameworks do whites require to begin appreciating the reality of racism? Such a cognitive development may be particularly important for the large majority of white activists who did not grow up in Laurie's radical family.

I found some evidence of the importance of racial analysis. Susan Sandler, for example, grew up in a very wealthy family in an all-white community outside of San Francisco. She attended predominantly white private schools and eventually Stanford University. She became involved a bit in student activism and then read Paolo Freire:

> It just completely spoke to me. It dealt with lots of questions I had around power and change—the idea that people who are oppressed are doing their own analysis of conditions and making change based on that analysis. I loved doing that kind of thinking. And to think that you can facilitate that in other people, so it's not you being elitist. It just answered a lot of stuff for me.

Susan started social work school at San Francisco State and tells this story:

> At that time they really had a commitment to racial justice. They had a policy that 50 percent of the students were people of color, 50 percent of the faculty were people of color. They had a year-long sequence called Ethnic and Cultural Concepts and Principles that was really a lot about racism. I was lucky because the professor I got for that is just this incredibly brilliant person, Margo Okazawa-Rey. So that was all very powerful. The class was very powerful. This whole sense that there is something structural, there's something systemic, and this is what it is, and this is how it's operating. She combined that with just really challenging us to take it to heart and internalize it and live it,

and she had very high standards that she set. So it was just a very deep, powerful experience.

During this time, Susan says she came to understand white privilege and how whites through their actions can reproduce racism even unintentionally; she also began to see racism as an interconnected web of institutional processes. Susan talked about a specific meeting in which Margo had questioned the purpose of integrating kids' culture into a school's curriculum. Susan had felt that it was an important way to create a bridge to the dominant culture. Margo argued that a dominant culture shouldn't exist in the first place, and that "shook things up" quite a bit for Susan.

Racial awareness grew, though, when she met her activist husband:

> It's a context where my eyes are opened to racism and where the people of color in my classes are talking about it in a way that I had never experienced before. Just at that same time I met my husband, who is committed to racial-justice work. That's how he sees the world. He had a multiracial group of friends, most of whom were doing racial-justice work. So it was a watershed year that just changed everything.

By the time she left graduate school, Susan had acquired a racial justice lens and had decided she wanted to work on racial justice issues. She started working in public schools around equity issues. Later she came to direct Justice Matters, an advocacy group whose mission is to bring about racially just schools by developing and promoting educational policy rooted in community vision.

While many activists in the study talked, like Susan, about the importance of acquiring a racial justice lens, only a couple spoke to the cognitive side as an important route into activism.[9] Rather, many develop and strengthen their understanding of racism as they practice their activism, not before they start. Indeed, it is striking how minor a role the cognitive aspect played in the development of their commitment.

For Emily Zeanah, in fact, learning about racism and oppression at Guilford College actually led to a sort of paralysis. She was inspired toward activism instead by working with activists of color at the Beloved Community Center in Greensboro, North Carolina:

> Guilford's really good at critical thinking and learning how to criticize all these things, but it's so overwhelming, and it's so depressing. You can get pretty cynical pretty quickly and apathetic and think, "What difference does it make? What difference can I possibly make in this?"

Being in the Beloved Community Center, I was treated like it mattered that I was here....They're pretty amazing people. Being around people who have been in Greensboro forever, number one, and been involved in all the civil rights struggles, like Mr. Brandon. Mr. Brandon was organizing a sit-in when he was at A&T in the sixties, all the stuff that I just read about. It's very creative here. There's a lot of creative energy, a lot of vision, a lot of spirit.

If anything, activists like Emily speak powerfully about how relationships with people of color taught them about racism, a subject I treat at length in the next chapter.

Speaking of the impact of his earlier work representing clients in criminal cases, Mark Soler underscores that, for him, understanding racism is not simply an intellectual project:

The prostitutes I represented were almost all black and Latino. For the most part they were prostitutes because they had no other options. Well, that was in part because of structural racism in society. They had gotten terrible educations, they had no job skills, and they believed they had one commodity that they could offer. But beyond the intellectual look at it was a very visceral, visual kind of thing. I kept seeing the system that was grinding up people of color, especially African Americans.

In the end, I conclude that analytical understanding plays a supportive role in the development of commitment. It is important, but it is not central. Learning in detail about the history of slavery or the workings of contemporary racism, however important for many reasons, does not appear to motivate white people to act. Direct experience of racist practices, by contrast, does move some people. When they interpret this experience as a violation of deeply held values, they feel the moral shock and anger at injustice that can start them down the road to racial justice activism.

College as a Turning Point

Susan Sandler's experience highlights the importance of college as a critical place for gaining racial knowledge. It turns out, not surprisingly, that time at college represents a key turning point in many activists' lives. I looked at the kinds of social settings in which people shifted toward racial justice and found college to be the one common place. Many people had a seminal experience at college, one that led them more directly to activism.[10]

For example, Roxane Auer grew up in a wealthy family in virtually all-white Malibu, California, just north of Los Angeles. Her parents were very progressive and often talked about politics with her when she was growing up. When Roxane was eleven, her parents hired a woman from El Salvador to live with them and help raise Roxane's younger sister. This new situation was unsettling to Roxane, and "it didn't seem right" that her parents weren't raising their own daughter. She felt uncomfortable that her parents didn't invite her Latina nanny to eat dinner with them. Nevertheless, Roxane remained largely apolitical throughout her high school years.

When Roxane went to UCLA, however, she began to connect with the activism happening all around her. She had long felt critical of the corporate greed that led to the kind of wealth she saw in Malibu. In the middle of her college studies (Roxane was majoring in English), she decided she was tired of reading the works of "dead white men" and changed her major to American Studies, which included African American studies. She took her first African American studies class as one of ten white students out of a hundred and felt uncomfortable in that situation:

> I do remember very vividly just thinking, "Wow, this is amazing. This is really uncomfortable, and this is how black people must feel every day in America."...I just felt it was important to expose myself to that discomfort because it must be what other people feel. You can't start learning about this stuff without realizing your own extreme privilege. You can't study African American history without feeling very white, very wealthy, especially if you're from Malibu.

One critical incident in a class opened her eyes to racism and her own privileged position:

> It was mostly the black students talking, and they were talking about how angry they were. They'd go into Westwood, and they would be turned away from restaurants and be treated like crap and given cheap tables. They'd experienced racism all over our little college town. At one point I raised my hand and said, "I wish I'd known. I'd never have gone to those establishments. I'm never going back." One of the students turned around and just screamed at me, "It's everywhere. Don't you realize it's everywhere? You can't not go to the places that are racist because it's everywhere." Like, "You idiot, how could you not realize that it's everywhere?"...I felt stupid and naïve about it and left that class flustered and bothered. I certainly remember that moment, screaming, vividly.

Roxane started looking around her with a new perspective and was outraged at the blatant racism she saw on campus:

> The feminist newspaper on campus got hold of some fraternity song-book lyrics and published them. They were just completely racist and sexist in a disgusting way. One of the lyrics talked about "you *puta,* my Mexican whore." There was a protest outside one of the fraternities. It was a Latino protest because a lot of the songs were expressly racist against Latinos. The frat party was a "wetback party." They had a bar that you were supposed to crawl under to get into the party. Then they threw water on you before you went inside. Horrible. A lot of students protested outside the fraternity and threw tortillas at them.

As Roxane gradually became more involved in activism, she supported the Justice for Janitors campaign, which sought to improve conditions for the low-paid service workforce of Los Angeles. After college, she went to work as an intern for Communities for a Better Environment, an environmental justice organization in southeast LA. Seeing first-hand the conditions in which poor Latinos lived made a powerful impact on her:

> I saw communities living right next to glass-crushing factories or concrete-crushing factories. The air was filled with glass dust and concrete dust, and kids were coughing up blood. I couldn't believe that I had never been to this part of LA, and here it was, twenty minutes away. Doing the work I did for that organization really showed me the racial aspect of environmental injustice.
>
> It was the first time I ever spent a huge amount of time in communities that were completely nonwhite. LA is a completely segregated city, and it's stark when you see it. I was completely naïve and privileged and sheltered from that and felt rather stupid that it was so shocking to me.

Wanting to be part of a larger movement, Roxane eventually took a position doing research for the union Unite HERE, where she supported organizing drives for hotel workers who were mostly Latino. Reflecting on her life, Roxane explains her activism this way:

> I felt like I was raised in the lap of luxury. I had everything I could have wanted and more. I mean like beach houses, a horse when I was growing up, and a car when I turned sixteen. Total spoiled brat. Yet my dad's income bracket could almost be called working class if you look at some of the corporate wealth and salaries that are on the books today. These companies are just hoarding everything, hoarding it all.

That always really bothered me, made me very angry in my late teens and early twenties. I was kind of very bitter, angry at the world.

When I first started doing this work, I felt this sense of hope that you could change things start creeping into my anger. It was just a better feeling. Starting to do the work just felt so right to me. It just felt so good.

Roxane has worked on a number of important campaigns, including a widely publicized effort to get the city of Santa Monica to pass an ordinance that would require employers in the tourist industry to pay a living wage to its largely Latino workforce. When she tells her union colleagues and members that she's originally from Malibu, a symbol of white affluence, "eyebrows go up." She jokingly calls herself "Malibu Barbie, my dirty secret." Harking back to her earliest memories of race, Roxane later found herself working side by side with a Latina staff person who was the daughter of a maid in Beverly Hills. "Here we are working together, side by side, sharing an office and organizing together for economic and racial justice. And it's so interesting we came to it from such different realities."

Like Roxane, many people in this study cited college as a turning point. There are several reasons for this. First, young people attend college at a time in their lives when they are open to modifying their worldviews. Late adolescence has long been recognized as a period when people are open to new ideas and ways of living.[11] Moreover, going off to college removes these young people from the immediate influence of their parents and home community. We have seen examples of young people who experience a moral shock in their teenage years, but at that time of life they may more easily be pulled back into dominant ways of thinking. At college, they are freer to explore new ideas and to develop new meaning from critical experiences. Taking courses and having teachers, sometimes faculty of color like Margo Okazawa-Rey, provide one source of these new ideas. Indeed, the growth of ethnic studies departments and courses on the history and culture of African Americans and other people of color increases these opportunities for newer generations.[12]

College also offers young people the chance to meet others who might share a racial justice perspective. For example, although Jim Capraro witnessed his neighbors riot against a housing integration march, it was only when he went off to college—and not to his factory job—that he found other activists who shared his views and pushed his justice activism along. Moreover, college is often the first time that many whites, growing up in segregation, find themselves in a multiracial setting, where they have a chance to build relationships with people of color. I treat the effects of these relationships in great detail in the next chapter, but suffice it to say here that relationships play a powerful role in developing an understanding of racism and commitment to racial justice, as they did for Susan and Roxane. College is not the only place that provides whites with this opportunity, but it is a key one.

Finally, college often provides young people's first opportunity for activism. Scholars of collective action have long noted that social networks foster participation. Students find themselves drawn into activism when friends or even acquaintances invite them to participate. Meanwhile, young adulthood has been recognized as a time of life when people are more likely to become activists.[13]

The student activism of the sixties provided a strong set of opportunities for baby boomers in the study like Jim Capraro. Yet later periods were not short of opportunities for younger activists. Some of the interviewees got involved in the Central American solidarity movement and the South African antiapartheid movement of the eighties. Although campuses were quieter in the nineties, young people like Roxane Auer still found opportunities to work on issues of environmental justice and ongoing struggles around diversity on campus.

In college, some people find an opportunity for their first activism on racial justice. However, a few of the interviewees became active in other issues, ones not directly focused on race. Nevertheless, these earlier activist experiences can be very important to the development of later activism around racial justice. People develop a sense of agency through activism. Like Emily Zeanah, they come to believe that something can be done about injustice when people take action together. If anger at injustice represents a key emotional component of activism, then hope for change is another. After all, it is not enough to see and feel injustice; one also has to believe that change can happen in order to take the risk of acting.[14]

Once involved in activism, some people then find themselves exposed to racial justice work. For example, Ingrid Chapman grew up in Yakima, Washington, near the Yakima Indian Nation. Her parents were liberals and opposed the overt racism she said was rampant in the city. Ingrid attended mostly white schools and had mostly white friends, some of whom were rather racist. She described Yakima as "a hard place to live" because of widespread poverty and violence. She went on to attend the University of Washington in Seattle, where she became involved in student activism around environmental issues.

The next year, the World Trade Organization came to Seattle for its annual meeting. Ingrid joined the protests against globalization and was inspired by the power of mass action to shut the meeting down. Ingrid herself gained notoriety as the first person arrested at the protests. Although her fellow protestors were largely white, she did meet activists of color with a racial justice lens for the first time. A publication by one of them, Elizabeth "Betita" Martinez, titled "Where Was the Color in Seattle?" deeply affected Ingrid. In it, Martinez asked why the protesters were so white when a multiracial movement was needed.

Excited by the success of the Seattle protest, Ingrid left college to become an antiglobalization activist and movement trainer. She went to a Ruckus Society training camp with a group called Freedom Rising to organize protests at the Democratic National Convention in Los Angeles in 2000. For the first time, Ingrid encountered a large number of activists of color. These activists challenged the way Ingrid and her white activist friends were operating. They felt white activists were trying to dominate the meetings, ignoring the concerns and needs of people of color. This challenge created quite a moral conflict for Ingrid between the professed ideals of her white activist circle and their actual practice:

> They showed us how white folks are perpetuating racism and privilege at this camp. I saw my own actions as part of that and saw how difficult it was for us to really be building trust when we were perpetuating all of the same privileged, racist crap that happens in society. We are saying that we are fighting for justice, and we are simultaneously oppressing each other.

Ingrid realized her group of six white activists had come to Los Angeles without knowledge of the local community and had in essence been saying, "This is the way to do things." She began to feel the need for a different kind of leadership that would be collaborative and connect globalization concerns with support for local organizing in communities of color.

Ingrid continued traveling across the United States, Canada, and Europe in order to train young organizers but this time seeking to bring a more consciously antiracist lens to the work. She ended up in San Francisco, where she participated in the Challenging White Supremacy Workshop led by Sharon Martinas, and helped found the Catalyst Project. She continues to work for the project, which trains organizers through its core workshop called "Antiracism for Collective Liberation."

Seminal Experiences Abroad

For a number of interrelated reasons, then, college provides a critical time and place for seminal experiences that can lead to racial awareness and activism. I was surprised, however, to find that many people in the study also reported that important experiences while traveling abroad had been influential in developing their understanding of racism in the United States. A few of the older activists recalled such experiences, but the younger activists were much more likely to mention them as such travel has become more and more common. Going abroad, activists are exposed to a more critical perspective on American society and its race relations. More generally, they discover other ways of looking at the world.[15]

During his sophomore year in high school, Seth Newton went on a service trip to Tijuana with a group from a friend's Catholic church. Growing up in a relatively affluent white community in Eugene, Oregon, Seth had had little direct exposure to poverty and exploitation. This trip made a powerful impact on him, but a second trip sponsored by Border Links in his senior year proved even more pivotal. Seth witnessed the terrible working conditions for Mexicans in the *maquiladora* factories along the border, but the home visits especially moved him:

> We had a home stay there. For me, not growing up in a really poor family or growing up with racial oppression, I didn't know very directly what that feels like. To encounter folks who do and did on a very personal level and have them explain what that feels like just really had an impact on me.

Seth went on to college at Stanford but continued the trips. On a Witness for Peace trip to Nicaragua in 1997, sponsored by his Presbyterian church, Seth sat down in people's homes; they told him how U.S. imperialism was affecting them. He was surprised that they were so open and welcoming to him as an American. "It really hit me hard to have that kind of direct connection to inhumanity and humanity at the same time." He says he broke down and cried in the debriefing session.

At Stanford, Seth took courses from Nadinne Cruz, the director of the Haas Center for Public Service, who profoundly influenced him:

> The first thing I remember her telling me was that we need to be able to stop and listen to people's rage of what it feels like to live in a highly stratified society. I really looked up to her. That struck me that

you should just listen to people's rage. I was in this mindset of thinking I have to do something, and she said you have to first understand where folks are coming from. The other thing she said was, you need to understand where you are coming from and how being privileged can shape and even deform a person in a stratified society. I think that kind of blew my mind.

Seth got involved in multiracial student activism on campus. Indeed, he says he got hooked on activism. Leaving college, Seth sought a job as a union organizer so that he could get training and work directly with low-paid workers of color.

As he organizes, Seth spends a lot of time in workers' homes and continues to listen to their stories. Such direct contact provides the experiences that still stoke his anger at injustice, but he is also moved by people's courage to organize despite the threat of being fired. Meanwhile, Seth asks why more white Americans are not outraged over racial injustice:

> There is this myth and theory that if you work hard, you will make it. That is what the U.S. is all about. You pull yourself up. But that couldn't be farther from the truth from all of the incredibly hard-working people I've met in my life. I'm outraged by that. . . . I think when a person like myself with privilege asks, it forces the question, why am I not outraged about this if this is happening? White folks should be outraged about racism even if they are not a direct target of it.

In Seth's view, the operations of our current system conflict with the values of humanity and American values as well:

> People with a lot of power have created the systems in which we live. For the most part, those systems tend to deny people their fundamental humanity and the chance to live out their full potential and live a fulfilled life with the kind of dignity that I think a person deserves. That is the connection for me. This is an aspiration that I have myself and for everyone I know. Most people have that same aspiration. It is in direct conflict with the way in which society is constructed and operates today.

Seth's story suggests how issues of injustice in the United States are seen more and more to be connected internationally. It also reveals several of the themes of this chapter. His direct experiences in Mexico shocked him out of the complacency of life in the progressive world of Eugene. Both anger at the injustice he saw and the hope and spirit he found among the people there moved him. Seth says it was the combination of these direct experiences and a broader political understanding of how imperialism works imparted to him by Cruz and others that combined to cement his commitment to organizing.

Faith-based Routes to Activism

Faith communities played a role in moving a number of other activists in this study toward racial justice. Seth was virtually the only person in the group, however, whose home congregation provided a direct vehicle into activism. Most of the others, like James Capraro, reacted against what they came to see as the racialized practice of their home communities in light of their professed faith values.

Consequently, a number of the activists I interviewed looked beyond their home communities of faith. They found racial justice voices and networks within their larger faith traditions or branched out into new faith-based organizations. For example, Kate Foran was brought up in a big Catholic family in the predominantly white suburb of Tolland, outside of Hartford, Connecticut. Although they were Catholics, her parents took her to a Protestant congregation while she was growing up. Because that church did not particularly foster a sense of social justice, when Kate arrived at Mount Holyoke College, she was eager to explore new faith traditions in a variety of interfaith religious activities. These spiritual networks led her to the Catholic Worker movement, which was organizing against the Iraq war at the time. After graduating from college, Kate joined the Catholic Worker house in Hartford. The Catholic Worker movement combines assistance to poor people with antimilitarism, and that's where Kate feels "her activism and her politics and her faith really started to come together."[16]

The Catholic Worker house served an all-black neighborhood. This became Kate's first direct experience with racism; seeing first-hand the conditions of the neighborhood and the schools affected her powerfully:

> One of the epiphany moments came because there was an African American woman who was a social worker. I'd see her every week, and we would sit down and chat, and she was very nice to me. I just asked a little about her life. She had been one of the first black students in an all-white school in South Windsor, Connecticut. So I asked her, "What was that like for you?" She said, "Well, it made me more comfortable

with white people. I'm talking to you, aren't I?" And that hit me. That blew me away because I had never conceived of myself as in any way threatening. I had no idea that people could be afraid to talk to me because I was white. When I moved into the neighborhood in Hartford, which was a high-crime, high-drug area, I was more aware of the threat to me being there, but I wasn't aware of my threat to them.

I started to see that this thing is deep, and this has nothing to do with my good intentions and how much that I can say I'm not a racist. We carry these things wherever we go without even meaning to, without being aware of it. So that was an important moment. I could have easily just gone back to the suburbs and gone back to an all-white community. But I feel like those experiences made me see that the question of racial justice had to be central to my life.

Kate and her husband, Steve, discovered Word and World, a multiracial, faith-based activist network. Kate began to feel it important not just to work in a black community but also to work with and learn from African American leaders. Consequently, she and Steve moved to Greensboro, North Carolina, to run the Word and World office there and work with the Beloved Community Center led by African American activist Reverend Nelson Johnson. The center fosters a range of organizing activity, including the Truth and Reconciliation Commission, set up to address the legacy of racial violence in Greensboro.

From her Catholicism, Kate takes a commitment "to the least of these." From the Catholic Worker, she takes a commitment to live in the "abandoned places of empire." But she has moved toward Word and World to find a faith-based opportunity to organize in collaboration with communities of color. In other words, Kate has been influenced by faith traditions and institutions, but she has also chosen to follow new paths based on faith values and action.

Seminal Experiences Late in Life

The large majority of the activists in this study began their racial justice activism in their twenties. A few, however, came to activism somewhat later in life, two in their late thirties and one in her forties. Molly Munger was a successful forty-two-year-old corporate lawyer in Los Angeles when the Rodney King beating occurred in 1991. It turns out that Molly had a personal connection to the beatings that made it a more direct experience for her: She and Rodney King had gone to the same high school. Molly's friends seemed more concerned about the subsequent riot than about the police violence and racism that had caused the uprising:

> I started hearing all this racist stuff from people at dinner, and I just thought, "That's it. That does it. It really has gotten out of whack. This is really wrong, and I just can't stay living like this anymore...." It's not about the African American enraged citizenry over these horrible things that have happened. It's about the leadership of the country causing those enraging things to happen. It's people like my friends.

Molly's discomfort with the priorities of her legal community had been growing for a while, but it took the King affair to crystallize it:

> For a long time there had been this kind of syndrome: I'd read the paper, and all these horrible things would be going on in the paper. So many big things in the society didn't seem to get any kind of expertise or attention, while a very able, well-trained cadre of people making hundreds of thousands of dollars did fine embroidery on little, tiny things. It just seemed wrong, it seemed disproportionate, and it just seemed unfair.
>
> I remember working on a case and looking out over the East River. I remember having this thought that I knew more about this particular manufacturer of leotards and her dispute with her designer at that point than I knew about the entire education system of my country. But ask me anything about that particular leotard problem! I just remember thinking, "God, I don't know, can this really be right?"

Molly's concern about racial justice did have some even earlier roots, too, however. Her mother's grandfather had supported black freedmen in Mississippi in the late 1800s and was attacked by the Ku Klux Klan. Her mother wasn't a "cause-y person at all," but she supported civil rights. The doctor she married (Molly's stepfather) won election to the school board and supported integration of the schools in Pasadena. Meanwhile, Molly attended John Muir High School, the same as Rodney King. Muir was integrated, and Molly's experience there gave her hope and faith that Los Angeles could be a great city as a diverse community:

> I got very lucky that I had this experience at Muir because it was a seminal, mind-altering experience in terms of the strength that there is in diversity. It wasn't just the negative message about people aren't being treated fairly. There was also this really positive energy that came through everybody working together to make Muir a great place.

Molly left her corporate job to work for the NAACP Legal Defense Fund (LDF) against Proposition 209, the antiaffirmative action initiative. Along with colleagues she met at LDF, Molly went on to found the Advancement Project, designed to develop a new model of legal work that focuses on racial justice advocacy and poverty issues in collaboration with community organizations. Through the Advancement Project, Molly has been working to get the state to set aside money to build schools and provide more preschool facilities in poor communities, among other equity campaigns.

Conclusion

I tell Molly's story at length because, although she is atypical in coming to racial justice activism relatively late in life, the processes that influenced her are quite typical: a direct experience that caused her to see racial injustice in a clear way, a recognition that her community of friends was acting contrary to its professed values, the ignition of anger at this injustice, which led to a moral impulse to act, combined with the hope of making a difference. Earlier "seeds" of racial justice concerns crystallized for her because of a critical event. She also had social connections that provided a route into activism, in her case through the Legal Defense Fund.[17]

As we have seen, seminal experiences tend to be abrupt events that change white people's racial perspective. The experience itself does not lead to commitment. Rather, the meaning that white people attribute to this experience matters, and that is a deeply moral issue. People appear to be led toward racial justice activism when they see a contradiction between their community's deeply held values and the reality of racism. These are the kinds of moral shocks that social movement scholars have begun to identify as catalysts for other forms of activism as well. I conclude that the initial move to racial justice activism comes from what I call a moral impulse.[18]

Indeed, not a single person in the study offered an interest-based account of the start of their journey toward racial justice. In other words, no one even remotely expressed thinking along the lines of "You know, I realized that to get what my white community and I need, I should work with people of color." Nor did anyone say, "You know, I came to see that black people and white people like me have a lot in common. I never realized that before." Development of a sense of shared interest and common cause comes afterward, as will we see in later chapters.

According to activists, they experience a moral shock and develop a moral impulse through direct experience, not primarily through reading, coursework, or the media. Traditionally, scholars of social movements have focused on these cognitive dimensions while exploring in detail the kinds of "frames" that movements use to recruit members. Critical and social justice educators, for their part, also emphasize the importance of white students' learning a racial analysis. I found that developing a racial justice analysis plays a supportive role in the development of commitment over time. It provides activists with the tools for deeper understanding, but it does not appear to provide the primary motivation to act.[19]

The moral impulse to act has important emotional dimensions. Emotions are too often distrusted as something dangerous and perhaps counter to rational thinking. Rather than counterposing emotions and rational cognition, they may instead work together. As James Jasper has argued, "We become indignant (emotion) when we discover information (cognition) that violates our sense of right and wrong, thereby jeopardizing our system of meaning (morals)."[20]

Indeed, the direct experience appears important for generating anger or outrage at injustice. Helen Haste has argued that "triggering events" like the seminal experiences of white activists create a moral affect that contributes to moral thinking. In other words, for people to act, they have to do more than recognize that racism exists. They have to believe it is wrong. Values, then, are closely tied to emotion. When we care deeply about our values, we are expressing an emotional connection to them.[21]

Uncontrolled anger, of course, can be dangerous. Some community organizers use the term *cold anger* as a way to combine passion with the kind of cold, strategic calculation necessary to be effective. Indeed, the activists in this study seek to channel their anger toward productive ends.[22]

Where do the values come from that motivate activists early on? They do not appear to be new or an alternative to dominant values in any real sense. Rather, activists speak passionately of carrying out the values with which they grew up at home, in their church, and in their country. Some put religious values first, but all seem to reference broader American values of justice and equality. Indeed, they perceive the reality of racism to be in conflict with these deeply held values.

As mentioned earlier, and this is a crucial point, the design of this study does not allow us to determine why these white Americans—and not others who witness racism directly—respond with moral shock, but it can show us how such shocks can move whites to work for the cause of racial justice. Understanding the way dominant ideologies work helps us see that these shocks may well be a necessary catalyst for whites in crossing over the color line. Moreover, since virtually all fifty subjects reported seminal experiences and derived moral meaning from them, we can have some confidence in the conclusion that the first step down the road to racial justice commitment comes from a moral impulse.

Colleges are key places for the early development of racial justice commitment. Young white people meet professors and students who can help them interpret seminal experiences and deepen a racial justice perspective. Many also find their first opportunities for activism at these institutions. But colleges provide something more as well. There, young people who grew up in white communities often meet people of color for the first time. It turns out that these relationships have a profound impact on white activists. In the next chapter I turn to a close examination of the effects on white activists of relationships with people of color.

CHAPTER THREE

From Do-Gooder to Deeper
Commitment
Relationships with People of Color

One of the most profound lessons that I've ever learned, and I use it in everything that I teach, and I learned it from the IAF culture, is that relationships are intentional and deliberate. Diverse relationships are not going to happen to me. If I want them, I have to create them.

—Tony Fleo

You've got to have the relationship with somebody to understand that what hurts you hurts me. If you don't have a relationship with people, it doesn't hurt as much.

—Janet Morrison

PENDA HAIR GREW up in an all-white neighborhood in Knoxville, Tennessee, during the sixties. In high school she had a powerful seminal experience that generated the kind of moral impulse we saw in the last chapter. Penda and her family attended a Southern Baptist church. Penda took the values her faith tradition preached seriously and joined a youth choir that sought to recruit new kids to their Sunday school. It turned out, though, that the congregation had an official whites-only policy:

A group of high schoolers in the church, led by a youth leader that the church had hired, formed a choir. We sang at other churches, traveling on a bus that we raised the money to buy. We decided we would use the bus to go out on Sunday mornings and bring children or adults to our church. We were going to be little evangelists. Well, we got a great response. We had all of these kids on our bus coming to Sunday school, and the majority were black. I don't know how long it went on before somebody invoked the whites-only policy that had been on the books for years. There was a vote, and this time it was much debated because our entire youth group was in favor of ending this policy and couldn't believe that they were going to cut off our bus. You know, we were doing what the church had taught us to do.

So the church voted again, and they voted to exclude African Americans again. And that had a huge impact on me. I would say that was probably defining. I'm starting to cry now thinking about it because we had to go tell those kids that we couldn't come and take them to church anymore.

I definitely remember thinking that this is unfair, certainly not letting these kids into the church is unfair and wrong, and that it was clear to me that black people were treated worse than white people and that that was wrong.

Shortly after the vote, Penda and her friends switched to another congregation and continued their bus evangelism. After high school Penda attended the University of Tennessee and was song leader on the bus all through college. She says, however, that her understanding of race didn't grow much during college. She graduated in three years, focused on building an academic record that would enable her to get into a top law school. In sixth grade she sensed that she could help people, so she decided to become a lawyer and never deviated from that goal.

Penda went on to Harvard Law School and was influenced by its progressive political climate. In her first year there she studied constitutional law and learned about the NAACP Legal Defense Fund (LDF). She quickly decided that she wanted to practice civil rights law. She clerked for Supreme Court Justice Harry Blackmun, who a few years earlier had penned the majority *Roe v. Wade* opinion on abortion rights. Eventually she landed a job teaching civil rights law at Columbia University. Through Columbia's connection with LDF director Jack Greenberg, she took a job at the defense fund and eventually went to work at its Washington, DC, office.

Penda credits her experiences at LDF with developing her understanding of and commitment to racial justice:

That's where I really learned about race. Before that I see myself as this do-gooder who had some instincts that were toward fairness, but I had no understanding of how race really worked in this country. There were a lot of personal experiences at LDF but also a lot of eye-opening ways of seeing how race has impacted people's lives.

Penda speaks powerfully about what she learned from her relationships with her African American clients:

My first case was a claim of promotion discrimination by the postal service in Jacksonville, Florida. My first client that I put on the witness stand was a person named James Douglas, who had applied for something like twenty-five or thirty promotions at the post office. He was a mail carrier, African American. I went to his house, met his family, and talked to him about all these jobs. He had been in the army in World War II. He had gotten a college degree and a master's degree, and the only job he could get was working as a mail carrier.

It occurred to me that my father did not have a college degree or a master's degree, was roughly the same age as Mr. Douglas, had come out of the army, and had gotten this nice job at Union Carbide. He worked his way up through the ranks. We always thought we were deserving because my father worked hard. He got up at 5:30 in the morning to make sure he was there on time. He worked the swing shift, which means that he worked one week 8 to 4 and the next week 4 to midnight and the next week midnight to 8. That was a hard life for us, we thought.

But when I saw Mr. Douglas's life, it was like, "Oh, I'm privileged." For the first time I understood in a different way that I was racially privileged. Because of my father's ability to get that job at Union Carbide, I got put in the best high school in the city where we lived and got the education that allowed me to go to Harvard. I could see that Mr. Douglas's kids probably didn't have as many of those opportunities. I saw the intergenerational effect in a personal way, but I also saw it in a structural way in all the promotions that he had been denied and the way that other people in the class action case were kept back.[1]

As much as she learned from her clients, Penda also mentions the power of her relationships with her African American colleagues. She often worked on cases as part of an interracial team of lawyers. She tells the following story about an event that occurred during the same class action case in Florida:

> One night we were in the car driving home from a class action meeting with a white man and black woman in the front seat, Sam and Barbara, and a white woman and black man in the back seat, me and an expert witness. We were stopped by a police car. I remember it was on a dark road, and there didn't seem to be much around. We were driving by railroad tracks. Barbara and Sam freaked out. We looked like two interracial couples. The tension and fear became so palpable in that car immediately. "Oh, my God, you know, this is lynching territory."
>
> At first I was totally oblivious. To me, policemen were benign. They give you speeding tickets every once in a while, but otherwise they protected you. I just remember that feeling of fear sweeping through that car, and I became afraid also. We were sitting there in the dark, and these bright lights were shining from behind. Then at some point I hear Sam, or maybe it was Barbara, say from the front seat, "The police officer is a brother," which meant he was black. The police officer was black. Then, of course, the tension all goes away. He gave us some routine warning. We had a light missing or something. But everybody else in that car knew to be afraid. I didn't even know to be afraid. So it was one of the first times I started seeing victimization from the other side of the color line.[2]

Penda built particularly close personal and political friendships with several black women lawyers at LDF, including Lani Guinier and Dayna Cunningham. Because of these relationships, she started taking racism personally. One powerful experience occurred when President Bill Clinton nominated Lani Guinier to be the assistant attorney general for civil rights. Conservatives immediately attacked her as a "quota queen." Clinton quickly withdrew her nomination in what many saw as a humiliating dismissal:[3]

> Lani was attacked because of her views on voting rights, and so it was personal in the sense that, well, I'm a voting rights lawyer. I have the same views as Lani. If she can be attacked and humiliated publicly, then that's essentially saying the same thing about me. And then it was personal in the sense that Lani was staying at my house part of the time when she would come down to do her DC round of meetings. I remember I had just had a baby. At the time, when the newspapers were writing all these things about how antiwhite she was,

I remember her sitting in my house in the rocking chair, holding my white, blond-headed baby. And it was just surreal. How can this happen? How can they paint a picture of her that is so beyond reality, and yet they get away with it?

The humiliation of Lani Guinier affected Penda deeply. Subsequent battles with the Clinton administration over both the welfare reform bill and affirmative action led Penda and a set of LDF colleagues to feel the limitations of legal strategies in isolation from organized power in communities:

We were very angry with the Clinton administration. Our thinking was, if this is what you get with Democrats who are supposed to be sympathetic, we need better. We felt like we didn't have any power to force the Clinton administration to be better. They could thumb their noses at African Americans, essentially, which they did on the crime bill, the welfare bill, and Lani Guinier's nomination. All of that turmoil made us think we needed to do something different.

Penda left LDF and subsequently formed the Advancement Project with Connie Rice and Molly Munger in 1999. The project aims to partner with community organizations, offering expertise in legal issues, communications work, and research to influence policy and public discourse and to foster the development of a new racial justice movement.

———

If white people do not personally experience racial discrimination, how can they come to an understanding of the reality of racism and develop a firmer commitment to work for racial justice? People of color develop their understanding of racism in part from their own experience and that of their family members, neighbors, and friends. But white people do not face racial discrimination. Given the high levels of segregation, the extended family and friendship networks of whites are typically also white. The media, meanwhile, continue to reinforce racial stereotypes. It is not surprising, then, that white Americans find it difficult to grasp the experiences of people of color in dealing with racism.

In the last chapter, we saw that many white activists start on the road to racial justice through direct experiences that generate a moral impulse to act. Yet, if we stop at a moral impulse, we are left with altruism. These are the do-gooders that Penda talked about, those who act for others. In this chapter we ask how whites can deepen their commitment by building relationships with people of color and working with them to address racism.

If chapter two shows that white activists can develop an ethic of justice, this chapter shows that they can also develop an ethic of care. Relationships with people of color are a key link in the development of an understanding of racism and a commitment that makes the political issue of racial justice personal. Penda's growth from a do-gooder to a committed justice activist illustrates this process. The first part of this chapter examines the various ways that relationships increase white people's understanding of racism. The second part discusses how activists create close bonds with people of color and come to care about racism.

Learning about Racism through Relationships

Virtually every white activist in this study—forty-six of fifty—mentioned learning about racism through relationships with people of color.[4] In chapter two Mark Soler talked about the emotional impact of seeing the horrific treatment of black and brown young men in juvenile detention centers. Here, he talks about what he has learned from his relationships with his colleagues at the Youth Law Center:

> I have a very close relationship with the guy I work with now. He's African American. We spend a lot of time in the car driving to work sites. We end up talking about everything, about our lives and our spouses and everything like that. Some of the most interesting conversations we've had have been about his son. He's got a six-year-old son. He's been dealing with the issue of what to say to his son about racism in this country. It leads my friend to talk about his own experiences when he was first aware of being treated differently. He has very black skin, so he is probably treated differently than African Americans with light skin and is comfortable with me enough to talk very honestly about those kinds of experiences. That's something I can't get from reading a book or from talking to white people.

With this colleague and others, Mark ran a series of discussions about race:

> We did a focus group in Baltimore of African American men and found that within five minutes every one of them had had exactly the same experience of being stopped by the police for no reason whatsoever. Every one! The person leading the discussion was a black man, and he also had had the same experience. These were middle-class men with college educations.

Like Penda, these relationships pushed Mark to compare his own experiences as a white person with those of his colleagues of color. He tells this story about his own son:

> When my son was in high school, they instituted a curfew in DC. If you were under eighteen, you had to be home at a certain time on the weekends. My son regularly violated the curfew, and I used to tell him, "If you get picked up by the cops, you're going to get in trouble." He looked at me, and he said, "The cops don't enforce the curfew where we live. We live in the northwest part of DC, which is a largely white area. They're enforcing the curfew in southeast, which is an all-black section. You know that's where the cops are going. They don't care about white kids walking around." That's absolutely true. And it was a good lesson. I knew it, but I hadn't realized it quite in relationship to my own life.

In chapter two David Utter, the head of the Juvenile Justice Project of Louisiana, spoke about the impact of seeing plantation-like conditions at the state prison in Angola. David's understanding of racism was also deepened by the experiences of clients he has defended:

> One of my very first capital cases was a guy named Tom Morrison, an African American out of Lake Charles, Louisiana. There's no question that Tom killed three white people when they were sleeping. We got a jury to agree to not execute Tom, but at the end of that case, I got a letter from Tom. He is depressed. He's going to die in prison even though there's strong statistical evidence that by the time he's forty or fifty, we could safely release him, and he would never commit another crime. He'll never hurt anybody, right? But he's going to die in jail.
>
> Tom grew up as a light-skinned African American in Lake Charles. His father was passing as a white man in Lake Charles and had three or four children. When Tom's brothers and sisters started to exhibit characteristics that indicated that they were black, Tom's father could no longer pass as a white man, and he left the family. Tom was five or six years old. The family went from middle class, passing as a white family in Lake Charles, to the depths of poverty. They went from having food on the table, clothes, and a decent school to picking food out of dumpsters to eat. Tom's mom lost it. Tom became a drug addict and started acting out in school. Smart kid but failed out of high school and just went into this style of cocaine addiction. He ended up killing

three people, taking their tools and hocking them for thirty bucks to buy crack.

I certainly couldn't look at it with any honesty and say that there's any justice in the fact that this guy is going to die in prison when there were probably a hundred different points at which society could have intervened and done something to save him.[5]

Union organizer Seth Newton, who spoke in chapter two about visiting *maquiladora* factories in Mexico as a student, works closely with workers of color on union organizing drives and listens to their stories. Seth learned about life as an undocumented immigrant through these relationships:

At one of the hotels I organized there was this woman who was a housekeeper in the hotel. I went and knocked on her door, sat in her house, and through the conversation she told me about her experience crossing the border and the tremendous adversity that she went through because she was committed to feeding her family. She said it very specifically that way—that she needed to feed her family. She climbed in a trunk stuffed with several other people. In one case the car actually flipped over while they were in the trunk. After being found a couple of times and brought back across the border, she made it across. She then sent for her kids. One of them crossed in the desert and was lost for a month in the Arizona desert.

He also came to see the strengths of people in communities of color:

After crossing the border, she spent years and years and years working for this extremely rich hotel company, cleaning sixteen suites in a day. After one of those days, she was willing to call five of her coworkers to ask them to stand up behind her when they went and marched into the boss's office. It was an incredibly scary thing, obviously, for them to do, each one of them being undocumented. Their boss had sent each of them a letter saying there is something wrong with your Social Security number, and you have to correct this or you're fired. That showed her leadership and readiness to stand up for herself and her coworkers.

Seth traces his passion and commitment to racial justice to these relationships:

As an organizer I'm learning the hell they've been through and also the dreams that they have for themselves and family. That is what secures my commitment over and over and over again to racial justice work and to grassroots organizing and worker organizing.

These relationships are not always comfortable. Sometimes they force whites to confront their own history of privilege and their racial blind spots, including their own stereotypes. When colleagues and friends of color directly challenge white activists, these incidents often prove to be particularly powerful learning experiences.[6]

Jim Schutze began his newspaper career with the *Detroit Free Press*. Prizing his skills of observation and his determination to be objective, the following incident with Sarah, a black woman reporter at the paper, as well as a friend and colleague, had a profound impact on his understanding of racism:

> I remember once we played this game. The building was an old-fashioned, thirties'-style high-rise in downtown Detroit without air conditioning. I remember we would raise the windows in the summer in the newsroom and play a game of observing people on the street. I was looking out one day, and I saw this old, old man who was so drunk I thought that he couldn't walk. I made a crack about how could you be that drunk and that old? He was black, and she came to the window, and she said, "Why do you think he's drunk?" And I said, "Well, come on. He hasn't missed a parking meter yet!"
>
> She said, "Well, we're both reporters. Let's go see." We went out, and the end of the story was that he was not drunk at all. He had not taken his medication. He'd wandered out of his daughter's home and gotten on a bus. He was lost. He was terrified. She called the daughter, who showed up in this Volvo station wagon and embraced both of us, saying, "You're such wonderful people." Sarah was almost saying, "Well, don't embrace him!"
>
> We went back across the street, and I wanted to explain myself. She said, "Don't. You have nothing to explain because you don't get this. You're pretty good at looking at people. If he'd been white, you would have noticed that he was well dressed, that he wasn't falling like a drunk. He was falling hard. He wasn't rolling. And he didn't have a slurred face. He had a frightened face." She said, "You just saw black skin, and so your powers of observation stopped. I'm not calling you a racist, Jim. I'm just telling you you're a white guy, and your perceptions have all to do with that." And those kinds of little lessons were really, really important to me, really helped.[7]

Later Jim moved to Dallas, where he became an award-winning reporter for his writings on racial politics. However, he attributes much of his understanding of race to the relationships he formed during the time African Americans were asserting their power in Detroit in the sixties and seventies.

The Power of Stories

Relationships are powerful because they take white activists beyond the cognitive dimension and connect them to the personal and emotional levels. In other words, they make a statistical understanding of racial discrimination direct and real in the lives of people of color that activists know personally. As Mark Soler says, you "can't get that from reading a book." One key way this occurs is through sharing personal stories.

Tony Fleo grew up in an Italian American Catholic family in a white township outside of New Castle, Pennsylvania, in the sixties and early seventies. His father was a union carpenter, and Tony grew up hearing stories of discrimination against Italian immigrants. His father called the rich whites "cake eaters" because they could afford to eat cake and not just bread. Speaking of the level of segregation in his life, Tony says, "I don't believe I ever actually spoke to a black person until I was a junior in high school." Nonetheless, his family always identified with the underdog and seemed to support the civil rights movement. Tony was brought up to believe that his family was on the side of justice and that racism was wrong. However, when he was nineteen, he got his first lesson in the deep-rooted nature of racism, a seminal experience for him:

> When I was nineteen, my oldest sister, who was living in California, sent a letter to my father telling him that she was going to marry a black man. I saw the excruciating, overwhelming pain that that caused my father. I saw what was an otherwise very religious, very good man, very hard-working man respond in a way that was very hard for me to fathom. My response to the marriage was, "Well, he's a good man. She loves him, so what?" My father's response was dramatically different. He was very angry. I heard words and language and descriptive words come out of his mouth that I never even knew existed. He refused to accept it, he refused to speak to her, and he refused to go to the wedding.
>
> I can remember having a conversation with him. I said, "Well, I don't get this, Dad. I mean, it was those white nuns that you sent me to who taught me that all of God's children are created equal. They taught me that there are no differences between whites and blacks, so this is hard for me to understand. Were they lying or are you lying?" That was the first experience where I really had to say, "Wow." I really had to look at this and see how deeply it ran and start to understand it, start to get an experience of it.

Tony went off to college, earned a graduate degree in counseling psychology, and took a job in a Fort Worth, Texas, parish that served many Mexican immigrants. Because of what Tony calls "the power of the immigrant story in my life," he wanted to work with an immigrant community. Needing a better-paying job to support his growing family, Tony took a position as director of family ministries at All Saints, a predominantly white and affluent parish in north Dallas. Through this affiliation Tony got involved with Dallas Area Interfaith (DAI), an affiliate of the Industrial Areas Foundation (IAF) organizing network. At DAI Tony began working with African American leaders for the first time. Few groups brought whites, blacks, and Latinos together in racially polarized Dallas. Tony recounted a personal high point when a group of DAI leaders came to lobby the city council. One councilor wanted to call extra security because he thought the three racial groups would end up in a fight. Tony said, "No, no, no. We're here together. But we're here against you!" Tony says he found the diversity and caliber of the DAI leaders "really energizing."

Tony built strong relationships with black leaders like DAI cochair Reverend Gerald Britt, but there was tension, too. Tony recounted perhaps another seminal experience when an African American religious scholar, Professor James Cone, came to speak to interfaith organizers and leaders across the state. Tony was angered by Professor Cone's blistering critique of the racism of the white church since it was the white nuns at his church who had told him to attend his sister's wedding:

> I can remember being very angry listening to him, talking about how the white church didn't do anything about race. I finally raised my hand and said, "That's just not my experience. It was the white nuns who started me on this whole path. It was the white church that taught me that racism was wrong." I obviously had to be attentive to their perspective of how the white church let them down, but on the other hand, in my own personal story it was the white church that really lifted me up in this regard.

However, when Tony tried to equate discrimination against Italians with antiblack racism, things came to a head. African American leaders argued that "the color of a person's skin really does matter":

> My story was, yes, there's racism, there's oppression. But my family was oppressed, they couldn't get jobs, either. There were issues in the school, and the teachers hated them because they were Italians and blah-blah-blah. At some point you overcome that. Well, their

response to me was, yes, at some point you can overcome that because your skin blends in with the dominant culture. My skin will never blend in with the dominant culture, and therefore overcoming that becomes more nearly impossible.

Tony slowly began to realize he had been in denial:

While I could relate to that paradigm of oppression, what I walk around with, in terms of blinders, is that this is America, and anybody can be anything that they want. The experience of interacting with African Americans in a leadership role and then in one-on-one conversations was that that's really not true. The color of a person's skin really does matter. Having to hear about how that matters really took down any denial that I had. There was a certain amount of denial about the American dream that I possessed that clearly is not the experience of a lot of African Americans.

...It's clear that you walk around with a denial of racism. Having those conversations over time diminishes that denial, and you start to see the world differently. You start to see it from another person's perspective, and you realize it is not the same. It's just not the same for me as it is for an African American.

The IAF network places a big emphasis on having people share personal stories as a way to build relationships. Tony believes that personal stories work because they engage the emotions, as well as the intellect. Even though Tony doesn't experience racial prejudice himself, he has found a way to connect to the pain in the stories of the people he knows. Meanwhile, the power of learning through relationship and of seeing racism from the point of view of people of color pushed Tony to make racial justice a central focus of his work. He later ran for Dallas city council on a platform that promised to bring the city's racial groups together.

Learning through stories emerged as a prominent theme with many of the activists I interviewed. Katherine Carter is the principal of a small, autonomous elementary school established in Oakland by another community organizing group, the Oakland Communities Organization. Katherine finds relationships and stories important for understanding the everyday experiences of people of color. She recounted an incident that happened when she and an African American colleague took the school's kindergarteners on a field trip to the wealthy community of Sausalito:

There was an African American male teacher with me at that time that was very well educated, extremely cultured. He is a professional actor. This is someone who grew up in an intellectual household. He happened to be one of the last people to get off the bus. The person who met us at the museum assumed he was the bus driver. He tried to correct her, and she still assumed he was the bus driver. It wasn't just a quick, honest mistake. It took her a long time to get it. It wasn't until I stepped in and said, "No, this is the other teacher." That experience stayed with me. It doesn't matter how much education he has, what his life experiences have been, what his background is. Would anyone ever assume I was the bus driver? No.

A lot of white people think that kind of stuff stopped happening fifty years ago. I think about my friend Adrianna, who was my college roommate. She is Mexican American. She told me stories of her family driving up into Oregon and not being served in restaurants. She is my age. I didn't think people my age experienced that.

Stories are powerful humanizers. If racism dehumanizes people of color, then relationships and stories provide a venue for white people to understand people of color not as stereotypical representations but as complex human beings. As young activist Emily Zeanah says, "Through stories, people become more human. You can begin to empathize and therefore bridge the gap that is in yourself."

Enhancing Conditions

Many whites can have interactions with people of color without being led to an enhanced understanding of racism. Whites can have various kinds of relationships with people of color at work or in school, for example, and only in some cases will these connections contribute to building the kind of commitment to racial justice that has occurred with the subjects in this study. Indeed, the design of this study cannot tell us why these whites rather than others changed because of their personal associations. Rather, from this study we learn how relationships can have the impact they sometimes do. At the same time, however, we can consider the kinds of conditions that appear to be more conducive to white people's learning from relationships.

First of all, whites will likely learn more if people of color are willing to share their experience of race and racism. Susan Sandler, an education advocate in San Francisco, said she really learned about racism the year she began a social work program at San Francisco State University (SFSU). In chapter two Susan talked about the impact on her of listening to Margo Okazawa-Rey and students of color talking openly about their racial experiences, making it a watershed year for her. Her earlier experiences with people of color did not teach her much because they had rarely discussed race with her:

> When I was twenty-six, the whole racial justice thing all happened that year. But I had several interracial relationships before then, and they didn't really affect my understanding of racism. The people that I was in relationships with, they didn't have an open politics about it. They didn't really share their experiences of racism with me in any systematic way, or maybe I just didn't have my antennae open.

Susan, like many of the activists in this study, did not want to assign to people of color the responsibility of teaching whites about racism. Nevertheless, the fact remains that whites can benefit from a powerful learning experience when people of color share their experiences of racism with them.

Second, learning appears more likely to take place in contexts of relative equality and through relationships with strong and assertive leaders of color. Madeline Talbott is the director of Action Now, a community organizing group in Chicago that works to build power in African American and Latino communities around issues like affordable housing and school reform. She spent her teenage years in an all-white community in Portland, Oregon, where she attended Catholic schools. She told this story of joining a social action youth group with black kids in the early seventies:[8]

> They put us in contact with African American teenagers who had been thinking about stuff and were angry and moving. It was really a jolting experience. We spent a weekend hanging out with some African American kids who were on the other side of Portland from where I lived, the east side. It was really exciting for me to meet kids who weren't taking the back seat at all. They were aggressive and smart, and they were really pushing us because we were kind of naive.
>
> I realized that my sole experience of black people was the couple who were very quiet in whatever class I was ever in, who never said anything, never did anything; you know, just tried to get through the day. I realized how dramatically different it was to be around kids who felt powerful and absolutely equal. I realized, gee, I had never seen black people as equal despite my purported commitment to justice, and it came as a jolt to me.

While a student at Harvard, Madeline got involved in a welfare rights organization and built relationships with an activist group of African American welfare mothers. She then joined the staff of the community organizing network ACORN and offered this account of her first assignment in Pine Bluff, Arkansas. The city was planning to take land owned by a number of black people to widen a road, and she had been working with an African American organizer, R. Walker, to bring black residents to a meeting. One of them, Theo Jefferson, had agreed to speak:

> This was my first ACORN action ever. I'd never been to one. I didn't know what they looked like. A white engineer got up to speak in the city council room. He took the oath, and he started to speak at the hearing. The questioner starting asking him questions, and he started giving his degrees. Mr. Jefferson stood up, and he said, "I know you got your fancy degrees, and I haven't finished the fifth grade, but I can't go to the bathroom on the highway. We need indoor bathrooms, and you can sit down." And the engineer got up and left. The place went into an uproar. It was just a priceless moment for me as an organizer to see the guy who didn't have more than a fifth-grade education take on the engineer and beat him.
>
> A lot of this antiracist work really comes down to white people figuring out what their role is vis-à-vis black people. That started to set the tone for what that role would be. I could support it. I could be in the background, but black people themselves had to lead it and were ready to and were capable of it, more capable than I would have ever dreamed, and that was important.

Madeline has continued to work and build close relationships with strong leaders of color, an experience she says most white people rarely have.

Finally, and perhaps this point is rather obvious, the white person needs to be open to listening and learning. This is not always easy, especially when people of color may express anger at their treatment by a white-dominated society. Working together for a common purpose, as we saw in Tony Fleo's account, gives white activists a reason to stop and listen. Indeed, these stories make it clear that, when white activists are working together over time with people of color, not just having superficial conversations, the personal relationships they forge have their strongest impact.

Reciprocity in Relationship

Working together suggests a degree of reciprocity in the relationships between white activists and people of color. Few white activists describe themselves as "sitting at the knee" of folks of color in a one-way relationship.

Indeed, if white activists do not come to the relationship with something to give, why would it be worth the time of people of color to share their experiences with them?

Industrial Areas Foundation organizer Sister Christine Stephens emphasized the importance of reciprocity:

> In my experience it really doesn't happen unless you meet people face to face and get to know them because it's all head otherwise. We're dealing with one another in a reciprocal way. I'm interested in them; they're interested in me. I listen to their stories; they listen to my stories. We're doing something together.

However, it took Christine a while to find a way to build those kinds of connections. Christine grew up in a working-class family in an all-white neighborhood in Houston in the fifties. She said she grew up "union first, Democratic Party second, and Catholic Church third" and always knew "that the Dixiecrats and people like that in Texas were enemies of the working class. More than Catholic, my mother brought me up to be working class." After attending a Catholic college, Christine chose to become a woman religious and joined the Congregation of Divine Providence. She was sent to teach at McGinnis High School in Oklahoma City, an integrated, co-ed Catholic high school. The midsixties were turbulent times, and the teacher Christine got a lesson in the black experience from her African American students:

> They talked to me about how they looked at the world, how they looked at the civil rights movement. As much as you can see things through another person's eyes, I began to see through their eyes. They talked to me about their struggles. They talked to me about what they were having to go through. What it meant. They liked politics, and they liked history, which were the things that I was teaching. They were interested in what I was interested in, too, but they were also giving me a broader dimension.
>
> They really took me under their wing and tutored me. I was teaching them, but they were also teaching me, and it was in that period of time that I decided that I wanted to do something full time in an African American community.

Christine turned down a prestigious offer to become dean of students at a Catholic college and went to Natchitoches, Louisiana, to run a school for African Americans. However, the school closed, and she was sent instead to teach at an integrated Catholic high school. At the time, whites were fleeing the neighborhoods they were living in to avoid desegregation in the public schools, and her parochial school began accepting many more of those white kids. So, instead of teaching black kids, Christine found herself teaching these white students. In protest, Christine and the other religious withdrew from the school.

Christine ended up back in Houston running a social service center, where she met Ernesto (Ernie) Cortes, who was building an IAF organization in the city. She now found her anti-Hispanic racial views challenged by her relationship with Ernie:

> In Texas the racism against Hispanics has been as virulent as the racism against African Americans, and my own internalization of that racism—having grown up in Texas—was something that I needed to deal with just like I needed to deal with it about African Americans.
>
> When I started going into organizing with Ernie Cortes, I got really challenged. Really challenged! Frankly, I was surprised at how smart Ernie was. I remember one time he went to some west side church—the west side is very white in Houston. Some guy really came after Ernie, and it was just clear that part of the offense that Ernie did to this guy was that he was smart. Mexicans aren't supposed to be smart. For me, that's how I change my own stereotypes. When people surprise me by not fitting my stereotypes, and I think, my God, where did I get those stereotypes? I can deal with the stereotypes and break them down when I deal with real people.

Christine felt that personal relationships within the context of organizing helped her to move beyond broad stereotypes:

> I know that there is a broad category. You can talk about the African American community. But it really is meaningless when you're dealing with this particular person and this particular congregation and this particular group of African Americans. I could still be in an all-white world, thinking just these wonderful thoughts about how we need to be more just and less racist. But if I were existing in an all-white world, I wouldn't be any closer to ending racism. It's all in the individual people that you meet and the work you do together to build power.

For Christine, the reciprocity in these relationships proved important to the learning that occurs through the sharing of stories:

> The only way that you can really go across differences that divide us is through the stories that we tell to one another about our

experiences.... I, too, have stories of pain and loss and sorrow and lost opportunities. I've seen my parents struggle. My dad because he was not very well educated and my mom because she was ill. And so it's accepting that I, too, have a story that can connect.

Reciprocity suggests an active engagement by whites in relationship. Teacher and activist Bob Peterson, like many others in the study, pointed out that, from his experience, people of color want to see that a white person is open to learning; however, they also want to work with someone who has integrity. Bob speaks of what he learned from Clara, an older black community activist, when he was involved in desegregation battles in Milwaukee public schools in the seventies. A different group of black activists challenged Bob's position on the issue, and he started caving in:

> Clara said, "Look, you've got to stand up for what you believe in. People will judge you on the basis of what you say and what you do. Don't be so obsessed with skin color that you actually do things that are racist because of skin color." And that's taught me well. One of the things I learned under her [Clara's] guidance was to not be liberal— not to be a racist in a liberal form of just agreeing with black people because they're black.

Making It Personal

Relationships do more than teach whites about racism. They create the bonds with people of color that help whites feel that the issue of racism is personal to them. The whites in this study speak about the power of relationships to create an ethic of caring, which helps promote commitment not just to a cause but also to real people.[9]

Josh Kern, founder of the Thurgood Marshall Academy, a charter high school in Washington, DC, has worked hard to build relationships with students, their parents, and members of the community around the school. In chapter two, he talked of his experiences teaching at Ballou High School, which led him to dedicate his life to this charter-school initiative. Here he speaks about the humanizing relationships that have helped him overcome his stereotypes:

> You can only maintain stereotypes if you keep an arm's-length distance. Once you've had sustained, intimate interaction with people, with African Americans, with poor people, whatever, it's just hard to

see them as stereotypically lazy, stupid, whatever, unmotivated. You see them for who they are: people who have issues like you have issues and are working hard to try to overcome them.

These relationships have not only challenged his stereotypes but also altered his own connection with issues of racism. He uses as an example his experience of being with other whites who were telling racist jokes:

Six years ago it wouldn't have affected me in any real way. It just would have been like, eh—it's neither here nor there. But now it affects me because I'm intimately involved with this community. So if it's hurtful, it hurts me because of how much time I'm putting in here. I also think it hurts me because it's an issue of integrity. I can't be doing this and then later in the day listen to an off-color joke about blacks. It can't be. It just doesn't work. That's obviously going to be uncomfortable for me if I just spent ten hours fighting the fight.

Lewis Pitts is a children's rights lawyer in Durham, North Carolina. He spent many years traveling around the South fighting civil rights cases with local African American leaders. In this story, he relates a little bit of the flavor of those times:

Sleeping in the home where Emma Gresham, the retired school teacher, and her husband live in Podunk, Georgia, outskirts of Augusta, it's 7:30 in the morning. She's making breakfast, and we're getting ready to go to some meeting about struggling to get the movement going. She's on the telephone, talking to maybe a state representative or a newspaper reporter, and stirring the grits, and leaning over and pulling biscuits out; she put sugar in the biscuits to make them good. You can't put a price tag on that. Getting to know her and be a part of that, and having her hug me, and me hug her, and replicate that with all these characters that are out there. That's what I've gotten out of this, man. So when I use that word "solidarity" with people, it really means something.

Because of these relationships, Lewis says he can "feel a little bit of that pain":

Surely the human is capable and programmed not to have to experience the oppression before it can respond to oppression. What's that saying, if somebody says that we won't get justice until everybody is victimized by it? Surely it's not that. Surely we can. By being in it with black people, we get as close as we can to feeling a little bit of that pain. You start to feel black or think black. Then it's not an academic understanding of inequality. It's as close as we can get to an actual experiencing of that inequality. Then you can respond to it more.

An ethic of caring is strong in the African American community, according to Lewis, and he picked some of that up "by osmosis," by being immersed himself in the community:

> I can be around and in these meetings and begin to see what it's like when they talk about working with children. I probably can't put words to it, but I have a feeling of that proverb, it takes a village to raise a child, and how that's being implemented. Because you hear, boy, the aunts are doing this, and so-and-so's not even an aunt, but gosh, she's feeding and taking care. It's a network there of connectedness that I don't think white folks have. "Save the kids"—that would be a lot different phrase to me if I'd only read about it and not felt like I'd observed it and then by osmosis picked it up.

Some of the white activists in the study had had romantic interracial relationships with people of color.[10] These kinds of relationships seem to lead to even closer personal identification with the plight of people of color. Educator activist Christine Clark, for example, is married to an African American man. She is careful, however, about disclosing that fact in her work:

> I often don't disclose my marriage because, if I do, it makes people think that that's why I do what I do. White students think, oh, she has a black husband. That's why she thinks this way. Certainly my knowledge or my understanding of racism has been profoundly deepened and broadened because of my marriage and my relationship to him and his family. I see things that I probably wouldn't have seen and learn things that I probably wouldn't have learned had I not had that intimate level of a relationship.

According to Christine, relationships, especially (but not exclusively) romantic ones, can lead to a profound identification:

> I think of making the other us, the quote by Richard Rorty, making the other us and not them. There's a part of me that really tries to look at it that way...Black people are members of my family. My family are black people, like in a personal way. I guess when people talk about black people, they're talking about me because it's my family.

Learning to Care

We have seen how white activists learn to care about racism through caring about real people of color. Nearly a third of the activists in my study, however, mentioned a slightly different connection to communities of color through their relationships. They said they discovered a certain warmth and community feeling that they found missing from their experience in the white world. Chicago community organizer Madeline Talbott calls it "enwrapment":[11]

> When I started organizing years ago, what I found knocking on doors and meeting new people in low-income communities, there are cultures in some neighborhoods that are so welcoming and so warm that it feels like a great sense of community out there. You don't really find that in many places in America, it seems to me. I grew up on army bases and military places, where there was a strong sense of community, but I don't find that anywhere else. Where I do find it is in communities of color, for whatever reason.
>
> There is a kind of joy of living in lower-income communities that doesn't seen to be quite as present in other communities. That's one of the very wonderful advantages of this kind of work for me. There's the anger about the injustice on the one side and the ability to move on that; that seems critical for me. Then there's this wonderful, warm sort of "enwrapment," I almost want to say, of having connections and networks and people who take care of you that I really love about it.

Christine Clark said that she's learned a lot about caring from her husband's African American family and from her work in communities of color:

> I learn a lot about what it means to be a good person, what it means to be a caring person, and to do that in a way that is not superficial but sincere. To understand that what you do is much less important in most African American communities, especially if they're economically challenged communities, than what kind of a child you are. Do you help your neighbors? Do you help your family? How do you treat people? My in-laws could probably give a shit about what I do for a living. But they certainly taught me a lot of lessons about how I treat people, how I treat them, what's acceptable in terms of polite, respectful interaction.

Ed Shurna, the executive director of the Chicago Homeless Coalition, was trained as an Alinsky community organizer. In an African American neighborhood on the west side of Chicago in the eighties he helped build a community organization that fought the construction of a new football stadium for the Chicago Bears. During this effort, Ed developed a close relationship with one of the African American leaders of the group, Mabel Manning, who was an elderly woman:

> There was something about her that was really powerful and really loving at the same time, really strong. I asked, "Mabel, how are you so fiery, and how are you so warm at the same time? Where did you come from? Where did you grow up?" She said, "I came over in the early sixteen hundreds on a slave ship." She was a poet, too, so she talked this way. I said, "No, Mabel, I am talking about where you actually grew up." She said, "No, you got to understand me. That is where I come from; that is where my roots are."
>
> What is the connection between people that really struggled really hard and overcame so many things and then had such grace? Is it something in their spirituality? I asked her what she did every day. She said she woke up every morning at four and read the Bible for an hour. Then she went outside to talk to the petticoat girls who were coming home from work. Petticoat girls are what she called the prostitutes. She said, "I would like them to come to some sense about what they were doing. After I talk to the petticoat girls I come back and make some sandwiches and cookies for the school kids because they don't have a good food program. Then I start cooking for the community meeting that night." I said, "Wow, Mabel you do more before I get started in the morning than most people do all day."

Alinsky organizers taught Ed how to be tough, but Mabel taught him how to care:

> I was raised in the Alinsky school, through Tom Gaudette. You got to be tough; you got to be agitational. But then how do you be warm and loving? How do you be kind and generous? I saw a whole bunch of people that had been through something way beyond what I have ever been through in terms of my life, in terms of obstacles. The fact that they came out not being bitter and just loving people was just amazing...It is the best of what humanity can be.

Limitations to Understanding

Although activists in this study spoke about the impact of relationships on their understanding and commitment, they also identified important limitations. First, they suspected that their friends and colleagues of color might not be completely open with them about their experiences and views on racism. Mark Soler, for example, has worked closely with African Americans in his juvenile justice work and built trust over many years. Earlier he talked about long car rides with an African American colleague, discussing very personal matters related to racism. Yet, he said there is no guarantee of openness:[12]

> Just because I've worked with somebody for twenty years doesn't necessarily mean that they will be honest with me about this issue. I wish that weren't true. It also tells me that this is a very powerful issue. I probably have a very small appreciation of it as much as I work on it. But I have to recognize the limitations of my own ability to understand the depths of how important this issue is.

In his view, people of color typically speak with each other and with him in different ways:

> We've had an experience with hiring a young lawyer here who is African American, who I trained because I'm the senior person on the staff. But unquestionably he was influenced at least as much, and maybe more, by another attorney not in this office who is African American and who he clearly saw as a different kind of role model. That's completely understandable. They have a different relationship between the two of them than I have with either of them. There are things that they talk about that are different from the things that I think they'll share with me.

However much white activists have come to learn about and identify with the experiences of people of color, they still do not really experience racism directly. Mark Soler talked earlier about his visceral hatred of the way the criminal justice system treats young men of color, yet he knows that the police will not pick up his own son even if he violates DC's curfew:

> I don't live in anybody else's skin. My good friends who are African American have taught me things that I would have never learned otherwise. But I still think if you're white, you cannot fully appreciate the experience of having dark skin in this country.

I don't pretend that racism in the criminal justice system is as important to me every day of my life as it is to my friends who are black. The presence of the criminal justice system, the juvenile justice system in black males' lives is just everywhere. The number of men affected by this is just astronomical. It's incredible. Half the men in Baltimore, half the men in DC are under the custody of the criminal justice system. I just think it's relevant to them in a different way because it is a part of their lives all the time.

Louisiana juvenile justice lawyer David Utter has developed close relationships with a number of his colleagues of color, so racism has become more personal to him. Speaking of one of his African American colleagues, David says, "I worry about Dwayne every time he gets in a car."[13] Yet he says this:

I think the experience of growing up black is just very different than my experience. One example is why Dwayne does this work. He says every time he meets with one of his clients, he sees himself in his clients. He figures that if he was worth fighting for, his client is worth fighting for.

Ed Cloutman, a Dallas attorney, understands the power of stories to help people emphasize with the plight of others:

I'm now doing this police misconduct case for this black guy who was just driving his car, not too far from where I live, a pickup, hauling some furniture. Cop pulls him over, suspects him of stealing the furniture in back. Cop assumes he's got a burglary suspect, treats him like one, has him down on the ground, face in the dirt, handcuffed. Wife drives up, she freaks out. He starts screaming at the wife, get back in the car or the cop is going to blow his f-cking head off. Cop thinks this guy is going to get up because he's saying don't hurt her, don't hurt her. So he gets mad at this guy on the ground and screws his shoulder all up—twists his arm and pulls it out the socket.

How are we going to let the jury know what he was feeling? How this was happening to you as a black man, with a white cop's foot on your back, screaming at your wife about blowing her f-cking head off. And you can't do a thing about it.

Despite his deep level of understanding of racism as learned through many years of legal practice, Ed still says he's "never going to be there" himself:

I could never know what they have experienced. I can get a sense of what they tell me, when they tell me and how they explain it, and how as you gain trust of someone, they tell you how much it hurt. But how do I tell my children that, no matter how talented or how smart they are, they'll be faced with a very racist decision maker in their lives? Not because you're not pretty, talented, and wonderful. How do I tell my kids? Damn, I don't know. I could only vicariously understand that because I'm never going to be there.

Conclusion

In the last chapter we saw how whites begin their journey to racial justice activism with a moral impulse. At that point they are committed to a cause and to doing good for others. As they begin their activism, they take steps to cross over the color line by building relationships with people of color. Commitment grows through those relationships as whites come to care more deeply about racial injustice. Activists do not necessarily lose their moral impulse or their anger at injustice, but through those personal connections they begin to see the world through the eyes of people of color and begin to identify with their plight. They are no longer working for others but with people with whom they share their personal and work lives.

Reciprocity in relationship is important. People of color may be more likely to take the time to teach and engage whites if they bring something to the table, like a commitment to work for racial justice. Although whites have learned from a variety of associations, certain kinds seem more conducive to such learning. These include sustained, reciprocal relationships in conditions of relative equality and in a context of working together for some common goal.

As discussed in the introduction to this book, some scholars suggest that cross-cutting cleavages reduce the potential for conflict across ethnic and racial groups and foster a shared sense of common fate. I found some evidence that shared experiences of class or religion tend to orient white Americans to seek out commonalities through relationships. Tony Fleo, for example, feels strongly that his family's immigrant experience opens him up to identify with the pain of others who have been excluded. Yet, the transition has not been straightforward. Tony had to undergo a sustained struggle before he was able to appreciate that racism toward African Americans is qualitatively different from the European immigrant experience. Working together with black leaders in interfaith organizing created a much more real sense that "we're all in this together." In the end, I find that a sense of shared identity is built over time through relationships with people of color and is not generated from prior shared characteristics.[14]

Vanessa Walker and John Snarey have argued that the African American community combines within itself both an ethic of justice and an ethic of care. The African American church, for example, has historically combined advocacy for racial justice with care for its community members. Rather than being in opposition to one another, these two moral stances may be mutually reinforcing. Certainly this is the case for white activists. They care about justice more when they are concerned about real people who are being affected by injustice.[15]

Emotions play an important role here, as they did in the previous chapter on moral impulse. In that chapter I demonstrated that anger or outrage at injustice leads to an initial motivation to action, while hope for change encourages people to take the risk of engaging in activism. Here, bonds of affection create solidarity and an ethic of caring, which strengthen commitment to action. Stories shared in relationship make the connection personal. In this way whites move beyond compassion for the "other" and toward interconnectedness and caring.[16]

Of course, personal relationships in and of themselves do not provide an antidote to racism. All of the whites in this study act in the public world to create change in the practices of individuals or institutions. However, their commitment to this public work is fueled by the personal relationships they have formed across racial lines.

Becky Thompson offers a way for us to think about the relationship between the personal and the political in white racial justice activism. She argues that one of the advances made by social movements since the sixties is the recognition that the personal is political and that the political is personal. In other words, people of color have a distinctive understanding of the politics of racism because they personally experience it. White people do not personally experience racism in the way people of color do. Nonetheless, as I have suggested, they can make racism and the struggle for racial justice personal to them through their relationships with people of color.[17]

In this way white activists begin to work less *for* people of color as do-gooders and more *with* them as collaborators. Yet, there is still another part of the development of commitment to racial justice. Whites do not yet work for racial justice for themselves and for other white Americans. That is the subject of the next chapter, where we see how working together in multiracial groups deepens a sense of shared identity and commitment across racial lines.

| Getting to the "Want To"
Moral Visions and the Purposeful Life

I call it digging toward the "want to." One of the things I used to teach a lot in Dallas with our partners is, "I would want you to want this." Until we really, really get to the "want to," it's a limited exercise in actions or thoughts. I feel it, you know, I'm not just thinking. You're not just going to get my head. I'm going to give you everything I can out of my head, from history to the Bible and experiences. But I want you to get my heart. It's when we can go to the depths of the "want to" that we can tolerate even anger because we can understand it better and because we are not processing that anger in isolation from everything else.

—Kathy Dudley

It's not really about contributing to someone else's cause. I feel that I'm contributing to the world that I would rather want to live in. . . . I think inequalities—extreme inequalities—hurt everybody. For human beings to be very complete and really experience the full sense of community or a full, happy life, there needs to be more equality in it. So I see it as serving myself. I see it as working for what I want, not just what they want or need. It's what we all need to be a little happier and more centered and fulfilled in this world.

—Roxane Auer

H OW CAN WHITE activists come to embrace racial justice as their own cause? With the kind of moral impulse discussed in chapter two, white activists believe they should stand for racial justice as the right thing to do. Through the relationships discussed in chapter three, white activists begin to care more deeply about racism as they take action with people of color. This chapter, however, is about doing racial justice work for yourself and for other white people—getting to the "want to," as Kathy Dudley put it. Looked at another way, if the moral impulse that injustice arouses reflects what activists are *against,* this chapter examines what activists are *for.* Here I examine the nature of the racially just society they are working to create, what I call their moral visions.

A few activists report having had a sense of a moral vision early on, usually one that their own activist parents inspired. However, the vast majority of activists reported developing a vision while doing their work, engaging with fellow activists, and connecting with institutions or networks that exhibit the values of a racially just society. The same appears true of the "want to," or their own direct interest. Not one of the interviewees in this study described their early activism as being for themselves. Rather, they reported developing a personal stake in racial justice through their participation in the work for racial justice.[1]

When I asked the activists whether they pursued their work as a job or a passion, not a single person said it was mainly a job. Of course, almost all of them need to make a living, so in that sense many said that their work is both a job and a passion. Still, they all said passion drove their activism.

What are these passions for? What does it mean to say "I do this for me"? Two main themes emerge from a close examination of the interviews. First, these activists find that they can lead a meaningful and purposeful life through this work and that it gives them a sense of personal fulfillment. Second, they say they are working for a better society for all, including themselves and their children. I will consider each of these themes in turn. However, they are profoundly connected in that the meaningful and purposeful life is one lived in pursuit of that better, racially just society. As Roxane Auer says, "I'm contributing to the world that I want to live in."

A Calling to the Purposeful Life

Virtually all of the activists in this study reported that working for racial justice provides them with a meaningful life. Perry Perkins, an organizer with the Industrial Areas Foundation (IAF) network in northern and central Louisiana, describes it as a vocation or a calling:[2]

The term I would use is vocation. I don't think you have to have a religious terminology, either. I would, but I don't think that's necessary. In the religious terminology, it's a calling. But there's a sense that this is around your lifestyle and around commitments and values, not around employment. So I don't see it as a job. I don't think you can do it unless it's around your values, how you want to live your life and how you want to engage people.

Perry grew up in a small town in Mississippi in the segregated fifties and sixties. His father was a Southern Baptist minister in an all-white church. He told Perry that segregation was wrong, a violation of the Christian belief that all human beings are created in the image and likeness of God. Nonetheless, his father would not speak out against segregation in public. Perry recounted this story of darkness and light:

> I was told by my parents that the notion of being created in the likeness and image of God meant that not only was segregation wrong but that segregation was going away. It would not continue to exist much longer. They told me that in a dark room. We lived in an older house at that particular time. This is when I was three or four. It was a very dark house. So I remember being told that story under the cover of darkness. I went to Sunday school in a room that had windows on all sides. That was the room where there was light. Well, that same story wasn't told in the room with light...So I never was comfortable with that. That was always the rub with my father.
>
> My father did some pretty courageous things, but he had to get forced into them. He wouldn't preach a sermon about the radical nature of the notion of being created in the likeness and image of God, politically what that says, racially what that says.

In the midsixties Perry's family moved to Greenwood, Mississippi, where Perry witnessed the rise of Black Power. In fact, Perry and his high school friends attended the 1966 rally where Stokely Carmichael made the first public call for Black Power. Perry went on to a Baptist college, where he began to connect with progressive networks in the church. He went to work first with the Southern Baptist Home Mission Board and then did neighborhood organizing in Washington, DC, with Sojourners, a social justice group of evangelical Christians. When he returned to Mississippi to organize black and white pulpwood cutters into a union, he discovered the IAF. Perry felt the IAF was one of the few organizations really committed to organizing cross-racially. He also found in the IAF "a real clarity about the centrality of political engagement in public life to faith." He joined the IAF in 1985 and has organized with them ever since.

Through his reflection on a broad range of Judeo-Christian theology in the IAF, Perry discovered that his parents had left out half of the meaning of the story of creation:

> The first half of the story was about being created in the likeness and image of God; the second half of the story means we're God's agents. God created us, and we have the capacity to create, the capacity to make history. God brought history into being. And that's the notion of the Genesis.

For Perry, Genesis requires action for justice in the world:

> We're never fully human until we feel like we can make a difference in the place where we are in history. We have some capacity to shape the world around us, maybe not in big ways but in ways that are meaningful.

Perry has come to a point where, although he does not justify his father's failure to speak out publicly, he does understand it:

> I've come to understand the victimology of my father. I read Charles Payne's *I've Got the Light of Freedom*. The first chapter tells about all the lynchings. I noticed that about fifteen of them happened between the time my father was about eight years old to the time my father was about fifteen, anywhere from three to ten miles from where he lived. So he was very, very clear that violence could come against him because violence was not used just against black folk. It was more prevalent against black folk, but violence and particularly economic sanctions were prevalent. Pastors that spoke out were gone.

This perspective on racism gives us another clue as to why Perry feels a direct stake in racial justice. He sees racism as a system that oppresses anyone who opposes it:

> Growing up in the experience that I grew up in, I did not in the directest sense experience racial prejudice. But I did experience the kind of stifling oppression and silencing that happened to white folk who dared to challenge the regime in those days.

Other activists in the study also mentioned a sense of calling or vocation in this work, which implies a sense of responsibility to act to address racial justice and work for a better world. Many of them mix religious and more secular, democratic, or humanist notions of this responsibility to act. Chapter three discusses the views on reciprocity held by Sister Christine Stephens, an IAF colleague of Perry. Expressing her Catholic tradition, she quoted the following biblical passage: "To whom much is given, much is expected." However, she also stated that she believes in civic and political responsibility:[3]

> We have a birthright in this country, those of us living here in the United States. There is a good part of that birthright, and there's a burdensome part of that birthright. Part of the burdensome part of that birthright is that we are a nation that has been racist. We have got to do something about that for the good of democracy. It's just not healthy for a democracy to have that kind of racism at its core. I think we're responsible for that. You can't say you're not responsible because you didn't do it. Well, we live in the United States, and we bear that birthright.

Responsibility is not the same as guilt. Although many say they used to feel guilty about racism, only one admitted to feeling guilty in the present, and even that person stated that guilt represents a small part of her motivation. Rather, activists speak of a willing acceptance of the responsibility to act. In other words, a calling is not something they feel they should do but rather something they want to do because it gives their lives meaning. In this way, activists appear to have embraced this duty or responsibility to act.

Kathy Dudley, who speaks about getting to the "want to," is an evangelical Christian who came to Dallas with a commitment to minister to the poor, following Jesus's example. She was more serious about this commitment, however, than many of her white Christian friends. She brought homeless black men to live in her house in suburban north Dallas—to the outrage of her supposedly compassionate neighbors. She and her husband then decided to move into the largely black inner-city neighborhood of west Dallas and raise their family there. She wanted to work with black pastors in that community, to work in and with the community as she feels Jesus would do. Although the ministers were initially skeptical, Kathy worked long and hard to build collaborative relationships. She adopted the Christian Community Development model developed by African American minister John Perkins and helped form Voice of Hope Ministries with the pastors. The group established educational programs, sponsored a dental clinic and medical services, opened a resale store, offered job-training programs, and built low-income housing. In recognition of these accomplishments Kathy won a "one thousand points of light" award from President George Bush Sr., although she points out she is an independent, not a Republican. She eventually founded the Dallas Leadership Foundation as a way to connect black pastors from the inner city with faith-based institutions across Dallas. Reflecting on her life, Kathy says she has gained a lot from her work:

> A better understanding of who we are and maybe who we're supposed to be, in a broader sense, that life does not revolve around my individual ideas, whims, options, privileges, lack of privileges, injustices. That's been really good. I think the belonging to a purpose that I believe is right and feeling like I'm making a difference on something.
>
> Had we stayed in business, continued to climb the corporate ladder, sent our kids to white Christian private school, lived in our all-white neighborhood, there's no doubt materially all of us would be better off. Maybe we wouldn't have lost all that income and had to go rebuild about three or four times. But I look back on my life, and I'm forty-nine years old. If I were to die today, I would have felt like I really lived and that I left a world more accurately reflective of God's purpose and kingdom to my kids than had I not made those choices. So that's a huge reward.

Kathy is a deeply religious person who brought her copy of the Bible to the interview with me. She places her life in the context of God's purpose. However, the more secular-based activists in the study also reported that they gain purpose in life through racial justice work. For example, John Affeldt is a San Francisco lawyer and the managing attorney for Public Advocates, the firm that filed the landmark Williams case requiring the state of California to ensure quality instruction to low-income children of color. Although he considers himself spiritual, John no longer practices the Catholic faith in which he grew up. His early religious influences have apparently blended into a more humanist language. John explains his commitment to racial justice work this way:

> At its simplest form, I think that we aren't here just to eat, drink, and propagate, but that we should use our time to try to reach out to those around us, to the community around us, the world around us, and make life better for those around us, and make the family and the community stronger. That's really what our purpose is here.

As we saw in chapter two, Josh Kern attended a Jewish high school that fostered social justice values, but after college Josh pursued a career in business consulting. Disillusioned, he returned to law school, found his passion for educational justice ignited, and ended up cofounding a charter high school in Washington, DC. Josh reflected on the trajectory of his life in this way:

Those high school years were years that I really felt myself develop and become my own person. It took me ten years to get that back. This time in my life and that time in my life were the only two times where I really felt alive, good about what I was doing, connected in a way that felt like I'm a whole person.

Although Josh is Jewish, he talks about meaning and purpose in more general terms:

I take it for granted this is what I do. I made the commitment a long time ago. I find it very fulfilling, very meaningful. It gives my life purpose, and it's something that I've come to feel passionate about as I've gotten immersed in it.

I actually think this work has been incredibly beneficial for me because it feeds me in some way. I believe in it in my core. I'm trying to articulate why I do it. It's not easy to say, but I know this. I wake up every morning, and I'm excited about the day's work. In three years of consulting, I never woke up and was excited about what I was doing.

Reclaiming Hope and Humanity

Perry Perkins said that we are never fully human until we participate in the struggle to make a better world. This theme of becoming fully human or reclaiming humanity resonates strongly throughout the activists in the study, faith based and secular alike, and for a particular reason. Many of the interviewees believe that racism undermines the humanity of white people. In their own personal experience, they have felt less whole themselves. Action for racial justice then becomes a virtual necessity. In fact, many of them say things like "I can't not do it," "I don't have a choice," or "it's who I am." Joanna Dubinsky, a community and labor organizer in New Orleans, echoes the sentiment of many:[4]

The only way I can live in this racist and oppressive society is to feel like I'm part of a struggle to build a more just world. I don't think I could be who I am. I don't think I could just feel comfortable passively living my life in a world that is as unjust as the one that we live in. I feel like I don't have a choice. I feel like I have to do this work. It's fulfilling to me and gives my life meaning.

Pursuing the struggle for racial justice in this way becomes "my struggle." Anthropologist and educator Laurie Olsen explains it this way:

I've become more and more clear in this work that it's not like this is somebody else's struggle. This is the world I want to create. It's like the vision I'm striving for, antiracism, really killing the racial system. I'm not doing it for somebody else—on somebody else's behalf. I feel like it is my struggle. It is white people's struggle. It's a system that is harmful. It's deeply, deeply, deeply antihuman. I have from my own need and from my own humanity a need to end it.

Similar to Laurie, many other activists characterized it as the struggle to save their own souls. Randy Johnson, a community and political activist in Greensboro, calls it life giving. Speaking of racism, Randy said:

I think it's the price of the soul. You're internally diminished when you dominate other people or when you're trying to convince yourself you're not dominating others. You think it's because poor people are stupid or white people are stupid or whatever it is—trailer trash. There are these rationalizations that we've created to disguise the domination and hide it and rationalize it and justify it. But people know. I think there's a real hunger among affluent people. They know something is missing. There are things missing in their lives.

Once you really get seriously down this road, you can't go back. But you don't want to go back.... It gives you energy and it gives you life. It's the way you live. It's a great way to live. I know people use the word "journey" a lot but it really is. It's an ongoing kind of journey that will never end.

Chicago community organizer Madeline Talbott puts it powerfully and bluntly with an analogy to Noah's ark:

I think being white and privileged in a racist society, you feel like you're one of the family members of Noah on the ark. You hear all the people beating on the doors trying to get in, and you've got to find a way to open the door. This work allows you to crack the door open, which otherwise you'd have to kill yourself. I mean that's the way it feels to me. You feel like that kind of privilege is killing you. It's one of the things that make white society less connected and less welcoming and less warm because it's constantly protecting itself from the people and the flood on the outside. It's a terrible way to live.

Even though I probably started in order to help, I'm here for me now. I'm getting huge benefits out of this myself. It helps enormously because I'm never resentful about whatever, you know, sacrifice [laughter]. There's no sacrifice. I'm doing what I want, and I get to experience change and wins and transformations and be a part of personal relationships that you couldn't get in America any other way. It's a great opportunity. I feel that very deeply.

As some of the activists have already mentioned, they find meaning through their participation in the struggle for a better world, usually in a collective setting. By working with others, they discover hope, a key emotion connected to moral visions. Cathy Rion, for example, is a queer-identified youth organizer in the Bay Area. After discussing the dehumanizing costs of racism to whites, she goes on to talk about hope and the power of working with others to create change:

> It's really powerful to me to be able to work collectively with other people. To make change happen is something that's going to help us all down the road. The way to deal with the crap in the world is to fight it because to work with other people is a huge way of dealing with the way that racism really impacts everybody....
>
> I've got to a point where it keeps me alive doing this work. It gives me hope. I've seen and come to understand so much of the crap and outright racism and hostility and violence that racism and imperialism cause. And it makes me sick. Doing this work is the way to not just crawl into a hole and shrivel up. And it's fun. It's inspiring and it gives me hope. I'm learning, and it's amazing to just be a part of working collectively to change the way things are....I can't not do this work.

Antiglobalization activist Ingrid Chapman stresses the connection between hope and community:

> I have been so inspired by the different work that people are doing. It gives me a sense of possibility and gives me inspiration to continue to struggle and continue to build my hope that another world is possible. For me that is really big. Lots of people that I know want to just disengage because they have no hope that another world is possible. They are disconnected from struggles for social justice and feel totally disempowered and have turned to drugs and alcohol to make it. That sense of community helps me keep going in a world that is really, really disempowering and really, really degrading in a lot of ways.

Laurie Olsen also talks about the excitement that comes from this pathbreaking work:

I try to help people get in touch with that part of themselves that wants it, that sees it as important work, and that recognizes that it's really the work that is part of giving birth to a different kind of society.

Visions of a New Society

Racial justice work is meaningful in that it "is part of giving birth to a different kind of society," as Laurie says. But what is this new kind of society? Virtually every activist in this study—forty-six out of fifty—expressed strong views about the kind of society they are working to create, the kind of society they would like for themselves and their children, for people of color, and for white people.[5] Out of their descriptions, I identified six aspects of this new society, which would do the following:

- provide a decent quality of life for all, a clean environment, and a more egalitarian distribution of resources in housing, education, and jobs
- foster true human community based upon care, respect, and reconciliation
- empower individuals and communities to have a say in the decisions that affect them
- include and respect all cultures and build upon their values
- treat all individuals fairly and provide an equal chance for all
- respect the basic dignity of each human being

I originally thought I would find distinctly different visions of the future among the activists, but I found in the end that, try as I might, I could not place the subjects in distinct categories. Rather, I found that most of the interviewees described the society they are working to create in a complex way that includes several, if not all, of the six aspects. Some of the activists led with or emphasized one aspect or another. And a few spoke to only one element. However, I feel confident that virtually every activist in the study would agree with all of the six features even if they did not volunteer them all in their own description.

Each of the six elements of the new society finds its roots in American ideological or religious traditions. Socialist and more moderate social democratic movements emphasized material well-being and a more equal distribution of resources. The King-led civil rights movement envisioned the Beloved Community, which emphasized love, reconciliation, and brotherhood through nonviolence. The New Left valued participatory democracy, while a newer movement promotes multiculturalism. We can point to a broader liberal democratic project that features fair treatment and equal opportunity for individuals, and we can identify Judeo-Christian and other religious traditions that stress the inherent dignity of each individual.[6]

Perhaps it is not surprising that activists would combine elements from these various traditions into their vision of a new society. We have been living in an era that lacks a unifying movement offering a single vision under which we can all come together. In this more fluid and pluralist age, the activists in this study are influenced by a number of institutions, ideologies, and belief systems.

Indeed, we live in a time that lacks grand ideologies and a coherent social movement for racial justice with visionary leaders. When Martin Luther King Jr. called people to build the Beloved Community, he spoke to a large civil rights movement. However, of course, King's vision of that community involved all or most of the aspects that contemporary activists continue to name. He led with the vision of a community based upon love and reconciliation, but certainly that community treated each individual fairly and provided people with the kinds of economic and educational opportunities through which everyone could develop to their full potential.[7]

The people in this study are not primarily visionaries but activists. Most work in their own locality or domain and with their own particular group or network. They are not focused on the task of developing coherent visions. In periods of heightened movement activity, activists might clash over alternative tactics and competing visions, as advocates of Black Power and of integration did during the mid- to late sixties. However, during our present, quieter ideological times, few spend their days defining visions that somehow mark them as distinct from others.

Nevertheless, the theme of forming a more human community rings throughout the visions of almost all of the activists. In fact, it is the leading aspiration expressed by white racial justice activists, faith based and secular alike. In the following sections I present the visions of several activists in this study. I start with some faith-based activists who explicitly work to build a Beloved Community. I then consider the visions of a variety of other activists and show how different versions of human community weave throughout the group.[8]

The Beloved Community

Z. Holler is a retired Presbyterian pastor and a leader at the Beloved Community Center in Greensboro, North Carolina. He grew up in Greensboro in the thirties and forties under segregation and tells this story of separation:

My mother used to have what we'd now call yard sales. She'd go park the car at the underpass. The Southern Rail line went over this underpass. On the east side of that was the black community, East Market Street, we called it. And that's all the little stores and the jive places. It was a real culture over there. She would come and sell the clothes, and I would go with her. It was our used stuff. The people would come to that dividing place. They were always very pleasant, and she was very pleasant with them. But taking your used stuff and selling it at the boundary between black and white. What more can you say after you've said that? That's the way it was.

Later on, Z. left Greensboro for college and eventually became a minister in a small town in South Carolina just as the civil rights movement was emerging. He began working for desegregation and invited freedom riders to stay in his home. He served as associate pastor of the Central Presbyterian Church in Atlanta between 1966 and 1968, and "that's when everything happened." He said, "I was with King," and I think he means both physically with Martin Luther King Jr. in Atlanta and with him in his thinking. In addition, Z. worked closely with the Southern Christian Leadership Conference, which King led. After King's assassination, the church fed five thousand people and put up hundreds of mourners who came for the ceremony.

Throughout the seventies Z. remained active and in 1979 found himself back in Greensboro, where he pastored a declining congregation. This was a quieter time, and Z. concentrated on the internal rebuilding of his new congregation. However, 1979 was also the year that a combined group of Ku Klux Klan and Nazi Party extremists shot at anti-Klan demonstrators, killing five members of the Communist Workers Party. One other party leader, Nelson Johnson, was wounded. Johnson, an African American, was later jailed for inciting a riot. The killers went free even though television cameras recorded the shootings in broad daylight.[9]

In the late eighties Z. met Nelson Johnson after Johnson had found his own religious calling. Johnson had become a minister and established the Beloved Community Center with his wife, Joyce, and other community activists. In 1989 the killing of a black girl on a street in Greensboro put Z. back on the road to racial justice activism. Throughout the nineties Z. worked with the Beloved Community Center to support union organizing at a K-Mart distribution center and to deal with a variety of community and educational issues. In 1999 Z. helped launch the country's first truth and reconciliation commission on racism. Modeled on the South African commission, the group worked to foster an honest examination of the hate killings in 1979 in order to move the community toward racial reconciliation.

When interviewed, Z. said he is "hooked on Jesus of Nazareth," which has led him, via King, to the possibility of creating the Beloved Community. For Z., Jesus is an activist, inclusive leader guided by principles of love:

> What an astonishing leader, and what an astonishingly kind person to his enemies! He never, never pulled back a minute's worth on what he understood to be the reality. But no violence, no denigration of the person that he was dealing with.
>
> The people who are in power don't want somebody who has a following among the masses and who is willing to stand up to them and tell it like he saw it. He started this movement. And it was very difficult for anybody to go with it. But it was utterly inclusive. Women were his disciples, which was insane from the standpoint of patriarchal society. Children were welcome, taken as models of the kingdom and the kind of community where people are learning and moving ahead, not stuck on the way it was.

For Z., Jesus's life shows the possibilities of hope and change:

> That's what Jesus was up to, showing the world the graciousness of the creator and the possibilities of life lived in that spirit, the Beloved Community, to use Martin Luther King Jr.'s translation of the kingdom of God. That's the possibility always before us. It is also a judgment on what's going on. It's an exposure of all of the things that divide us. There is the possibility, if we take one another as seriously as we take ourselves and believe in the goodness of God, that we should be coming together. Then there's some future. That was Jesus's hope, and he gave his life gladly in that hope.

In Z.'s view, the struggle to redeem humanity is a common one for blacks and whites:

> It's a common struggle, which King well understood. The liberation of blacks would entail the liberation of society. He was working for everyone's liberation. We're as much caught in our box as the blacks are; it's just not as painful a box. And we've got a lot more room to operate in it. So, yeah, I think that it's a common struggle when one finally recognizes that we all have Pogo's thing. The enemy is all of us in the way that we in our various ways are twisted and broken and not able to be available to one another as friends and as brothers

and sisters. That's the common struggle. And that's, of course, Jesus's struggle, the redeeming of the human family.

Bringing whites and blacks together requires reconciliation through listening to and forgiving each other:

> If we are willing to listen to one another's stories and understand the pressures under which you are operating that brought about your behavior, then we begin to get the larger picture of what happened and why it happened. It's truth in that sense, the largest understanding of what's going on. It's related to the known facts but not mistaking those facts with the larger thing, which is truth. Why did people do what they did? If we understood, we'd have a chance of forgiving one another. Then we can move into the future with greater hope and greater capacity for dealing with issues that arise.

It turns out that everyone is for reconciliation in the abstract, but the struggle to come to grips with the history of racism and the particular events of the Greensboro killings has not been easy. Many whites in Greensboro prefer to think of the event as a shootout between outsiders rather than an incident that reflected the history of racism in a Southern place:

> The truth is bitter. People don't like bitter; it tastes bad [laughs]. We had a service on reconciliation. Well, reconciliation of what? That's hard for us. We want to be for good things—reconciliation and forgiveness and so on. It sounds like a good thing, but then there's a question: What is it that needs forgiving? What is it that needs reconciling?

Although Z. leads with a vision of the Beloved Community, he understands that it has to be founded upon social and economic reform. He argues that racial reconciliation with the Beloved Community requires justice not only in human relationships but also in public policy and the economic structures of society. He's working toward a society

> Where everyone is honored and respected for who they are, where the brokenness and the sins are recognized. We help one another see our weaknesses. Others help us see what we don't see. We help them see what they don't see. Together, if what we see in each other is grossly unjust, we call it by name. We try to come to grips with it. We forgive one another. We move ahead as best we can. And that means policy; that means the structures of government; it means what you do with the economy. The goals you pursue. I think that the economy is now

for the few and corrupts the many for the sake of the few. It excludes growing numbers.

Although Z. works day to day fighting issues of injustice and wrestling with the hatred that divides people, he says this:

Love is the real power. There is no power more powerful than love. It outlasts death. That is what the Resurrection is about. It's a reality of what Jesus had with us through the power of his spirit, the thing that he gave. The complete giving is stronger than all of the opposing forces that would keep it down and keep us separate and control the situation. You can't really stop it.

That's my hope—that in all this craziness we have the possibility related to the things Jesus did. It is quite available to anybody of any faith. It's not exclusive. It's there. God is as Jesus showed God to be. God is for Islamic folk as much as for us, the Buddhists, the animists, the new age folk. It's not a matter of getting it right. It's a matter of being available for the spirit of hope in the universe, the spirit of love, of creativity.

For Z., anger at injustice must be tempered with love for humanity in the effort to create the Beloved Community:

"Anti" sort of sets the stage for a good old American adversarial relationship. I do not believe in racism. I do not think it is true to the Christian situation. If we want to say "antiracist," yes, I am. I'm opposed to that kind of thing. But "anti" is basically what I'm against. I'm for community. I'm pro-mutual respect. And I'm pro-brotherhood and sisterhood.

Building the Beloved Community Today

Visions for a better society turn out to be powerful forces for commitment to racial justice. But this commitment does not appear to be to some abstract, faraway future. Rather, the commitment of people like Z. Holler comes with the effort to implement this vision today in both small and large ways. Other activists also stress the close link between their vision for the future and their work today. Joseph Ellwanger is a retired Lutheran pastor of a predominantly black church in Milwaukee and one of the leaders of a faith-based, community-organizing group called MICAH (Milwaukee Inner-city Congregations Allied for Hope). Joseph grew up in Saint Louis and went south with his father, who was also a Lutheran pastor. Joseph followed in his father's foot-steps and pastored his first church, a black congregation, in Birmingham, Alabama, in the sixties.

It was in Birmingham that Joseph was "transformed, changed, and gelled." The father of one of the four black girls killed in the infamous 1963 bombing of a Birmingham church was a member of his congregation, and Joseph participated in the funeral service. It was a seminal experience for him and left him with a haunting question: How could the Ku Klux Klan get away with murder? Joseph came to see that racial violence depended on the silence of good white people and their churches.

Joseph committed himself to ending the silence of whites. He came to see nonviolent resistance as both an effective and a biblical method of speaking out. Joseph led the Concerned White Citizens of Alabama in the first white march to support civil rights in the South on the day before the infamous Bloody Sunday. Seventy-two people marched in an "air of danger" to show that some whites also supported civil rights. Although a white mob threat-ened the marchers, no violence occurred.

Joseph moved to Milwaukee in 1967 and kept up his activism. He par-ticipated in open-housing marches in the late sixties and continued his com-munity organizing work for nearly forty years. Most recently, he has worked to acquire greater funding for public education in urban communities and participated in MICAH's campaigns for "treatment instead of prison" and for immigrants rights.

Like Z., Joseph explicitly mentions King's Beloved Community in his vision while his practice focuses on "dismantling the structures that racism built":

> It is practicing antiracism and insisting that we work together across racial, ethnic, denominational lines. That in itself is a living out of what King describes as the Beloved Community. So we're not just working for the ultimate goal of social justice, which certainly is what we're working for. But we're also working at building community, and in the process we have to dismantle some of the expectations and the fears and the structures that our society has built.

In other words, Joseph works to build the kinds of interracial relationships and social policies that reflect his future vision. His work today is a fulfill-ment of his vision:

> The way I live my life is that I do believe that I have a purpose to live out here on earth and that is to relate to people and to bring wholeness

and healing and justice and peace to the human family. And to do that overtly and intentionally and not just by osmosis via personal relationships. I do believe in the necessity of working together to bring about social change and transformation.

Moral Visions and Economic Interests

We have seen that efforts to build a human community involve the improvement of the social and economic conditions of people of color. Activists see that white people also have a stake in that human community, and they see their material interests improved by more egalitarian policies as well. Jim Capraro, for example, says he believes in "race-plus," that is, dealing with both racial and economic issues. Jim is the Chicago community developer whose story of witnessing the race riot against an open-housing march in his own Marquette Park neighborhood is recounted in chapter two. Jim has fought to open up housing opportunities in Marquette Park to Chicago's African American community and has sometimes encountered physical threats. Yet he consistently insists to the neighborhood's working-class white residents that integrated housing will be to their benefit as well. His Greater Southwest Development Corporation is committed to promoting economic and commercial development along with racial integration. In Jim's view, whites and blacks have a common enemy in block-busting real-estate developers. These people have not only exploited the fears of working-class whites, whose entire savings are wrapped up in their modest homes, but also taken advantage of African Americans seeking a better life for their families. Too often, Jim has seen racial turnover destroy a neighborhood's economic vitality.[10]

From this understanding, Jim works to create an economically healthy neighborhood that will be attractive to middle- and low-income families of all races. Low-income blacks need the resources such an environment offers, and so do middle-class whites and blacks. He uses a baseball analogy to explain his values:

> I used to say that winning the pennant would be to have some long period of time go by and have this neighborhood be middle class but inclusive of low-income black people. This way the poor people who lived here and the kids who live in poor households would have the benefits of living in a middle-income economy. There may be a bakery on the street because there's enough money to support the sale of

baked goods. The little kids would know that some people could bake for a living because it was in their environment.

Although economic development provides the necessary foundation for racial integration, it is not sufficient. To accomplish racial integration and, more specifically, to change the way white people in the neighborhood think about black people, they have had to find a place to meet and build relationships. Speaking of Western Avenue, a commercial avenue that included the boundary between blacks and whites, Jim says this:

> We had a DMZ, which was a dividing line. In a very simplistic way we said, "It is a dividing line. Couldn't we imagine that it could also be a meeting ground?"

One can understand Jim as being simply about the hard interests of economic development, but this idea of a meeting ground begins to hint at his other side, his more humanist and communitarian approach. Jim was raised in what he felt was a strong community in which people cared about each other and the Catholic Church taught the value of compassion:

> I always had a nub of Catholicism way down deep inside of that ember. It might not have been flaming at the time, but the ember was glowing. I never lost that. You know how, when you're a kid, you played tag, and you always could go to home base. That was my home base, way back down deep inside. I could always say this is my compass, and I know it's right because I have this home base inside it to keep me centered.

The problem was that his white, Catholic community cared only about itself and was hostile to African Americans. Nevertheless, Jim feels God called him to re-create a caring community that is open and inclusive right in Marquette Park. Part of what God and Catholicism taught Jim was the power of love. However, Jim was also taught that lesson by his daughter Betsy, who was born with a profound mental disability:

> I'd come home from a really terrible day and close the door. I'd hole up with Betsy, and I was in the presence of somebody who could never perceive of a utility for telling a lie, who had no ability to hate. Couldn't understand why anybody would ever wish harm on somebody. Just wasn't there. God didn't make that part of her, didn't allow that part of her to develop. That's what motivates me, is to make this world a better place. If I could bring one tenth of a percent to anybody's life what my daughter brought to my life, I'm going to go to heaven. I'm

going to help create a little bit of heaven for people. That's what it's all about.

In a comment that echoes the theme of personal benefit from participation in the struggle for racial justice, Jim refers to an earlier conversation with his close friend Jack:

For a long time I really believed that God put Betsy with us because we can be a really good family for her. It's what we're called to be. Later in life, before Betsy moved out, I had a long heart-to-heart with Jack. I said, "Jack, you remember a long time ago we had a conversation about my daughter?" He said, "Yes, I remember." He remembered it really well, and I said, "I've changed. I don't think that's the reason anymore." He said, "What do you mean?" I said, "I think God put Betsy with us because she's so good for us."

Although he does not use the term, I think it would be fair to say that Jim Capraro has a vision of the Beloved Community, one firmly rooted in the hard economic realities of life in Marquette Park yet looking to create true brother- and sisterhood across the color line. In other words, he works to integrate economic interests into a broader human vision of a truly inclusive community based upon authentic relationships. Achieving that goal would be like winning the World Series.

Solidarity Politics

It is not just activists from the civil rights movement of the sixties who embed material interests in a vision like the Beloved Community. Seth Newton is a young union organizer now working in the San Francisco Bay Area for AFSCME, a union of public employees. In chapters two and three Seth described the development of his commitment to racial justice while on church trips to Central America, his experiences with activists of color at Stanford University, and his relationships with the workers he organizes in the service industry. Seth calls himself as a "cultural Presbyterian," one who is no longer active in his faith, and he describes his politics as anti-imperialist. He works hard to improve conditions for low-wage workers and has a strong vision of a future society that meets people's material needs in a more egalitarian manner. He believes in

big principles of equality where people are really treated equal and where privileges are not ascribed to some and denied others, where people have the ability to live a fulfilled life and their necessities are met and where they can achieve that and not harm other communities of people. It is like the equality and justice side of things. It is pretty straightforward but hard to imagine.

Nevertheless, he has a strong humanist vision as well, as he sees racism as a dehumanizing force:

> I can't be very free living in a world even if I have individually what I need if other people don't have what they need and don't have the humanity they deserve. I'm dehumanized in that process. I get choked up even talking about it. A lot of it came from direct experiences with a lot of poor people and working-class people and folks of color very honestly talking about what it feels like to live in this society.

Acting for racial justice represents a humanizing process:

> I feel more like a human being. I really mean that because I think racism really strips everyone of humanity. In the process of standing up against that system, I feel like I can live. It is like a weight off my shoulders even though I'm not the only one carrying most of the weight. I stand up for and speak about what I believe to be true, and that is changing that system.

For Seth, racial justice represents both a political project and a way of relating to people today:

> A lot of what defines the way I live my life is based on my political identification. It breaks down to the projects that people have, the say over the decisions that affect their lives, and the ability to live with humanity and dignity. It's a political identification, but it really drives how I want to operate in my work and also just with my family and friends and the people that I encounter.

Seth speaks passionately about his efforts to build "real relationships" in community. He sees himself as part of a new, multiracial movement of young organizers in a variety of fields who are committed to working together for racial justice as a central component of progressive change:

> I think just building real relationships with other leaders from other communities is for me the most important thing there ever is. Building relationships based on compassion and interest in that person and in the struggle that they are a part of and the experiences they've had rather than for the benefit or gain of potential power. I think that

mutually respectful relationships are what built this dynamite coalition and campaign for me and for the other people that were in the core group.

Seth sums up his approach with the word *solidarity,* which suggests he works with people of color on the basis of his own direct stake in racial justice:

I generally consider myself to be in solidarity with people of color. It reminds me of the quote that is often cited by a native woman. "If you have come here to help us, you are wasting your time. If you've come here because your liberation is bound up in ours, let us work together." This is the perspective of a person of color saying it's not about helping. That is really how I identify with it. Even if I haven't had the conditions of oppression that others experience, I'm still not a free person, a whole person, until that system falls.[11]

Seth is a committed labor organizer, but he also plays the guitar:

If I didn't pick up the guitar in the morning and play something, I wouldn't be able to function the same way....It helps me because I have a hard time sharing very specific poignant stories, and I think that the song-writing process helps me focus. For me, those stories are what is most powerful a lot of the times when we organize folks.

Radical Visions

In addition to Seth, a number of other activists in the study also consider themselves to be radicals or revolutionaries.[12] Some trace their activism back to the radical black and brown movements of the sixties. Sharon Martinas, for example, is the cofounder of the Challenging White Supremacy workshop in San Francisco. Since 1990, nearly two thousand activists have taken the workshop, including Seth Newton. Sharon says her politics were forged during the San Francisco State University strike in 1968–1969. Led by the Third World Liberation Front, the strikers demanded a black studies department and an end to the Vietnam War. Police in tanks occupied the campus, and hundreds were arrested before a compromise was reached.[13]

Sharon considers herself an "antiracist, anti-imperialist, solidarity organizer." This is how she describes the purpose of her workshop:

If you're working with a majority white group, if every single thing you say and do doesn't have antiracism as its core—because of our white blinkers as white folk—it's going to uphold the white supremacy system because we will forget that racism is involved. So everything I have any control over in that workshop focuses on racism. We can talk about heterosexism, we can talk about class, we can talk about Iraq, we can talk about bunny rabbits! But rarely do we do that. The language that I use is analyzing with an antiracist lens. If we don't do that, we are by default analyzing with a racist white privilege lens, and doing that upholds the system that we're trying to undermine. So everything is connected. Yeah, this is where I get called hard assed!

Sharon has perhaps the most radical political critique of anyone in the study, although her views are shared in broad terms by many. As "hard assed" and political as she is, however, her goal is to create a peaceful and loving society:

We're talking about systems of oppression. White supremacy is a system; capitalism is a system; patriarchy is a system. We're talking about building grassroots revolutionary multiracial movements led by organizers of color that can, over a long, long haul, bring that system down and create a just, self-determined, peaceful, and loving society. I won't see it in my lifetime. But that's what it is about. This workshop is a building block in the foundation of a revolutionary strategy. That's all it is. As white folk, if we don't do it, nothing else we do will be moving toward what we believe in.

In describing that future society again, Sharon places material needs at its center but includes love as well:

In terms of how I see my life, my vision, I work for a goal which I will never see in my lifetime, which is a time when every human being has nourishing food from before birth to time of death, has shelter that is warm and clean and not for profit, a free education from the time of babyhood through the time of death, free medical care. I'm a socialist in terms of wanting a society where the air is breathable and the earth is producing healthy food. My belief is that the accumulation of vast amounts of wealth, more than what people need for simply having a productive, creative life, is more than obscene. Speaking in terms of how I try to conduct my life, it's "do unto others as you want them to do unto you." Act toward people with love and respect, and you get love and respect back. It's kind of old fashioned but basic.

Sharon believes that racism divides and disrupts the creation of a common progressive movement that would be to the benefit of all but those of the wealthiest capitalist class. Yet when asked about the benefit to her, she turns to a humanist explanation:

This work allows me to have a glimpse of what it might be to be a human being, which is really, totally beautiful. It means to understand that love and justice and freedom are like breathing clean air. It's hard to describe. I know that before I began this work, I didn't think there was any reason to live. And I do now. I look back on my life, and I've made huge mistakes with it, but I'm essentially pretty proud of it. I don't hide in a corner. I've been able to use whatever the creator gave me to make some changes in the world so that some other human beings have been able to have a little more than they did before. That is an incredible, incredible benefit. The other thing is, I'm never, ever bored! And I'm blessed with knowing absolutely beautiful, committed human beings.

At the time of the interview Sharon was closing down the workshop she had spent many years building. In part, she has found it more difficult to connect with a younger generation of activists. She has not yet decided which new path to follow in her work for racial justice, but at the age of sixty-eight, she still has no plans to stop:

Retirement is something for people who have had horrible jobs all their lives and want to relax. But how the hell as a white antiracist person do you retire? You can't!

Sharon's comment suggests what other activists feel—that working for racial justice is not a job or an activity per se. It's a way of life, or, as Sharon puts it, "It's life's work":

I personally believe that the creator created us as an act of love to live our life by loving others. Somehow or other I was able to tap into what I should be doing. I consider that a blessing. So that's kind of on the human-spiritual level. Politically I cannot imagine if I weren't able to do something positive to change the horrors of the country I live in. So it gives me a reason for being and doing each day. It's life's work.

Sharon's comments are representative of those of other activists who take a socialist position and even of those of a more moderate social democratic persuasion. They stress an egalitarian vision, and they see racism as preventing whites and people of color from joining in a common struggle to the benefit of all. Yet when asked about the effects of racism on whites, they stress a humanist critique and offer a humanist vision.

The Strengths of Multiculturalism

We have already seen evidence of a multicultural vision in the accounts offered by these white activists as they speak of building a community that learns from and builds upon different cultures. A few activists in the study led with or emphasized this kind of vision.[14] Molly Munger, for example, is one of the founders of the Advancement Project in Los Angeles, a group of civil rights lawyers who seek to partner with community organizations to address issues of racial equity and justice. In chapter two we saw how the Rodney King uprisings had shocked Molly out of her career in corporate law and into a life committed to working for racial justice.

Molly was part of the early wave of women who entered corporate law and focused on succeeding as a woman in what had been a male domain. By the early nineties, though, she had arrived at a point where the practice of law had lost its meaning for her:

> I got to where I felt that practicing law was like playing a video game, and I was really spending my days, "Oh, God! Get to the next level! Oh, yes! Got the golden key! Pow, pow, pow." It's kind of like that practicing corporate law. It's very much like that. And it had about that much content.

Even prior to the nineties, Molly had been developing a commitment to multiculturalism. While many of her white friends became fearful of communities of color, particularly after the Los Angeles riots, Molly articulated a vision of a new Los Angeles made strong through the contributions of diverse communities:

> I went out to lunch with a guy who was very upset by the whole thing that happened in town, and I said something like, "You know, it's going to be okay. It's going to be okay. There's nothing you can't do with a diverse group because you have so much depth on your bench. Everything you want to do, you find that you've just got fabulous people to come forward." And I really have great confidence in L.A., which was not a common view at that particular historical moment.

Molly's confidence in this vision came in part from her experience at John Muir High School, which she attended in Pasadena. When the school was integrated, some affluent whites left for a white enclave called La Canada, although most stayed. Molly talked about the response to this white flight:

La Canada had left, and the black kids and the white kids basically had this mentality like, "Oh yeah? Well, you watch." So the school in the years that I was there was just this incredible place. The athletic teams were tops, the music was great, the plays were fabulous. Everybody just excelled, and we had the most marvelous mixed group of talent at the place. It was just a really very healthy experience.

This healthy experience gave Molly an enduring belief in the strength that can come through multiculturalism. Like other activists in this study, Molly integrates her multicultural beliefs with material and moral concerns. She feels that addressing racial justice is central to achieving a broader social and economic justice agenda. Molly calls racism, particularly against African Americans, America's "founding sin":

> Social justice and wanting to get rid of racism are so very close. I have a pretty strong conviction that there is a sort of a founding sin, and I don't blame the people who did it. I don't think that's productive, but I do think it's something that happened that we should all be regretful for. That we should all acknowledge this was not a good thing to have happened, and it wasn't a good foundation for a country. It has shaped our country in distorting ways ever since its founding, and that's an important fact to me. That's something that's very bedrock.

Molly feels an obligation to model her vision of the multicultural life today. She lives in an integrated neighborhood and sent her children to integrated schools. She works in a multiracial legal/advocacy group that partners with leaders from communities of color. While other activists stress the challenges of building some version of a Beloved Community through relationships, Molly presents an air of naturalness. In other words, she wants this kind of life for herself, and she just makes it happen:

> It just seems like there have been things that have come along that are opportunities to have an interracial life, and it's just a matter of saying yes instead of no.

Values and the Liberal Democratic Vision

A number of activists in the study, particularly lawyers, emphasized equal opportunity and fair treatment of individuals in their description of the kind of society toward which they are working.[15] For example, earlier in this chapter we saw how John Affeldt finds purpose in his life through his work with

Public Advocates. Many people and institutions have influenced John. His father, an antidiscrimination lawyer, believed in "the dignity of the common man." His Jesuit teachers in high school stressed commitment to the poor. John has weaved these influences together and developed a complex and rich vision of the future. According to him, his "underlying philosophy is aimed at trying to make sure we have strong and healthy families and strong and healthy communities to live in," which to John means combating unequal opportunity and poverty. Nevertheless, he appears to root himself primarily in a liberal tradition, which he describes this way: "Part of being a progressive is a belief in the basic worth of every human being and enabling them to realize their potential and achieve a full life with dignity."

Despite John's emphasis on the individual, he is well aware of the structural and institutional processes that perpetuate racial and economic inequality. Meanwhile, although he argues for racial justice in part because of individual notions of merit and fairness, he also adds a more spiritual and even multiculturalist rationale:

> It accords with the fundamental principles of our constitutional democracy. From an economic rationale it would be a more rational system if the benefits of society were distributed in accord with merit and the quality of the person and not according to some arbitrary feature. From a spiritual-health perspective, our social order will be more harmonious if there are not underlying racial tensions and occasional race riots and all the bad things that happen with that. Theoretically, our economy would function better. Our society would be smoother, and our democracy would be more just.

While John's father addressed employment discrimination against African Americans, John himself focuses much of his work on education. He believes that today education is the key to the development of a person's human potential and to the possibility of achieving full participation in society:

> Education is fundamental for everyone. Giving low-income students and students of color, who have real disadvantages, a place and then giving them the opportunity to have a decent education can really, more than anything else, open up doors to economic security. It will ultimately help them to lead a life where they can achieve their potential and maintain their dignity.

Like other activists, John finds that this work is a way to live out his values. He sees meaning and purpose in life to be the biggest gains he receives:

This work fits with my personal beliefs, that it's important to use our limited time here to try to make the world a better place. I wouldn't be satisfied just working on increasing my own personal wealth so that I could leave more for my family. That won't satisfy me. I really do want to get up every day and be able to say, "Okay, what am I going to put my energies in today that's going to help move the needle a little toward making this world a better place for all of us?" I get to do that in this job.

Like other activists, values drive John's activism:

I think the biggest gain is being able to feel that you are leading a meaningful life, that you're living your life according to your values, and that's priceless.

Prefigurative Politics

Visions are not solely an end that activists work instrumentally to achieve. Rather, they shape the way activists live their lives today. Activists attempt to prefigure a future just society as they build meaningful relationships with others in the struggle to create a more humane community across racial lines. However, I noted earlier that these activists are not primarily visionaries but practitioners. Rather than understanding these visions as predetermined or fully formed, we may find it more helpful to see them as works in progress. In other words, activists develop their visions for the future through the kind of work they do and the way they live their lives in the present. Teacher activist Alex Caputo-Pearl explains his work building multiracial activist organizations this way:

Some of the project is trying to figure out what we want the struggle against racism to look like. A lot of the understanding has to be forged in multiracial settings, where you have people from different ethnic and racial backgrounds and language backgrounds—working together over an extended period of time, sharing life together, sharing work together, sharing political projects together—to create those small models of multiracial settings that I think we need in order to explore more deeply what do we want race relations to look like?

In a new body of research, scholars have begun showing how activists in a variety of social movements derive meaning and purpose from their activism. The activists in this study are similar to other activists in that way. However, there is something different about white racial justice activism that makes this kind of prefigurative politics and personal action so central. In most other forms of social activism, the "enemy" is someone else or some institution, for example, the government or big corporations. White Americans, however, are themselves profoundly implicated in racism. As Z. Holler puts it, "The enemy is us." Of course, activists seek to change institutions and government policy. Racial justice activism does not represent primarily a self-improvement project. Nevertheless, white activists feel a profound personal responsibility to think and act differently in order to participate in the struggle for racial justice.[16]

Youth organizer Cathy Rion wants to fight institutional racism yet struggles with her own role in the system:

> I've come to a place of really trying to understand an institutional framework and that I'm a white cog in this wheel. It's a huge, huge wheel, and I don't have a choice about jumping off of it. I can try to slow down that wheel. I think for me that sense of responsibility around swimming upstream is critical.

Ingrid Chapman works to bring an antiracist perspective to the antiglobalization movement. In chapter two we learned about the development of her understanding of racism after her arrest at the World Trade Organization protests in Seattle. She described the approach of her network of activists this way:

> This is about prefigurative politics in trying to bring into the organizing and the political work the vision for the world that we are fighting for. If we are fighting for a world where people are empowered and have decision-making power, then we operate that way within our organizations in order to empower as many people as possible. If we are fighting for a world that empowers women, then we don't disempower them in our organizations. We practice the culture that we want to see in the world. If we are fighting for a world without racism, then we don't perpetuate it in the organizations that we are working in.

This approach has implications for how she operates:

> I am in struggle for social justice in all parts of my life, in the way that I relate to people and then in the political work that I do and the work that I do for pay. I build relationships with people that are honest and empowering. I try to do that. Figure out how to do that on a national level and then international level. How we can be empowering each

other in a way that is struggling to make real changes in this world and not be so disempowered by the Bush administration and by corporations but see ourselves as connected and as agents of change.

It turns out that personal growth in the struggle for prefigurative politics provides part of that meaning and purpose in activism and strengthens commitment. Perry Perkins, IAF organizer, explains it like this:

A colleague of mine said that he used to be working on changing the world, and finally he'd given up on that and decided that the real work was on changing himself and see how the world reacts. I like that. I think that's right. There is a high premium in IAF, particularly this part of IAF, for personal development. The colleagues and the leaders you work with, they stay around not because of the issues. They stay around meaning and around their own growth and development.

Conclusion

All of the activists in this study have found a way to make the cause of racial justice their own. If they started with a moral impulse to act for others, through their activism they came to see racial justice as essential to their own humanity and to the well-being of all Americans. Indeed, far from seeing their efforts as altruistic, several activists volunteered the view that they consider it an insult even to suggest that they make sacrifices by doing this work. John Heinemeier, who pastors black Lutheran congregations and has been a leader in several community-organizing groups, says he might have thought that way early on—before he found his own stake in making this kind of life:

There are still some of my colleagues who would like to sustain the notion that to be a pastor in the inner city, cross-culturally, is a kind of self-chosen sacrifice and even martyrdom influence. Man, I object to that. I *really* object to that kind of thinking. I resist it from every which way. No, no. That notion is so demeaning both to the profession, as well as to the people, that it's unspeakable. Just the opposite: I feel the beneficiary. That's been my constant feeling in this ministry: being the beneficiary rather than a sacrifice.

As John's strong words illustrate, emotions feature prominently in these motivations as well. If the driving emotions of the moral impulse are anger and outrage at injustice, the driving emotions in this chapter are love, hope, and a feeling of personal fulfillment. Activists speak of creating caring relationships today as they seek to reorder society away from exploitation toward the principles of love. In the face of the dehumanization of racism, they find hope through working together. These emotions do not precede racial justice activism. Rather, love, hope, and a sense of fulfillment emerge when working with others to create change.

Activists develop a strong sense of identity as a racial justice advocate, someone committed to building the future today. As Christine Clark says, "It's who I am." The findings of this chapter are consistent with a growing body of literature that considers activists to be moral agents. Unfortunately, value-based activism has been improperly understood as altruism. I have tried to show that activists develop a personal stake in racial justice through the meaning it offers in their lives. As Nathan Teske has argued, acting morally is not a denial of self but rather enriches us and allows us to live meaningfully and according to deeply held principles.[17]

Compared to other forms of social justice, racial justice activism perhaps has an even stronger moral edge for white Americans. Whites historically have been the architects of the racist system, and many continue to be complicit in its operation. As a result, white activists feel compelled to fashion a life that responds to the demands of racial justice not just as a strategic end but also in their day-to-day relationships. Few see this as a burden. Since racism undermines white humanity, activists find that by participating in the struggle for equality and freedom they gain the opportunity to become more fully human.[18]

Other studies of moral meaning in activism focus on the personal level but surprisingly few address moral vision. Indeed, scholars of social movements and social activism have largely ignored the role of moral visions in motivating activists. Yet I find that personal meaning and moral vision are connected. The purposeful life is one lived in pursuit of that racially just society. In other words, activists are working to create the society they want to live in, and they find meaning in working for that society today.[19]

I have shown some of the variety of visions that activists work for today. Despite different emphases, though, the most common and overarching theme can be found in the creation of a more human community that extends across racial lines. Many describe this as the Beloved Community, whether conceived in a specifically Christian or broadly humanist way. Indeed, activists share a vision of a society that is a caring community based upon human relationships, one that takes care of people's basic needs in housing, education, and income. They incorporate into this vision their concerns for fairness, equal opportunity, multiculturalism, and the inherent dignity and worth of every person.[20]

I call these visions moral, but they could be understood as political as well. I stress morality here because activists seem to be talking about the principles around which they want to organize a just society. Their visions include how people should live their lives and treat others, which are profoundly moral concerns. Even the activists most focused on material improvement in the lives of people of color and on a more egalitarian distribution of resources also have a moral project in mind.[21]

By describing these projects as moral, I do not mean that interests are not important. Rather, as I have shown, activists embed their notions of the interests of people of color and of white Americans in their vision of the Beloved Community. When pressed about the interests they and other white people have in racial justice, they rarely give a narrowly material account. Instead, they emphasize that racism undermines the humanity of white people and blocks them from achieving human community. Their future society would treat people more humanely and create the conditions for true brotherhood and sisterhood across racial lines. In that context, it would provide better and more equally for the social and economic needs of people of color and of whites.[22]

I do not mean to portray white activists as moral crusaders or out-of-touch dreamers who care less about the material well-being of people of color (or of white people for that matter). Nothing could be further from the truth. Even the activists who focus primarily on a humanitarian vision or the Beloved Community work day to day to improve the material conditions of people of color—in education and housing, for example. Some are astute political operatives and legal advocates; others are savvy educators who work the system to improve conditions for students of color. Many believe that racism blocks a more progressive social and political agenda that would materially benefit the vast majority of white people as well. Nevertheless, what inspires activists and sustains their commitment is a vision of a new kind of society based upon compassion and community. What fulfills them is working to build that kind of society today. In that sense, these activists get material interests and morality working in the same direction.

White activists have found a way to solve the paradox between universalism and race-specific policies identified in chapter one. In that dichotomy, whites work either for universalistic ends, that is, for policies that would benefit everyone across racial lines, or specifically for policies to benefit people of color. The universalistic program has been criticized for sacrificing the specific needs of people of color on the altar of cross-racial unity. On the other hand, the race program has been criticized for its appeal to whites on the weak basis of altruism. The activists in this study have found a middle path that fuses the two approaches. They work for a society that is good for all precisely because it places racial justice at its center. Paraphrasing Perry Perkins, race is real, but in the end we have a common humanity together. This is not an excuse to avoid dealing with race, but it is precisely a reason to address racism since it blocks the achievement of our common humanity.[23]

We have seen that white activists are not only inspired by the future vision of a common humanity; they also pursue their work and fashion their lives in an effort to begin bringing that community into the present. Two kinds of action appear important to activists. First, activists take on the responsibility of engaging with other white people to change their racialized ideas and practices. Second, they work to build respectful relationships with people of color. How they pursue each of these tasks is the subject of the next two chapters.

| ## Working with White People
Challenging Racism in the Context of Inclusion

If you walk up to any white person on the street and ask them if they oppose racism, they'll all tell you yes. But I think it's important for people to step back and really assess how well we're doing with it. What's the next step after that? So you oppose racism and...? What is it that you're doing to create better opportunity or to do something to correct the injustices that racism can lead to?

—Roxane Auer

A really important role for white people to play in the process is to engage with other white people who are at the very early stages of their understanding about these issues. We serve to challenge the stereotype that this is only about and for people of color as opposed to it also being about us and our mental and physical health.

—Christine Clark

A T THE HEIGHT of the Black Power movement in the sixties Stokely Carmichael told white activists that if they were serious about fighting racism, they should go back and work in their own community. Carmichael reacted against white liberals coming to the South to help out blacks in the civil rights movement. In his view, the problem of racism lay in the immorality of the white community—its unwillingness to live up to its stated principles. If white activists were serious about achieving racial justice, they should work in their own communities, confronting racism there.[1]

Forty years later, the large majority of activists in this study speak passionately about their special responsibility to address racism among white people. Forty out of the fifty interviewed in this study said it is a very important part of their work.[2] Indeed, many feel it should not be the responsibility of people of color to change other whites. Community activist Kate Foran puts it this way:

> Young white people need white role models to hold each other accountable and to call each other out because in a lot of ways the onus is on us. This is our work to do. We can't put it on black people and say, "Okay, tell me how to be your ally" or "Tell me what I'm doing wrong." That's not their responsibility. There's plenty of other work that they have to do without having to try to reform me. I think it's for white people to hold each other accountable.

Whites can perhaps be more effective than people of color in moving other white people forward. According to educator Phyllis Hart:

> White people have an obligation to talk to other white people. I think that it may be harder for people of color to have those conversations because they may not get people's real thoughts. It may only go so far because people get polite. Because white people tend to be in rooms with other white people, they can hear things that might not be said to people of color.

Challenging white racism was difficult in the sixties; it remains a difficult, if somewhat different, challenge today. White activists now face less overt racism. As Roxane Auer noted earlier, all whites, except for a small percentage of avowed white supremacists, will state their opposition to racism. Yet the actions of many white people nevertheless perpetuate racial inequality and injustice. We now live in what some analysts have called the era of colorblind or laissez-faire racism. In this era, most whites are unaware of their unconscious prejudices and stereotypes and fail to recognize how their actions perhaps unintentionally perpetuate racial injustice.[3]

For example, white teachers who have low expectations for students of color teach down to them and thereby contribute to poor schooling outcomes. Yet in this era of colorblind racism, as Eduardo Bonilla-Silva has shown, many whites don't see these attitudes as a form of racism and don't like to talk about them. For many whites, a certain kind of paternalism masks racism. In other words, many teachers believe that their low expectations come from a realistic appraisal of their students' abilities given that the youngsters live in poverty and have not had many chances to develop intellectually. They fail to see how expecting less of black children constitutes a form of prejudice and how action on that basis perpetuates racial inequality in schooling.[4]

Most activists in the study believe that whites have both a moral responsibility to oppose racism and a direct interest in promoting racial justice. Racial injustice is wrong, and whites have an obligation to implement their stated values of justice and equality. At the same time, activists believe passionately that racism harms whites, too, and that whites would benefit from living in a just society. The problem, however, remains that racism does not harm whites as much as it does people of color. Lewis Pitts expresses this point graphically: "The guy that took the rope and lynched the people ain't hurting as much as the cat that died or his family." As Janet Morrison puts it so succinctly, racism hurts white people, "but I don't think anybody ever feels it."

In fact, even if whites have a larger moral and long-term interest in justice, many nevertheless acquire short-term benefits from their position in the racial hierarchy. This is what many scholars and activists have come to call "white privilege." Some whites benefit, for example, by the ability to live in more affluent suburbs, which offer better schools, safer environments, and better-quality housing. They benefit from easier access to home loans. They benefit, in the end, by not having to think about race at all as a factor in their lives even if it lies unacknowledged beneath the surface. Consequently, as we will see in the comments that follow, many activists use the phrase "challenging privilege" somewhat interchangeably with "challenging racism."[5]

Most whites can continue to live their lives in comfort without addressing racism. As Penda Hair notes:

> I think most whites are probably more oblivious than aggressively hostile. They just don't have to deal with it. They don't want to deal with it. Their lives are fine. They can ignore it and live perfectly happy lives.

Indifference, in that sense, poses perhaps the key challenge to confronting whites. But whites can also resist discussions of racism. Confronting racism is uncomfortable at best and can even be painful to many whites. According to Roxane Auer, "most people tend in the comfortable direction."

White activists who want to advance racial justice, therefore, face a difficult challenge. They need to move whites out of passivity to take up the cause of racial justice. They need to convince them that a racialized system creates injustice even without racist intent. In many cases, they need to challenge more covert racial attitudes, like low expectations, and show that certain kinds of behavior by whites can help perpetuate inequality.

Despite the general state of white passivity and resistance, activists find reason for hope. Many whites have some sense that racial injustice continues in this country. Activists, moreover, say they perceive a yearning for racial progress, a sentiment that likely helped Barack Obama win election to the presidency. Many whites are searching for a different kind of life for themselves as well, one that is more authentic, connected, and truly diverse.

Activists in this study are engaged in an ongoing search for effective ways to work *against* racial indifference and resistance and *with* the positive impulses of other whites. Rose Braz puts it this way: "I have certain things that work, but I don't have an answer." I think that represents a pretty fair summary of where activists stand. If changing whites were easy, racism would not continue to be such a force in American society.

Indeed, I find that white activists face many tensions and dilemmas in trying to influence other whites within a system that perpetuates racism on a daily basis. This chapter starts with a key dilemma faced by all white activists who try to influence others, that is, how to challenge a white person's racism in a way that moves them forward rather than causes defensiveness and retreat. The chapter then turns to a close examination of how activists seek to influence other whites in the three different fields of action represented in the study: community organizing, education, and policy advocacy and criminal justice work.

I have not interviewed the other whites these activists try to influence, nor have I directly observed their efforts myself. In other words, this is less a study of effective strategies; even less is it a "how-to" chapter. Rather, I report on how committed white activists experience and understand this work, which lies close to the heart of what it means to be a racial justice activist. Nevertheless, I hope it will contribute to our understanding of the processes that can help move whites from passivity to action.[6]

The Danger of Self-Righteousness: Challenging Racism in the Context of Inclusion

Ingrid Chapman identifies a common dynamic that white activists face in addressing the racism of other whites:

A lot white folks who are in the process of trying to dismantle their internalized racism and privilege oftentimes have a tendency to want to distance themselves from other white folks and to be self-righteous, even within progressive organizations. They say, "Hey, I am not racist. Those are the racist people over there." I think a big thing for me that I have learned is to cut the self-righteousness.

Jim Capraro puts it more bluntly when talking about white activists who posture toward other whites:

We called it masturbation. A lot of energy spent. You feel good at the time, but there's really not a net result at the end. I challenge racism when there's a purpose to doing it.

Racism is a deeply moral issue for Americans. As noted earlier, few whites believe they harbor racist views or act in ways that perpetuate racism. Even fewer consciously want to be racist. To accuse someone of racism can appear to represent a moral and personal attack and provoke defensiveness, which can freeze a process of change and even set things back.

This situation creates a dilemma for many white activists. How can one address the racism of other whites without moralizing and without creating a defensive reaction? In this section I discuss some strategies used by activists in various fields. In the end, the activists reported that these strategies can be effective, yet the basic dilemma remains.

First of all, most activists are careful not to accuse a white person of being a racist but rather focus on the specifics of behavior.[7] In part, this appears to be a pragmatic approach, but it also reflects a particular understanding of racism. In this view there are no "good" whites who are free from racism and "bad" whites who are racist.[8] Rather, all white Americans grow up in a racialized system that socializes people into stereotypical thinking and perhaps unconscious prejudices. Consequently, racialized thinking lies inside all whites. The white activists in this study have come to recognize this reality and so work to combat their own racist thoughts and actions. From that point of view, they see themselves as fundamentally in the same place as the other whites they are trying to influence. Rather than seeing the issue as black and white, so to speak (i.e., you are either a racist or a nonracist), activists find that the willingness to confront internal racialized thinking is the most important thing. Rachel Breunlin puts it this way:

When I was involved with more direct community activism, you had people who were just getting involved in that kind of movement, and they would make mistakes in the way they said things. They would just get crucified for it. You know, "Oh, she's a racist after all." I'm like, "No, actually, if someone is on a path of unpacking white privilege, that takes a lot of time. It's not just one conversation or one workshop. That's actually a lifelong project that all white people have to do."

In other words, white activists confront racism with the purpose of bringing other whites into the movement for racial justice.[9] They challenge racism in the context of inclusion. Christine Clark has worked with public school teachers and on college campuses for many years dealing with issues of race and diversity. She cites a poem by Edward Markham that hangs on the wall of her office:

"He drew a circle that shut me out. Heretic, rebel, a thing to flout. But love and I had the wit to win. We drew a circle that took him in."

Christine stresses the importance of inclusion:

Yes, confront all of these really complicated, painful things about what does it mean to be white, upper middle class, whatever your privileged identities are. But do that in a context that allows people to feel like they can do something about it. Not to escape feeling bad, not to escape privilege and understanding, but in a way that allows them to become a part of something that will solve the problem.

Christine cut her teeth on the racial justice movements of the late seventies and eighties, which she feels were overly confrontational. That level of confrontation drove many potential white allies away. By demonizing whites and shutting them out, it was exclusive rather than inclusive:

I mentioned earlier making the other us and not them. It is really important to draw white people in and make them allies, not enemies. That doesn't mean don't confront; that doesn't mean don't express anger as part of a pedagogical approach. But it does mean that your goal is to want people to join with people of color or with others against racism as opposed to being made the enemy.

Christine feels most whites want to be included:

Even though it's kind of privileged to suggest that white people feel like outsiders, I think that it's important to recognize that everybody wants to be included; nobody wants to be excluded. One could ask, "How can a white male possibly feel excluded in our society?" But the reality is that we're all alienated on some level. Racism even alienates white people even though they benefit from it. So the strategy has to be to make people feel like they're part of the family, the antiracist family.

The stance of inclusiveness also suggests a second aspect that many activists see as a helpful antidote to moralizing; that is, approach other whites by trying to understand where they are coming from.[10] Rather than denouncing people for their behavior, white activists have found it more useful to ask questions and enter into dialog. Oakland community educator Michael Siegel puts it this way:

> I ask my white colleagues lots of questions and try to represent alternate viewpoints when I notice that I'm aware of racial dynamics that they are not—whether they are questioning why a certain person dresses a certain way or they might be ridiculing how a person talks or lots of situations in the day-to-day perceptions that are really some of the backbone to institutional racism. I find myself in the moment challenging, asking questions hopefully in a nonconfrontational way representing a different viewpoint to my white brothers and sisters.

Michael also distinguishes between necessary confrontation and ridicule. Confrontation can be positive if we assume positive intent:

> I would say confrontation is good, alienation is bad. I am willing to be confrontational in the sense that I'm not scared to ask certain questions, and I'm not going to leave certain comments unnoticed. If so and so says, "Why is that person dressed like that? They look like a pimp" or something like that, I'm not going to let that comment go unremarked upon. But I'm not going to be confrontational in the sense of ridiculing or cutting someone down. A lot of the social change techniques of the previous generation, of my mother and father's generation, was about proving who is right and who is wrong. I feel like a more effective technique is dialog, assuming positive intent and working toward a common understanding.

Homeless advocate Ed Shurna also emphasizes understanding where a white person is coming from:

> It helped me in some ways to grow up in an area that was all white and ethnic. You get to know people in a deeper way when you live or work with them. I knew that people weren't simply bad people. "They are usually good people, but because of ignorance they sometimes have strange ways of thinking." As opposed to "They are all bad people."

You have to see that there is a lot of gray in understanding what motivates people.

And that means having a genuine conversation with whites:

If you are talking individually with people, I try to get into a conversation. My whole life has been challenging and making demands in order to change injustices; that is what community organizing is all about. You have to develop a relationship with the person. Some people I can't talk to. If they are real racist, I just have to walk away. But if they are ignorant, you could start to give another way of looking at things. In our very imperfect society, we are all in some type of recovery from racism, homophobia, or sexism.

Ed's comment highlights a third aspect of what many activists see as a more effective approach: addressing racism through relationship.[11] Relationships can help to mitigate defensiveness by building trust and creating the conditions where whites can feel more comfortable opening up. Roxane Auer tells this story of an all-too-frequent defensiveness:

There was a night where we were precinct walking on a campaign that was extremely important. It wasn't going well, and so there was stress about needing to make sure that we covered all the doors that we planned to cover and get everything done. It was dark out, and it was raining, and they had gotten dark-colored ponchos for people. There were people saying, "I don't feel comfortable. You're sending a bunch of brown people with ponchos out into a wealthy white neighborhood at night while it's raining. That's just completely insensitive." The white person who had been in charge that night was just so defensive. Later he said, "I was called a racist. I can't believe someone called me a racist."

Roxane took the time to talk with him one-on-one later. She appreciated that perhaps that night he was under pressure and just wanted to get his job done:

He didn't see it as a racial issue, but he also was not being sensitive to the fact that someone who is black or brown would feel a lot different about doing that than someone who was white.... That needed to be told to him from a very human being–to–human being perspective. When a person comes to you, one-on-one, and looks you in the eyes and says, "Look, sit down with me. You need to understand this." It's much harder to dismiss it than when there's a group, and you're letting your defenses get going.

Many activists find it helpful to use their own experience as an example to help other whites.[12] Susan Sandler says this:

> I try to raise an issue as something that I'm grappling with or I have grappled with. What I don't want is, you know, "I have it all down. I know how to do it. I'm right. You're wrong." That automatically creates a relationship of defensiveness. So as much as possible, I try to share how I am struggling around the same issue I am raising with them, rather than coming off with an air of superiority.

Many activists have also struggled with the issue of guilt. Most of them talk about guilt as inevitable at least at the beginning but then say that whites need to get beyond guilt to do something constructive.[13] Although guilt could motivate action, whites tend to get mired in and paralyzed by it. Many activists try to counter personal guilt by helping whites place their personal beliefs and behavior in historical and structural context.[14] If whites can understand that that their personal thoughts and actions come as the result of historical and structural factors, then perhaps they will not get stuck in self-blame. Seth Newton talks about the origins of racism in the development of slavery:

> Where I often start with folks is an anecdote that shocked me. In the Challenging White Supremacy Workshops I learned where the actual words "white" and "white race" come from in the history of the U.S. It can be traced back to the era of Bacon's rebellion in colonial Virginia. There were some extremely powerful rebellions that were very multiracial and that almost overthrew colonial power in Virginia. The ruling group looked at the statutes and the laws and also the sermons, and all of a sudden they used this term "white" where it used to be Irish American, Swedish American, Italian American. They changed the statutes to give specific benefits and privileges to white folks in order to try to change and stratify what was a movement of people from different backgrounds.

Other activists try to make the historical impact more direct by helping people see how they have acquired racial stereotypes. Educator Bob Peterson asks whites to look at their racial memories:

> One of the things we do with staff development and I do with workshops is for people to examine their racial history and racial memories. One of my first racial memories is my mother, bless her heart. She's still alive, telling me and my two brothers, who were pretty much out of control some of the time, "You people are as wild as Indians."

Activists feel there is no one magic strategy that will work in all cases. Rather, they need to listen to each individual and try to move them a step forward, particularly by connecting to people's core values and identity. Educator Alexa Hauser puts it this way:

> There's nothing at this point that I can say I know this is not going to work or I know that this is going to work. It's much more negotiated. I will say that listening really carefully is a key piece of my approach. Listening for what it is I think the person sees as their core identity and trying to connect into that.... Who do they see themselves as in their best, and how does antiracism connect to that?

But the tension and the dilemma remain. White people need to feel comfortable in order to open up and move forward, but challenging deeply held beliefs and behavior is inherently uncomfortable. Alexa puts her finger on the contradiction:

> A lot of people talk about how people have to be trusting and comfortable in order to do the work. They're not going to learn from you if they don't trust you and if they don't feel comfortable. Well, antiracist growing is never comfortable for me. If I'm waiting for it to be comfortable, I'm never going to grow. So in some ways I reject that. But on the other hand you do have to have some level of comfort because, if you don't, you just have no place to stand.

In the end, many activists feel that talking with whites about racism is inadequate. Rather, getting whites to start taking some action creates a better context for development.[15] Working with people of color and building cross-racial relationships appear to create conditions in which whites can change, at least according to the community organizers in the study, the group to which we now turn.

Community Organizers: Building Relationships through Action

The first part of this chapter focuses on challenging whites through talk. The tacit assumption here is that if activists can get whites to change their thinking, their actions should follow suit. Many activists, though, have come to realize that the educational piece, however important, is not sufficient. Rather, thought and action interact in complicated ways. Indeed, if the goal is for whites to change their behavior—to move from passivity to action, as I term it—then the focus should appropriately be on action. Although many activists in this study hold these views, the community organizers place the strongest emphasis on action and relationship building.[16]

Community organizers work typically at the local level to build power in communities of color and to forge alliances between whites and people of color in order to create policy and institutional change. Within this context, organizers also work at the personal level. One key hallmark of community organizing is its focus on one-on-one relationship building among community leaders. Organizers appeal to people on the basis of their interests and values. Indeed, many of the organizers in the study work through faith networks, engaging whites through their membership in religious congregations.[17]

"STRAIGHT TALK ON RACE GIVEN IN LOVE AND RESPECT"

Perry Perkins, as we saw in chapter four, found his calling as an organizer for the Industrial Areas Foundation (IAF) network. He now works in northern and central Louisiana, where he builds biracial organizations in areas historically and deeply divided by race:

> When I walk into a place in north central Louisiana and people say, "Oh, what are you doing?" the first thing I say is, "I deliberately attempt to cross the lines that divide this community. The first thing that divides this community is race. There are other divisions, but the central division is race." And, you know, that is a critique that resonates with people, both white and black. They really understand it because the places that I work in now barely felt the civil rights movement . . . In Monroe I couldn't find white pastors and black pastors that even knew each other.

Perry brings together whites and blacks from religious congregations to build relationships in order to work on issues for which they share concern. Perry appeals to black pastors by offering them a route to power through alliances with whites. He tells them:

> You're not going to get anything seriously done around things that you care about if you don't have any ways to cross race. If you don't have white allies, I don't care how much political power you're going to have, the economic power ain't in the black community. And that's what controls the strings. Unless you have some capacity to break into

that, you ain't going nowhere, which strikes in the face of nationalism but is very politically realistic.

Perry appeals to whites to come to the table in part on the basis of their religious values, which lead them to engage in public life and to work for social justice, and in part on the basis of their interests. He says, "The black community really isn't interested in paternalistic responses to them":

> In our language of organizing it's really around building power, and race is the predominant tool that's been used in this country to maintain various political and economic power arrangements. Most black folk are not interested in being helped. They are interested in solving some things, and the notion of power usually rings truthful.

Working together on common interests does not mean ignoring race; in fact, it means precisely addressing the differences that have long divided people:

> We're very clear from the beginning that at the heart of our community there is this barrier of race and that we are deliberately crossing the barriers of race. So there's an analysis, a critique, right from the beginning that we're going to do that. If people don't want to be a part of crossing barriers of race, they don't come to the table.

Perry is quite critical of some kinds of antiracist efforts that focus solely on the personal thoughts of white individuals. In his own early days of activism, Perry used to "want to convert people and preach people into it and beat them over the head," but now he does not see that as very effective because it doesn't necessarily lead to real change for racial justice grounded in the realities of political struggles. Perry now says, "I'm not a personal crusader trying to get people to see the light. To me, that's not where it's fought out."

Nevertheless, in the context of relationships across racial lines and of working together, Perry says racism must be directly confronted. He talks about approaching whites with "straight talk that is given in love and respect," a phrase he borrows from Johnny Ray Youngblood, a black pastor who is a leader of the IAF network in New York:

> We need straight talk that is given in love and respect. It is being unabashed and clear about where you are about race and your analysis or feeling about its centrality to the problems that we face in this country and particularly those that we face in the regions that I work in. I think it's central in the whole country, but it has a particular history and culture that plays itself out in a much more pronounced way

in the South. You need to be very, very clear about racism but not lose respect for most of the other white people you deal with.

In Perry's view whites have an interest in racial justice in part because racism blocks any progressive effort to address their own family and community needs. Understanding the role of racism and the need to address it, however, often develops through collaboration and relationship, not before:

> The context of relationship and work is critical. Relationship where there is some engagement, where you understand each other at least on some basic level where work is possible and that, as you work, people really change.

He gives this example:

> I was at a meeting last night in Shreveport, where there was a middle-aged white businessman who had lived in Shreveport his whole life. He said the city is still racially segregated, and it's a cancer on the city. It's important to me to change it because my kids are not going to want to live in a place that is like this. He goes on to say that the engagement here in the sponsoring committee over the last two years—in getting to know and work with African Americans from all different parts of the city, both middle class and poor—has helped him grapple with his own struggle and just really opened his eyes to what people face.

In order to counter guilt and moralizing, Perry keeps the focus on action. Speaking about himself, he says:

> Oh hell, I've been working at this stuff for a long, long time. I'm clear that I benefit from notions of white superiority that have been inculcated in this culture from the founding of the nation, and I don't feel good about that. But I don't think hand wringing and feeling guilt personally about that is very helpful. What I have to do is be real clear about that and then say, "What can I do in a day-to-day way that allows people to cross racial barriers in ways that are meaningful at a personal level and that are meaningful at a communal and political level?"

He sees the results as having a profound effect on both blacks and whites as they build relationships:

> I think it changes the quality of people's lives. There's a spiritual quality to that. It's not ideological. It doesn't get lost in lots of definitions. It's really in and around relationship and exchange of culture and experience and interest.

Although many organizers would agree with the need for "straight talk," exactly how much to talk about racism at the personal level remains an enduring tension. Sister Christine Stephens, Perry's colleague and the Texas state supervisor for the IAF network, offers a cautious view. As we saw in chapter three, Christine came to racial consciousness and activism in the sixties. However, during that time, she says, many whites who were working with African Americans were "beaten up" about their racism. She feels this approach is too moralizing and guilt provoking and therefore uses a different method when organizing:

> When I started organizing with the IAF to build power, I began to deal with leaders around their interest and around my own interest and tried to build multiracial coalitions. That's where I saw relationships develop that I thought were healthy public relationships, where we were actually able to do something together. Everybody came to the table with their own concerns, and it was legitimate to come to the table with their own concerns. That becomes the basis for negotiation and deal making between leaders. There is a lot more dignity in that than in feeling that you're in it because you feel guilty about what's happened in this country.

In fact, Christine even insists she doesn't care what whites think—as long as they act. Referring to a passage from Jesus's Sermon on the Mount, Christine says this:

> I come from a tradition that says, "By their fruit shall you know them." It doesn't matter how you feel about something, how you talk about something; if you're not doing something, to hell with you! It's easy to talk about it. It's easy to say "Ohhhh, isn't racism terrible!" But it's in the doing that's the hard part. That translates in organizing to the IAF universal, "people do the right things for the wrong reasons," and that's okay.
>
> You can have endless conversations about racism, and then the whites go back to their little white world, and the African Americans go off to their world, and the Hispanics go off to their world, and they don't ever do anything together. They just talk about it.

Christine sees her work as being about "building organizations with some real power that allows people to work together on justice issues on an interfaith and interracial basis." She wants whites to come to the table on the basis of their own interests because she believes this approach is essential to establishing relationships with people of color that are respectful and reciprocal:

> If I were to go to a wealthy white community, I'd say to them, come to the table with your own concerns so that you're not there as some paternalistic, "Oh, you're so poor." It's far better to build relationships based on the fact that we all have concerns. We all are concerned about our children. We're all concerned about our families.
>
> The poorest communities have the talent to do something about their concerns. It's not talent that they lack. They lack power. They lack anyone investing in leadership. They lack allies. So our struggle is to build some real allies for poor, working, and middle-class African American, Hispanic, and white communities.

In fact, Christine says not to lead with race:

> I don't think you deal with it by dealing with it as racism. I think you deal with it by putting people into relationship with one another. Have them bridge their differences by working together in organizing. It's the only thing I've ever seen in my experience where you don't have to talk about racism; you actually do something about it.

Through that process of working together, issues of race arise:

> Ordinary struggling people are trying to deal with the fact that they've never had the opportunity to meet other people and to get rid of their attitudes. When you put them into organizing and give them an opportunity to meet other people, they're able to deal with those attitudes because they're able to meet people face to face. You don't have to beat one another up over racism. You just have to work side by side together to build power. You just have to show that you're a good ally. It helps both sides, all sides.

Christine even felt cautious about participating in this research project, fearing that too much of an emphasis on race could essentialize racial differences. She feels that everyone has a story and that it is through sharing stories that people can make connections.

This kind of organizing strategy has sometimes been criticized for ignoring issues of race.[18] However, Christine does believe whites need to own up to the history of racism in the United States and address the racism that persists. She just wants to ensure that that this is done through coalitions for action:

> I've seen groups that do discussions. They're exhilarating. I would not say that we won't do that kind of thing about the history of racism

and own up to the fact that there is racism still. There're still racist attitudes in many of us; you have to confront that and weed that out of yourself. But the best way, ultimately, to weed it out is to try to build coalitions where you come with your own concerns and not, well, "I want to help. I'm guilty, and I'm here just to help."

Christine served as the lead organizer for the founding of Dallas Area Interfaith, a multiracial organization of African Americans, Latinos, and whites in a city deeply divided by race. She speaks with great pride that the relationships she helped build have become strong enough for the group to publicly address issues of racism in the city. The organization criticized the racism of the school committee for its unwillingness to fund after-school programs in black and Latino communities as part of a campaign to expand those programs.[19]

In the end, Christine attributes this accomplishment to the building of power. Indeed, she believes power lies at the heart of racial justice work:

> Walter Brueggemann, who's a scripture scholar, talks about "Insight never liberated anybody." I think insight is useful, but the work has got to be the hard work of trying to build something that brings communities together.
>
> I'm in organizing to build power. That's what poor people need. African Americans need power. Hispanics need power. It's about giving people enough power to change the effects of racism. The effects of racism are in poor education, poor housing, and poor jobs. If people build enough power to change these things, it can be transformative not just to people who did not have power in the first place. It's also transformative to those who now have to treat people of color with respect because they are organized and powerful.

"A CONVERSION OF THE HEART"

Tony Fleo is a pastoral associate at St. Elizabeth Ann Seton Catholic Church in Plano, Texas, an affluent suburban city north of Dallas, where he works to develop parish and community leadership. He's also a key leader in an organizing effort in the Collin County section of Dallas Area Interfaith, an affiliate of the Industrial Areas Foundation organizing network. Although Plano is overwhelmingly white, in fact because Plano is so white, Tony sees racism strongly implicated in the community:

Plano is an original white-flight community. As the schools were being integrated in Dallas, people were looking for suburban communities to move to. This is a very affluent, predominantly white community. It's very well laid out. It's very controlled. It's rated one of the top places to live, yet it also has high rates of divorce, teen drug overdose, and teen suicide.

Tony believes in the power of relationships that cross racial lines and particularly in the sharing of stories, as we saw in chapter three. He gives this example:

> In our work around what happened in Katrina, we talked about it in terms of race, and we asked, what does it say about race relations in the United States? What did we learn? We invited a family here that's in the community now, an African American family who is an evacuee, into the conversation. They talked about their experience of it, why this would occur, and how this would occur to them. Then we do some kind of concrete work, which we have done on large scales with the evacuees, and then coming back and evaluating it and talking about what we learned.

Through his work he learned that Mexican Americans often face harassment by the police in Plano:

> I was working with a young Hispanic couple in marriage counseling, and the husband was late for a session one day. He was apologetic for being late, and I said, "What happened?" And he said, "Oh, I was pulled over again by the Plano police." I said, "What do you mean?" And he said, "Oh, they pull over the Mexicans all the time who drive pickup trucks because they want to harass us."

Tony arranged for the man to speak to a group of parish leaders and talk about his experience:

> He told them, "They don't want us in Plano. They don't know I was born here in the United States, as opposed to an illegal immigrant. I'm working and supporting a family, and my children are going to school, and I'm trying to be a standup kind of citizen. But I still get regularly hassled because I'm Mexican and I drive a pickup truck even though I own my own construction company."

After the session, Tony organized a group of parish leaders to take action. The group met with the chief of police to complain about the harassment of Mexican Americans. They received a commitment for fairer treatment, and since then harassment has significantly decreased.

Tony feels that whites can come to care about these issues of racism through caring personally about someone they have now met. This is what he calls "a conversion of the heart":

> You connect at a different place with people when they're telling a story rather than when they're giving facts. A story has the power to transform us. It engages us. It connects us to the universal truths in a way that reading facts and figures could never do.... As soon as somebody's telling their own story, there's a conversion of the heart of the listener that takes place. You can't help that.

Tony is not hesitant to raise the moral issues to his white community because he sees them as central to his goal of building leadership. He says that "racism is a clear evil" that "diminishes all of us" and undermines the humanity of society as a whole. "It's all of our work" to combat racism as part of developing the leadership we need:

> The whole issue of racism is taught by asking ourselves, "How are we leaders in the community? What kind of leader are we?" Leadership is about raising people to a higher moral calling. So becoming aware of racism and being able to speak to it is a way of lifting people up. It's a way of developing a higher moral calling, which is the kind of leaders that we're trying to become.

"YOU'RE COMING TO VOLUNTEER *WITH* US, NOT DO *FOR* US"

A few of the community builders in this study work more in the social service field than in organizing, where many struggle directly with paternalistic attitudes among other whites. Like many of the organizers, they emphasize reciprocity in relationship as a powerful way for whites to come to terms with racism—and overcome paternalism. For example, Janet Morrison came to south Dallas to run a food pantry sponsored by the faith-based Central Dallas Ministries. When she arrived, she found a fence literally dividing the white suburban volunteers from the poor black applicants:

> There was a metal fence like you would have on a porch. Not iron, not that thick, but it was a fence. It was an outdoor fence inside the food pantry. There was a gate, and it separated the interviewers from the applicants. The white interviewers were always behind this gate, taking in the applications for food. Very symbolic. "This is us. Here's us and there's you."

One of Janet's first actions as director was to tear down the fence:

> The fence drove me absolutely nuts. So all of a sudden I said, "This has got to go." I started ripping up the fence. I got to the wall, and it was embedded in the sheetrock. I started pulling, and I was like, "It's got to go!" I hollered at one of the community volunteers, one of the guys, and I said, "Let's get this out." We literally ripped it out of the wall. There were holes we had to fix in the wall. But we took the fence out because it was very symbolic.

Janet proceeded to make radical changes at the pantry. First, she brought in volunteers who lived in the neighborhood to work side by side with the white suburbanites, and then she reorganized the pantry into something that ran more like a grocery store:

> Most food pantries, you walk in, maybe you're interviewed or whatever, but then you are handed a sack of groceries, and you walk out. You're expected to appreciate those groceries. If people said, "Oh well, I don't like peas," these white people would tell them, "If you were hungry, you'd like peas!"
>
> We came up with this idea of God's Grocery Store. Instead of us deciding what you like, we would create a list—two vegetables, two fruits, soup, whatever. You choose off of the shelf that is designated the "soup shelf." So, basically, you're going to the grocery store. You're purchasing what you like and what your family will eat.

Janet found that many of the suburban volunteers resisted the change. It challenged their superior position as the charitable giver:

> Change doesn't come easy. One of the suburban volunteers told me, he said, "If you change this to a grocery store," he said, "I will never come back."

Many of the volunteers left, but this man did in fact come back, as did several others.

Educators: Connecting with Core Values

Community organizers and activists in education work in different contexts. In this section I focus on the educators who address racial inequality in public schooling.[20] Many find themselves working with white teachers to change and improve the work they do. As might be expected, educator activists believe in the power of education as a force to change whites. Perhaps surprisingly, though, many of the themes they stress are similar to those the community organizers emphasize: the focus on practice, the tensions surrounding how and how much to address the racism of whites, and the power of direct experience and relationships.

"AN ADAPTIVE CHALLENGE"

Oakland principal Katherine Carter understands racial inequity in public schooling as both an institutional and an interpersonal phenomenon. She believes that the large, impersonal schools that low-income children of color in Oakland used to attend did not teach them well. As a teacher in one of those schools, she participated in an organizing effort with Oakland Communities Organization and the Bay Area Coalition for Equitable Schools to create a set of small schools in Oakland. She became principal of one of the forty-eight schools created, Manzanita SEED Elementary School, serving a diverse population of students, about 45 percent Latino, 25 percent African American, and 25 percent Asian American. The school has incorporated a number of institutional features that are designed to mitigate racial inequity: small class sizes, an expeditionary learning curriculum that is project based and uses a hands-on approach, dual language immersion, which is meant to respect family and community culture, and strong connections between families and the school.

As principal, though, Katherine also sees the need to confront racism on a personal level with her predominantly white teaching force. One key issue is the teachers' low expectations. Although teachers can be trained with the best methods technically, they won't use those methods if they don't believe their students can learn at high levels. Katherine recounts this example:

> One of my teachers, Emily, has many years' teaching experience, but she has some of the lowest expectations. There are parts of her that are really strong, but she is not incorporating this new pedagogy. I've done all of this training on writers' workshop and rubrics, and she is not doing it. Fundamentally, it is because she thinks her kids can't do it. She has even articulated that to me. One of my drama residents reported to me that she once said out loud in the class, "Well, these kids aren't getting it because a bunch of them are English language learners, and the rest of them are Special Ed, and it is really only these three students who will be able to follow you," and had them stand up.[21]

Racialized fear of black children, especially boys, also affects teaching. Referring to another teacher, Katherine says this:

> This is going to sound very candid. I'll just say it. I can't worry about how I'm going to sound. She doesn't know how to teach African American students. I don't like to say that because it sounds like African American students are somehow different. They are not. But this is a second-grade class, and she was actually afraid of them. She wouldn't assert her authority. It goes deep, and it comes out in different ways.

For these reasons, Katherine sees changing white teachers as an adaptive, not primarily a technical, challenge:

> I think of it as a belief system. There was a framework that we were introduced to in my administrative training that was about looking at a challenge as either an adaptive challenge or a technical challenge. Technical is you can just give someone an improvement plan. Adaptive is actually changing their belief system, and this is adaptive work.

Change of this sort starts with data and confronting a teacher's values with the reality of racial inequity:

> What we are talking about is wanting equitable outcomes for our students. We look at data and disaggregate that data, looking at the fact that right now our outcomes aren't equitable. You really have to look at your own belief system and say, "Okay, if my students' outcomes are different, and I can almost predict it based on what their ethnicity is, what am I going to do about it as a teacher?" If I accept that it is just the way it is, then what am I buying into? A bell curve theory that says race predicts that? Well, no. It is making that explicit.

Change requires more than being presented with evidence that children of color at other schools can learn at high levels. Katherine finds that teachers need a direct, first-hand experience:

> I don't think people change their belief system unless they have an actual experience. You can give people articles, and you can talk to them about theory, and that helps, but it doesn't really change your belief system. If we can identify one high-leverage strategy, focus our coaching on that, do a preconference on that strategy, and keep with the teacher on that so that they are constantly looking at the students' results, that is what we are going to do. It is kind of based on some of what Enid Lee does, and some of it is on more of an inquiry approach.

I say, "So what is it your kids can't do? Okay, let's identify that thing they can't do, and now we are going to teach them how to do it. Let's assess beforehand. Oh, only 10 percent of your kids can do this? Let me show you how to teach them so that they can do it. Would you like to learn that? Sure, let's do it. Let's assess afterward. Wow, 90 percent of them can do it now."[22]

Katherine typically does not address teacher's negative attitudes as racism although she challenges the particulars of comments and actions:

> There was a student this year, actually, who is a first-grader. He was in Emily's reading group, and she was really negative about him. "Oh, he's just slow." I was like, "No, he is a first-grader, and he is six. This is what they are supposed to be doing right now." Not necessarily bringing it back to the issue of race but more calling on it, then again trying to come back with the concrete evidence.

Change comes slowly, but Katherine does get to see the fruits of her hard work:

> Jamal is reading now. What do you know? The last time this teacher tested his fluency level, he is reading like forty-five words a minute. He is six. The benchmark is like thirty something.[23]

"THAT'S WHAT I WANT FOR MY KIDS"

Laurie Olsen raises issues of race explicitly with white teachers. Laurie is the executive director of California Tomorrow, a policy research and advocacy group that addresses issues of diversity and equity, especially those that relate to immigration. An anthropologist by training, she is the author of *Made in America,* a critical study of how schools work to assimilate the children of immigrants. Laurie works closely with schools and school districts to address the practice of teachers, most of whom are white, as a key part of institutional change. She wants schools to help create a future society that values different cultures and languages and thereby open up possibilities for the full inclusion of immigrants.[24]

Like Katherine Carter, Laurie starts by using data with teachers to identify racial inequities. She finds, though, that although teachers might recognize the reality of racial inequality, they often resist seeing their own personal responsibility for this. Laurie's approach is to have teachers work collectively to look at data and reflect on their own practice:

It's a process of coming to see and, as you're coming to see, making decisions about what you're going to do about it. Ongoing learning and ongoing reflection is a really, really, really key piece of it. Even with the best of intent, people often don't see. That's where the team issue, the shared observation, the creation of these communities that are reading together, that are talking together, looking at their practice together becomes so important.

Laurie is careful to raise issues of race in an inclusive way that respects where teachers are coming from yet offers them a chance to move forward:

Some of it is the forgiveness piece, of recognizing that we're all trapped in this. We've all been schooled in white supremacy, and you know what? That's what we're given, and it's a question of what we do with it. We try to help white people feel they have some agency. That's really, really crucial. It's not where you've been so much that is the issue; it's what you're doing with it and where you're going.

This requires creating a safe space, sometimes in an all-white setting:

I feel it's my role to create space where white people can really work through some of their confusion and stuff safely, not around people of color. I mean safe for everybody involved, both for the white people who are trying to really understand it, muddle through it, and be able to say what they need to say. And I mean for the people of color, who have a right to be protected from that, to not be subjected to it.

Changing deeply held stereotypes that lead to low expectations also requires direct experience to ignite a sense of the possible:

We do a lot of taking people physically to other places to see schools where the kids are thriving or using our videos to show it because a couple things happen. When people see young people that have that strong sense of self, thriving, working in and across multiple communities, there's something that gets unlocked in them. "Oh, that's what I want for my kids. Oh, it's possible?" But they have to see it.

Just as organizers work to get whites to build relationships with people of color, Laurie asks teachers to listen to their students' stories and try to immerse themselves in their community. To teach children well, educators need to understand their culture:

In most schools teachers do not share a cultural, language, or racial background with their students right now. Part of my background, by the way, is in anthropology, and this comes into it. How do you come to understand a culture that is different from yours? There's a lot of support for teachers around that, and some of that is student voice, some of it is observation, some of it is immersion in the community of the kids.

Teachers have to get beyond the school walls to build relationships with parents and community leaders:

Typically it's often students taking teachers on excursions into the community. It's home visits. It's a lot of different things. It's trying to connect the teachers with people who are community leaders in different ways. It's often brokered through the students and the parents, the immersion of the teachers in the community.

New kinds of relationships with families and community leaders can challenge stereotypes:

People may make assumptions about so-and-so sitting there. It's not until they hear a lot more of their story that they realize the complexities, the complications, the overlays of different kinds of cultural experience, the fact that we don't all necessarily show visually who we are and what our life experience has been. So the telling of personal stories is a really crucial part to build those relationships.

The collective aspect of the approach to teachers is important because people need to feel they are working together and supporting each other:

I always have people do their own personal journey maps and share their stories with each other. The focus in the personal journey maps includes what are the things that opened your eyes? What are the moments of real fear in entering into this work, and what got you through it? What's gotten you to this point, telling their stories to the group about what kinds of things move people. Then our role is to try to move each other and others.

Like many of the community organizers, Laurie works to bring teachers into a collective process that taps into their core values and interests. In this case, most teachers want to be successful at their teaching and to help their students succeed; that is why they entered the teaching profession in the first place. However difficult the process of change, Laurie finds that teachers are energized by the opportunity to actualize their values:

I think another thing is just evoking in people that part of them that really wants to be on a cutting edge of breaking through racial barriers. Having people see themselves that way, having people feel that sense of the importance of being in that role, and picking up that charge.

Policy Advocates: The Search for New Approaches

In this chapter I have focused so far mostly on working with whites at an interpersonal level. Of course, the objective of most of this interpersonal work is to change the operations of institutions. In this section I discuss the views of legal and policy advocates, particularly in criminal justice, whose work focuses on changing both public policy and the operation of public institutions. Since white people are typically in power in legislative bodies or other decision-making entities, these advocates address other whites. Whites also constitute a majority of the broader polity, whose support is needed for policy change. Compared to organizers and educators, however, policy advocates try to affect other whites at more of a distance—through the media or in lobbying efforts, for example—rather than face to face. Many though report feeling frustration at the effects of working at a distance. Indeed, the policy advocates in this study stated that they were searching for new strategies, and many are struggling with the dilemma of whether to frame their efforts explicitly as addressing racial justice. Many are also finding that local work may be more conducive to building relationships that can move people toward racial justice.[25]

"WE DON'T TALK SPECIFICALLY ABOUT RACE"

David Utter is cofounder and director of the Juvenile Justice Project of Louisiana (JJPL), based in New Orleans. David and JJPL work to reform juvenile justice procedures and facilities and promote alternatives to incarceration. The JJPL is best known for its successful effort to close down the Tallulah juvenile detention center. David describes the conditions there:

> In the first twenty days of August in 1997, twenty-eight kids at Tallulah went to the hospital for broken bones or sutures due to injuries from violence. The kids were fighting over clothes. Doctors reported seeing in one single day eight perforated eardrums. The guards would put on a black glove and smack the kids so hard on the side of the head with the cuffed hand that the kid's eardrum would burst. They reported seeing eight in one day—in one day!

David is certain that the situation at Tallulah represented racism:

> There is absolutely no question that if the child of [State Corrections Secretary] Stalder, a white guy, was in one of those facilities, if your kid was in that facility, if my kid was in that facility, there would be no hesitation to fire somebody that perforated my kid's eardrum. There would be no hesitation to step in and do something dramatic if you had twenty-eight children go to the hospital in twenty days. But because the children are 80-to-90 percent African American, because the children are 99.9 percent poor and had no advocate short of JJPL, it was completely acceptable. That is pure and simple racism.

David and JJPL use a combination of strategies to shut down institutions like Tallulah, but they do not address the situation as racism:

> We found at least in Louisiana that if we don't lead with race, if we don't point out that this change in policy is going to help poor black kids, that policymakers are much more willing to engage and discuss changes. When you look at all of our literature, it's all about effective juvenile justice systems. It's all about wise expenditure of dollars. It's about basing policies on best practices and research. We don't talk specifically about race.

Such an approach, however, does not preclude shaming people about the situation in order to get their attention:

> First you highlight the problem, and that's the shaming part, and then you propose solutions. You've got to get policymakers and society to a place where they acknowledge there's a problem before you can start having them actually engage or honestly think about changing the policy. We definitely pointed out that twenty-eight kids went into the hospital in twenty days, 90 percent of the children in the facility were black, and they're all poor, and shame on you for brutalizing this largely voiceless, helpless group of kids.

Once he has their attention, David moves on to nonracial, efficiency arguments tied to their self-interest:

> When we talked about closing Tallulah in 2003, when you look at the literature that we gave to the legislature, there might not be any discussion of the demographics. It might all be about how much money we're spending, how ineffectively we were spending it, and why a policy toward community programs is the wise thing to do.

David has seen explicit talk about racism lead to defensiveness and resistance:

> When they were doing their stuff on disproportionate minority con-finement, the Casey Foundation was showing statistics to this prosecu-tor in Jefferson Parish that said, "Look, you've got all these black kids for the same charges as all these white kids, yet the black kids are get-ting secure care." This is just what the numbers show. The prosecutor just went off the charts crazy, just completely off the rails. "You called me a racist. That's bullshit. We're not racist here. The reason those kids are there is that they did the charge." It just completely shut down any dialogue about how to fix the situation.

Although David worries about avoiding the tough race discussions, he believes that building up victories increases the long-term capacity for change:

> I definitely understand the possible long-term implications of not leading with race. My response has been to get a shift in policy and bring dollars to communities and families and to fight to have com-munities and families at the table. That builds a base that has more potential to change the dialogue and to change longer-term policy on other issues. Once you win on juvenile justice, the community can shift to schools or wherever the community wants to go. They've got a win under their belt. That's a more strategic way to go about changing public policy on this issue than leading with race.

Still, the treatment of black residents in New Orleans after Hurricane Katrina, as well as white Americans' general passivity to their plight, leaves David apprehensive about how to proceed on race issues. Advocates seemed powerless as public authorities proceeded to rebuild white communities in New Orleans to the exclusion of African Americans. In fact, David feels he's part of a search for new strategies. "We've got to think differently about this stuff. We have to figure out a different strategy because what's happening isn't working."

"RACE HAS INFECTED POLICIES"

Louisiana may represent a particularly tough place to lead with explicit reference to racism, but David's views speak to concerns echoed by policy advocates elsewhere. Penda Hair is cofounder of the Advancement Project in Washington, DC, which addresses issues like quality education, ending "the schoolhouse-to-jailhouse" track, immigrant rights, and the rebuilding of New Orleans after Katrina. The project also works with community-organizing groups to address voting rights and to create majority-minority voting districts as a way to empower communities of color to effect change.

In the Advancement Project's broad policy work with moderate whites, Penda stresses the need to show whites their own self-interest:

> One of our solutions is to try to build multiracial coalitions around an issue that's been, as we call it, racialized, and also to show members of racial groups, especially whites, how these racial policies impact them and impact society as a whole. A quick example of how whites are impacted that even racist whites may understand is that it costs so much more to send a kid to prison than it does to give them a good education. If we can convince people that it's worth it to invest more in education because it saves money, then we're willing to make that argument.

At the same time, Penda feels that, because of racism, many whites don't see their self-interest in policy change:

> We also know that the reason that some of them haven't figured that out themselves and on their own decided to vote for more money for schools is because they're scared of these kids, and they want them locked up. So it's a very complicated racial analysis that we're dealing with.

Indeed, Penda believes that "race has infected policies" and that racism underlies much of white opposition to racial justice policies. This leads her to a complex strategy that addresses self-interest and morality:

> That's a fine line to walk because you don't want to walk away from the morality or in any way deny the injustice of what's happening. So we're always trying to proceed on multiple fronts. We would never not put in the racial statistics in our presentation on school discipline. We would always hit people with what's happening racially because we think it is important for people to have the real information. But we would also try to show the public, including whites, how it is in their own self-interest to change this policy.

Penda has a deep belief that racism harms everyone and that it serves as the critical block to achieving public policy that would benefit most whites, as well as people of color. Yet she and her colleagues continue to struggle for effective strategies because the issue of race is so deeply entrenched:

> It's also about moving this country to adopt more progressive policies generally that will affect everybody and make the country better

for everybody. If you can somehow deal with race, you will remove a blockage to progressive policies. I would say that those two are both very important. Race has infected policies. Race also has to be dealt with on its own terms. If you accomplish dealing with race on its own terms, we think it will unblock progressive policies.

"YOU HAVE TO HAVE BROADER GOALS"

Rose Braz stresses a racial analysis in her advocacy work on criminal justice issues. Rose is director of Oakland-based Critical Resistance, a group that has worked to stop the massive building of prisons in California and to create alternatives to incarceration. Using the example of their work around curfews in Oakland, Rose highlights the group's explicit strategy to address racism:

> We specifically try our best to make it clear in the work we do that we see it as fighting racism. We point out why it's racism. One example is our "esteemed" mayor here in Oakland—and I say "esteemed" with big quotes around it. Jerry Brown proposed recently to place people on parole and probation on a curfew from 10 PM to 6 AM. We organized a large demonstration against that curfew. We held it in front of Jerry Brown's loft at 10 PM. We specifically pointed out where this curfew is going to be enforced, who was going to get stopped and accused of being on a curfew, and made the connection to the black codes, where people of color were prohibited from moving freely in a community.

Rose does recognize the pragmatic need to advocate for issues in any way that works, but that creates tension with the goal of combating racism:

> If you're an organization like us, you go in with multipronged goals. Your goal is to get some piece of policy changed, and your goal is to educate people about racism in the criminal justice system. There's a bill that just died to equalize those sentences, to reduce crack cocaine to the level of powder cocaine.... It serves the policy purpose to talk about the disparity in sentencing. But in every case it doesn't necessarily help you in terms of getting the policy changed to say, "Look this thing is racist, and this is why." Other kinds of argument can be more persuasive. You have to have broader goals than just getting the piece of policy changed.

Rose believes that the larger agenda can suffer if advocates fail to address the racism that underlies injustice in criminal justice and other fields.

Advocates will have to keep fighting each and every battle until broader racial understanding starts to shift. So, in the end, the larger goal demands explicitness on race even if a particular short-term effort might suffer:

> To us it's very important to bring that race analysis to the forefront, including putting racial justice into legislative work, which I think is a challenge. A lot of folks doing policy work get very focused on getting the end result at any cost. For us, the end result is important, but so are the reasoning and rationale and everything else behind it.

"RACE IS EVERYPLACE"

Chester Hartman is research director at the Poverty and Race Research Action Council (PRRAC), based in Washington, DC. The PRRAC's mission is to connect social science research to advocates working on structural racial inequality and, more broadly, to foster understanding and action on racism and poverty. Chester has helped to sponsor and publicize research on a wide variety of issues from racial discrimination in housing to reparations for slavery. *Poverty & Race,* the newsletter he edits for PRRAC, includes:

> Symposia and articles aimed at an understanding of racial issues by all people. We deal with reparations. What does that mean? Why is it inadequate to say, "Hey, I wasn't around during slavery period, and my grandparents came here in 1903. Don't bother me." Challenging that kind of reasoning. A lot of it in good, good writing. What white privilege means, why you benefit from being white regardless of whether you intend to or not. We deal in that way with whites' understanding of racism, trying to make them more progressive in their views.

However, Chester feels it's a struggle. Often, whites just don't get it:

> It's really understanding the nature of the system and what white privilege is all about. That's a hard thing to do for most people. It gets back to arguments I've had on the reparations question. People just don't get it. "That's history," they say. "Nothing to do with us. There's Colin Powell, there's Michael Jackson. Don't worry about it. People just have to get their act together." Whites just don't understand that it isn't a question of bootstraps for most people. And they don't understand the bootstraps that they were born with.

Whites readily look for explanations for inequality other than racism, so Chester focuses directly on the role of race:

I see race and racism everyplace. When I was teaching a graduate seminar in sociology at George Washington University, every week I would ask the students to bring in what they saw in the *Washington Post* newspaper that had race about it. It's everyplace. To get people to understand that race is everyplace and is an explanatory variable for so many things—I think that's a good start. I would really want whites to see that and not look at other explanatory variables. It isn't only a race thing, but it's so frequently about race or that race is a large component.

Chester copublished a K–12 teaching resource called *Putting the Movement Back into Civil Rights Teaching* with Teaching for Change, a nonprofit group led by Deborah Menkart, another activist interviewed for this study.[26] The editors felt that progressive teaching about the civil rights movement often treated it as dead history. Their book helps show that change is possible and connects teaching to action. According to Deborah Menkart:

> We feel that the way the movement is taught now becomes disempowering to young people. The story that should be the most empowering story in this country's history has become disempowering because it's taught as if we just have to wait now for another messiah to come along and have another dream and rescue us. It was ordinary people that built that movement. It wasn't just a few mass protests, and it wasn't just a few leaders. It was a big movement.

Chester says he does not focus on addressing race with whites at the interpersonal level, although he appreciates the importance of the work some activists do in this area. Nevertheless, the *Putting the Movement* teaching resource has brought him into more direct connection with educators, and here he has found himself engaged in relational work. Pat Cooper, a white school superintendent in McComb, Mississippi, asked PRRAC and Teaching for Change to use the book and help him develop a curriculum for the district. Chester traveled to McComb and met with educators and community residents:

> When we were down there last, we were meeting with about forty people, school administrative staff plus principals and assistant principals. People were starting to talk a little bit about their own history in McComb. An African American woman talked about how she helped to integrate the movie theater in town and people threw popcorn at her. A white administrator got up and said, "I was one of the people throwing popcorn at you." They've never talked about this. It was a really emotional moment. It's coming to grips and to terms with that history that we have to do.

Although Chester remains focused primarily on research and education, he has come to see the power of the kinds of relationships that happen through dialog and personal connection. He understands that this kind of work takes time and patience:

> You got a feel that the place really wants to understand and live down that past. It was just quite remarkable. But Cooper knows that he's got to go slow with the community. He told a story about something that happened in the schools that he hadn't prepared the kids for. The kids went back and told the parents, and the parents got hysterical about it. It's one thing to work with the kids in the schools, but they've got parents and family. So you need to deal with the family and community, too. That's why he thinks it will take a two-, three-, or four-year process to do this.[27]

"YOU HAVE TO BE ABLE TO TALK WITH PEOPLE ABOUT THEIR LIVES"

There seems to be a growing appreciation among the policy advocates in this study that, in order to change whites, something more than media-based educational strategies is required. Like Chester, Mark Soler has also come to see the value of building relationships at the local level focused on practice.[28] As the president of the Youth Law Center in Washington, DC, Mark has helped lead a new initiative on juvenile justice reform called Building Blocks for Youth.

Mark points out that, although black and Latino youth represent one-third of the adolescent population in the United States, they make up two-thirds of the youth confined in local detention and state correctional systems. Confronting the institutional racism that produces this disparity requires confronting the racial stereotypes held by institutional agents:

> For example, some people are perfectly willing to believe that a child who comes before them in court wearing baggy pants that are set low and a big T-shirt and has his hair in dreads is more likely to have been involved with drugs than a child who comes into court neatly dressed, clean cut, and wearing a shirt with a collar. The kids who come in like the first kids are disproportionately kids of color. Part of what we are trying to do is isolate that decision making, see where it's based on stereotypes, and then try to make it more objective.

As Mark and his colleagues began looking for effective ways of engaging people, including whites, around racial disparities in the juvenile justice system, they came to focus on fairness:

Most people feel that they believe in fairness, and if you push them, they're not bad about that. That seems to be a more strongly held belief than sympathy for kids in the system. The problem with sympathy is that these kids have committed crimes. For many people, the fear of juvenile crime trumps the sympathy they may have for kids who are in the system.

That's why we framed our work in terms of children who are similarly situated, where children of color will get treated much more harshly at every single stage of the system. That seems to fit in with what people see as their own beliefs.

Demonstrating the overrepresentation of youth of color alone is not sufficient:

I found, when talking to reporters, editorial writers, conservative groups, police, public officials, if you talk about overrepresentation, their first response is, "Well, of course they're overrepresented because they commit more crimes." You need to be able to counter that.

The project sponsored research that focused on the treatment of similarly situated youth by race. It showed, for example, that when white youth and minority youth were charged with the same offense, African American youth with no prior admissions were six times more likely to be incarcerated in public facilities than white youth with the same background.[29] The report clearly shows that "the difference is the color of their skin." The project launched a national media campaign to publicize its findings and tried to engage national constituency groups. It got a reaction. But Mark still sees resistance:

The racial disparity bothers people, but I think people don't know what to do about it. People in this country don't want to talk about race. Not in these kinds of conversations. People who are public officials do not want to talk about the impact of race in the way that they do their work. A big challenge is getting them to find a way to talk about it in a way that's not threatening to them.

To get people to talk about race and develop alternatives, Building Blocks piloted local initiatives that brought a variety of stakeholders together for face-to-face conversations. These local projects focused on changing the practice of police officers and court officials in specific places while engaging a variety of organizations in developing community-based alternatives to incarceration. The local work was more successful than Mark expected:

If I was going to do it all over again, I'd put more money into the site-based work because I think that this is a local issue. You have to be able to talk with people about their lives and about people's real lives rather than on the abstract level. It just doesn't work on the abstract level.

In order to combat the operation of racial stereotypes, Building Blocks worked with local stakeholders to develop objective standards by which to make decisions:

On pretrial detention of kids the traditional standard is very broad, whether the child will commit another crime before the trial or whether they'll flee the jurisdiction. What that really means is, is the kid dangerous or not? If that's the only question you ask, and you put children in front of judges, judges act out the stereotypes. We try to come up with objective standards for dangerousness. Have they had an offense within the last two years, and have they ever failed to appear in court? Things like that, which are yes-or-no questions that are much more objective.

Building Blocks piloted local work in Seattle, led in part by James Bell, an African American leader in the project who proceeded to launch the W. Haywood Burns Institute to concentrate on this strategy. Mark describes the kind of detailed and sustained process that is necessary to make changes at the local level:

It turns out there were three neighborhoods that were contributing most of the kids to being locked up. So they took a very hard look at what was going on there: What were the kids having police contact with, who was arrested, what were they arrested for, what were the crimes, and what happened to them? They also did community mapping of those three neighborhoods. Where were the problem areas? Was it liquor stores or vacant lots or drug corners? Where were the strong points? Where were there recreation organizations and churches and community programs? From that, they have spent time working to try to strengthen the community in ways that would keep kids occupied and reduce the amount of police contact. They've had some success, although it's taken a long time.

Although change is slow, Mark feels the project has finally gotten people talking about race in juvenile justice:

We really made it acceptable and helped to define some terms that people could use to talk about this issue. Talking about it is the first step to doing anything about it. Nothing happens until people can at least identify what their problem is. I think that if we had never done the Building Blocks project, I think that there would to this day be very few places in America where people in the juvenile justice system actually talked about race.

Conclusion

In order to change white people's behavior, one can pressure them to change or win them over to change willingly. Undoubtedly both strategies are useful and necessary. Pressure can begin to force change. Nonetheless, for it to be thoroughgoing and sustainable, whites must come to accept and even embrace the change. Many of the activists in this study work to create pressure. However, they also feel the necessity and responsibility to engage white people around issues of race in order to win their hearts and minds.

Education plays an important role in changing white's beliefs about people of color. The activists in this study certainly work to educate other white people, but many see education as insufficient. If we want to change behavior, they argue, we need long-term engagement through relationships that focus on practice, which will, in turn, challenge stereotypes and change thinking.

In fact, the experience of these white activists lends some support to the key themes developed in the first three chapters of this book. As Mark Soler put it so clearly, it's not the facts of racial inequality that move white people; they can always turn to cultural or other factors to explain these inequalities. Numbers have limited power to pull whites out of their passivity and their normal routines. Rather, whites appear more influenced by concrete evidence of racially discriminatory treatment. This can happen at a distance, for example, through the reports of studies on police officers' differential treatment of white and black people. However, the more direct the experience, the more powerful effect it appears to have on whites in schools, in community organizations, and in local stakeholder coalitions for advocacy work. Direct experience of the violation of deeply held values stokes the moral impulse against injustice.

Some of these activists emphasized the material self-interest of other whites by showing, for example, the cost savings of educating rather than incarcerating black children. This strategy appears to have some positive effect. Still, in failing to get beyond the "head," it seems insufficient on its own. Rather, notions of direct interest appear more compelling when tied to people's core values like fairness.

Activists work hard to appeal to whites by giving them a chance to live out their values. Some of these values find their roots in faith traditions; others in ideas of American democracy. Activists may not present a full-blown moral vision, but they do push in that direction. They ask other whites questions of the following sort: What kind of community do you want to raise your children in? What kind of teacher do you want to be? How can we work together to create the kind of community, school, or institution that treats all people fairly?

Indeed, activists try hard to give other whites an opportunity to "join the antiracist family," as Christine Clark succinctly put it. Many whites greatly value equality and justice. If they can be helped to understand that these principles are being violated in practice *and* be offered an opportunity to work with others to put these values into racial justice action, they are more likely to move from passivity to action.

Action provides perhaps the best context for "straight talk on race given in love and respect," as Perry Perkins put it. Activists struggle for ways to effectively challenge whites on the issues of racial prejudice and racist behavior. In that they face a fundamental dilemma to which there is no easy answer. Too much challenge too soon produces defensiveness and loses people who might otherwise be moved. Too little talk might generate a short-term result but fails to create the deeper understanding needed to achieve the longer-term goal of racial justice. Focusing on behavior, listening to where whites are coming from, and challenging them with a firm inclusive approach all represent important aspects of the strategies these activists have developed. The context of action keeps discussions of race focused on both a desired outcome and behavior. It helps counter the moralism and self-righteousness into which challenges of white racism can easily degenerate.

By working together for institutional change, whites build relationships across the color line. These connections help white people learn and care more about racism, but they are not easy to create. In the next chapter we take a closer look at the efforts of white activists to build collaborative relationships with people of color.

CHAPTER SIX

Multiracial Collaboration

Creating "Right Relationships" under the "Weight of History"

It's absolutely a collaborative, experimental, trial-and-error, learn as you go, depend-on-each-other-throughout experience.

—Alex Caputo-Pearl

There's always a lot in the moment. I guess that's part of the learning. You're never just two people going about life. The weight of history and institutional arrangements is always there.

—Laurie Olsen

MULTIRACIAL VENUES REMAIN elusive in America. Forty years after the height of the civil rights movement, we remain a country still largely segregated. After some progress in the seventies, segregation appears firmly entrenched. We live in largely separate communities while our children attend separate schools by race and economic status. Some growth has occurred in multiracial religious congregations and interracial marriages, but these remain rare, as are cross-racial friendships. Perhaps just as rare are venues for multiracial collaboration, that is, places where whites and people of color work together on common projects.[1]

The large majority of white activists in this study work hard to build these venues, and they do so for two related reasons. First, most see them as necessary to advance the work for racial justice. By combining talents and resources from multiple communities, activists can build a stronger force for change. However, they have a second reason to build multiracial groups as well. Multiracial collaborations represent ongoing experiments in creating the new kind of multiracial society to which they are so committed. In this way multiracial collaboration is important to advancing immediate objectives, but it also represents an effort to prefigure the future.[2]

As we saw in chapter four, white activists work for racial justice in order to pursue a moral vision of the Beloved Community, a multiracial community based upon respect, equality, and caring. They construct this vision with others in their day-to-day work for racial justice. How they operate multiracially today and build relationships with people of color represent profoundly important questions to them. Building respectful relationships with people of color is necessary to advance racial justice work, but it also represents a test of an activist's own personal integrity.[3]

Activists confront deep challenges in trying to develop these new models of multiracial relationships and organizations. One problem is sheer inexperience as most Americans have little opportunity to learn how to collaborate across racial lines. A second challenge is perhaps deeper, as alluded to by the quotation from Laurie Olsen at the beginning of this chapter. How do you work together across racial lines in a way that does not replicate racialized patterns in the larger society? How do you create a model of that future society based upon equality in the context of today's continued racial hierarchy and the country's racialized past? Even as activists struggle to change those structures of racism, how do they prevent the "weight of history and institutional arrangements" from undermining their efforts?

Activists can bring into the movement all of the prejudices, behaviors, and inequalities that come from their membership in the larger society. Just because they have committed themselves to racial justice does not mean they are incapable of racialized thinking and behavior. They may act in ways that can undercut the participation and leadership of people of color, for example, by dominating decision making. Moreover, since white people continue to have greater access to education and employment experience, there will often be an imbalance in skills and experience across race in multiracial settings. Activists of color, for their part, may distrust the motives and the commitment to racial justice of their white colleagues. Although the roots of these issues lie in the history and current perpetuation of racial inequality at a structural level, much of the work to confront these challenges takes place at the interpersonal and relational level in multiracial settings. Multiracial collaborators have to work hard to forge trusting relationships and equalize participation toward the goal of true collaboration.

Leadership in multiracial organizations poses a particular dilemma. Should people of color be afforded a special leadership role in the movement for racial justice, or should collaborations seek equal coleadership across race? On the one hand, one could argue that those most affected, that is, people of color, should lead in order to keep these efforts closely aligned with the cause of racial justice. After all, white activists may not understand the issues as clearly as activists of color since they do not directly face racial oppression and its consequences. Indeed, white activists can walk away tomorrow and escape racism's direct oppression. On the other hand, many white activists have proven their commitment to racial justice over many years of hard work. Moreover, they have talents and skills the movement needs. If the ultimate goal is the creation of a community that values everyone equally, then should there not be full coleadership across race in the multiracial experiments of today?

Activists grapple with these challenges not only in the face of contemporary racial dynamics but also in the shadow of the civil rights movement. King's effort to create an interracial Beloved Community ran aground in the midsixties as younger and more militant black activists challenged whites who, they felt, were dominating the movement or were too moderate in the face of the new militancy. A rising Black Power movement pushed white activists out of groups like SNCC and CORE and led to the creation of all-black organizations. Meanwhile, African American communities demanded black control of institutions like schools and often challenged white principals to step aside.[4]

Today's activists have not given up on the goal of multiracial community, but they have learned from the experiences of the sixties to make a more conscious effort to address the inevitable tensions that underlie multiracial work. Many have also learned from practices in the women's movement that challenged male-dominating behavior or from New Left movements that promoted attention to interpersonal dynamics and behavior as part of movement building. Nevertheless, the "weight of history and institutions" remains.[5]

This chapter concerns how activists attempt to address these challenges and negotiate these dilemmas. What lessons have they learned in building multiracial collaborations capable of working toward racial justice? This discussion is necessarily limited because I have not interviewed people of color or other whites with whom these activists collaborate, nor have I directly observed the dynamics in these venues myself. I can only reveal the issues that the interviewees feel have been salient. In other words, this is less a study of effective strategies for multiracial collaboration and more a report on how committed white activists experience and understand this work, which seems critical to what it means to be a racial justice activist for most of the whites in this study. Nevertheless, I hope it will have much to offer to our understanding of the processes involved in creating truly collaborative multiracial relationships.[6]

Building Trusting Relationships

For the activists in this study, multiracial collaboration is built upon a foundation of relationships. In order to get people to work well together and to build and sustain such collaboration over time, people have to get to know and trust each other. Yet multiracial efforts often begin in a context of initial and perhaps to some extent ongoing mistrust. Segregation itself breeds mistrust. More than that, people of color are well aware of their long history and the contemporary reality of discrimination at the hands of the white majority. They may even have had direct experience with well-meaning whites who have done more harm than good in their view. People of color may suspect white people's motives. Certainly, activists in this study report that trusting relationships are crucial to multiracial collaboration and that mistrust is a pervasive problem. In this section I trace the activists' experiences in trying to develop trust and the lessons they have learned in doing so.[7]

PROVE YOURSELF "NOT JUST IN WORD BUT IN DEED"

Perry Perkins, an IAF community organizer in Louisiana, works to get white and black faith communities to form relationships in which they can find shared concerns and act together. However, segregation and a history of racial oppression have bred mistrust. Perry knows that black pastors are suspicious of white organizers like him; he accepts that as part of the context of the situation. Perry has learned that it takes time to cultivate trust. He has also learned the value of going to black pastors first—before engaging white faith leaders:

> The first black pastor I met with listened to me and said, "I like what you're saying. That sounds real good. But you are the craziest white man I have ever met. That will not work here." He was dead serious. I said to him, first, there is nothing in your history that tells you that you ought to trust me, so don't. Trust is developed over time. Second,

I told him that I won't do anything if there aren't black pastors who will do this. This will not start in the white community. Hopefully, we can start it simultaneously. But if there is no group of black pastors that endorses this and says this is theirs, it's gone.

Perry spends a lot of time in the black church, learning about the culture of the community with whom he wants to collaborate. He appeals to common values in the form of religious faith to find some basis for relationship building. He believes that, in the context of a segregated Christian church, stating your belief that all people, black and white, are children of God is a radical antiracist statement:

> Peter Paris, in his book *The Social Teaching of the Black Churches,* says that the paradigm of the black church is that we're all children of God, created in the likeness and image of God and that that is a nonracist statement. He says that's at the heart of black theology. Whether it is fully expressed and even understood and articulated, it is at the heart of the black community.

But the real test comes through practice. Lots of white people can talk a good game. Whites who want to build trust must prove themselves through their work, not just in what they say:

> We're all kin. A very radical notion in this country. But what I've come to understand is that when black folks really, really believe that you believe that and you demonstrate that to them not just in word but in deed, you're in. It takes time, but *you—are—in*. Not in every place, but you will be accepted in places.

The challenge to trust is ongoing, and you need to "earn your stripes" repeatedly:

> Look, there's the notion that I said you can be accepted in. But that's some people accepting you in and in some particular communities. You got to earn your stripes all the time, over and over again. It does not end. You have to be tough. You have to not feel uncomfortable being the only white person in a black church service, where the pastor talks very frankly about race. I mean that's kind of symbolic, but it's relentless. You have to constantly prove yourself.

After thirty years of organizing Perry has come to have faith in the process and in himself. He can accept mistrust as a reality because he knows it will change if he is able to prove himself over time:

If somebody says to me, "Well, I don't trust you," I'll say, "You know, fine. I know a lot of people who do, and I'm sorry that you don't." And I don't worry about it. But that's taken time. It has taken energy and growth to be able to have that kind of confidence.

Given the racial polarization in American society, Perry feels he has to take sides sometimes to demonstrate his firm commitment to racial justice:

Sometimes it really is an issue of choosing sides. There is a point where you have to say, all right, what has happened to the black community, the way they've been treated and screwed over, over four hundred years in this country, I got to choose. My tendency is going to be to side with the black community, not in an indiscriminate way without thinking. It doesn't mean that the black community always makes the right choices. So there are times where you say, that's ridiculous. But there has to be sensitivity to what folks are up against.

In the end, Perry finds that if whites don't take mistrust personally, accept that it is a legitimate result of historical oppression, and work to prove themselves in what they do, then trust can increase over time. Sometimes this means taking a clear stand with the black community. As a result, "It doesn't mean African Americans will always like me or think I always do things right, but there's a trust for the integrity of where I come from."

"TO BE COMMITTED TO A PARTICULAR PLACE"

Rachel Breunlin is a New Orleans teacher and community activist in the Porch, a multiracial, cultural organization in the city's predominantly black Seventh Ward, where she lives and teaches at the local high school. Rachel works with residents in a community storytelling project as part of mobilization efforts around racial justice issues in the rebuilding of New Orleans in the wake of Hurricane Katrina. Not unlike Perry, she feels that it is important for white activists to make a commitment to a place in which to create relationships with people of color. Perry worked closely in and with the black church, while Rachel focuses on the Seventh Ward. She is critical of many young white professionals who move into urban neighborhoods but do not share institutions with the local community:

Young white people move into a neighborhood like the Seventh Ward, but will they send their kids to the same school that their neighbors send their kids to? Do they share PTA meetings? Are they shopping at the same places? Are we investing in the same networks? Over and over again, the answer is no, we're not doing this. The way that I see my project is trying to invest in a way that we share. We have joint investment, and we have accountability to each other. But that's hard, that's a struggle.

Rachel's approach is different from that taken by many other white professionals in that she has made a commitment not to racial justice "in the abstract" but to real people:

It's important to know your neighbors and be committed to your neighbors, not to people in the abstract but to actual people. You love them as full people—not because they're black people or not because they're white people. I don't believe in a color-blind analysis, either. We need to really understand who we are and what our experiences really are. We need to learn to live and care for each other in deep ways, so that our kids will grow up together. That's the place where I'm at. I've got a deep commitment to the Seventh Ward. I have a deep commitment to working in public education, and I really love being a part of the Porch organization.

She finds that the basis for these relationships has to be genuine reciprocity, not charity:

If you're going to work in a predominantly black space, you need to think about what your motives are for being there. You need to be really critically reflective of your place and where the reciprocity is coming from. Cultures all over the world don't like people just to give them things and not be able to give back. If you just come into a neighborhood and say I'm here to help and help and help, but people don't know where you're coming from or what you're doing with yourself, where do you go? You're up here in my personal space. Who's up in your personal space, you know?

Although people build relationships in order to work together, they are not just working associations. Like Perry, Rachel believes trust can be created by getting beyond superficial conversations and connecting at a deeper level. Community implies that people develop caring, multifaceted relationships:

Getting dirty together is a very good way of building trust. We have a community garden. We had a block party in support of Ed's second line [a parade band], and everyone cooked together. We do these interviews for the poster project together. We just follow through for one another. We call each other. Not just for meetings, you know. These are basic things, but sometimes people don't do those things. We also want to have a good time together. We don't want to just be so serious about our cultural organization that we have no time for being able to enjoy one another.

Whites and blacks also need to learn how to have strong disagreements without breaking trust, and that requires this kind of long-term commitment to each other:

We want to actually know each other, and that's hard. We need to learn to fight with each other and make up. And say I made a mistake, and say that's okay, I still love you. That's where we get real trust instead of the superficial conversation that we have about race all the time. We don't have a very complex or nuanced understanding because we don't really invest or share anything together.

Like Perry, Rachel wants racial differences to be recognized and openly discussed. Yet when people focus solely on race, differences can be exaggerated. When they develop well-rounded relationships and work together on a variety of issues over time, commitment to the collective creates a positive dynamic where race issues and tensions can be worked out:

The dynamics are really great in the Porch because people have a commitment to racial justice, but they have a commitment to each other. They're not essentializing race. They're committed to working it out in practice rather than just in theory, and that feels really good.

"PEOPLE KNOW THAT I'M NOT JUST A FLASH IN THE PAN"

Katherine Carter also stresses the importance of a long-term commitment to an institution and a community through which she can develop multi-faceted relationships and build trust over time. As principal of the Manzanita SEED Elementary School in Oakland, Katherine strives to create a multiracial teaching staff committed to racial equity in education. She collaborates with community organizations in the Latino, African American, and Asian communities from which her students come. Like Rachel, she made a commitment to live in the neighborhood of the school in which she works. Like Perry, she stresses the importance of not taking mistrust personally.

Katherine experiences an "anger and a judgment" particularly from African Americans, which she understands as coming out of the history of racial oppression that communities have faced. Although she cautions about generalizing from her experience, she feels that the school has been able to generate trust more quickly with immigrant families, while African Americans have more suspicion:

> If you are talking about an African American community, you have to understand their experience of being disenfranchised in education and in the parents' experience themselves of going through a racist educational system. Nevertheless, they are telling their kids the same general message that school is really important, and you should do well in it. Really all families want that. Yet there is still so much personal negative experience to work through, and it is real. It is very real. We are seeing it play out in our small school in Oakland. The trust we are able to get and the buy-in from the immigrant community is instant. In communities that are more predominately African American, it really takes a different approach. There needs to be more time spent on that trust building.

Experiences with racism continue to fuel mistrust not just among parents but also among her staff. Katherine finds that people of color will not always assume positive intent on the part of whites like her. She recalls this incident at an equity retreat:

> I remember we were putting up what our norms were going to be. The norms would be like, speak your truth. Another one would be like, assume positive intent. I really loved both of those. I remember a woman of color stood up and said, "I don't know if I can really say that I will go by that norm of 'assume positive intent' because I don't know you people. I don't trust you yet, and I have had a lot of experiences, particularly with white people, that showed me that I can't really trust them. So I can't really assume positive intent right now."

She knows that many white people have trouble dealing with that kind of mistrust:

> Some white people were very offended. They said, "What do you mean? For me to participate freely in this discussion, you have to assume positive intent about me. Otherwise how can I speak my truth?" I see both sides on it. But for myself as a white person, I trust people very easily, so I expect people to trust me very easily. That is not always fair.

I should be able to earn people's trust, but it is not always fair for me to expect that they will give it without knowing me.

Consequently, Katherine spent eight years working hard first as a teacher and then as a principal to earn the trust of the staff and community. She has spent time meeting with parents and community leaders and collaborating on school and neighborhood issues. As a result, she feels she has been able to demonstrate a commitment that has fostered trust. Now, Katherine says, "People know that I'm not just a flash in the pan."

Katherine agrees with Rachel that multifaceted relationships and friendships can develop over time as people get to know each other in a deep way. However, she cautions that the goal is not friendship per se. She finds that too many whites come in looking for personal relationships rather than a basis on which to address justice issues together:

> One of the main things is not getting defensive when somebody doesn't want to be your friend. It is not about someone being your friend. At the last meeting of the equity retreat, one member of my team, who was a white man, went through some very interesting stuff. He felt very rejected by the African American people there. He didn't realize he wasn't there to prove himself by making friends with the black people. They weren't there to make friends with him. They were there to explore the issues.

Like Perry, Katherine has found that whites need to prove themselves by more than their words:

> I think it is easy as a white person to want to prove yourself: "No, I'm not that racist white person. You should like me. I'm different." You need to realize that it is not always about you. People will realize that about you over time if you really are committed to the work.

"YOU CAN ALWAYS STEP ON A LANDMINE"

Madeline Talbott has organized for ACORN and Action Now in Chicago for many years. She forged close relationships with many African American and Latino leaders in the organization by working together on tough campaigns and being honest and open when discussing racial issues:

> I tend to be blunt and just say anything. Part of building a relationship with me is, "Here I am." But to some extent I'm sensitive to the dangers. It's important to get over all those humps. If we're building

great relationships, we have to be able to talk about everything. But I'm still sensitive to when is the timing right, when are people ready, and when do they trust each other enough that we can go there? It's a tricky area.

Madeline is constantly aware of the possibility of "stepping on a landmine" where race is concerned. She gives the following example:

> Barbara and I were talking recently about our backgrounds and where we came from. I said there was some folk history in my family that an ancestor of mine was one of the kids that was put into a barrel and sent over to America to get away from the slave rebellion in Haiti. Otherwise they would have been killed. It's part of this great slave rebellion history that Haiti has. But our side was on the wrong side in my family. It was a slave that put the kids into the barrels and sent them over.
>
> We were talking about how far back she could trace her background, which wasn't that far, and how far back I could trace mine, which was pretty far. I detected that a wall went up. I was on very shaky ground. It was too new in the relationship for me to be talking about ancestors who may have been slave owners. I quickly backed off. I sensed that I was still too new in the relationship with Barbara to speak openly and ask, "Have I gone over some line here?" I just sensed trouble and moved back for awhile.[8]

These tensions and limitations remain troubling, but many activists come to accept them as inevitable. Racial mistrust is a fact of life. Trust can be built if white activists don't take mistrust personally and rather work to prove their commitment in practice over time while they build meaningful relationships focused on common action for racial justice.[9] As Reverend Gerald Britt of the Dallas Area Interfaith organization says, "It's kind of like a marriage. The question is not whether there'll be tension and conflict but whether you'll stay through it."[10]

Addressing White Privilege Behavior

Just as the history of racial oppression brings issues of mistrust into the effort, so, too, do the racial dynamics of the larger society infect interpersonal relationships within multiracial organizations and institutions. White racial justice activists are not likely to bring overtly racist views and actions into an organization, but there are many more subtle ways that white prejudice and behavioral patterns can lead to white domination of multiracial groups, crowding out the participation of people of color. Highly educated white activists, who are used to being the experts, can run roughshod over the views of people of color. They can tend to dominate conversations. A large and growing literature now documents what are called "white privilege behavioral patterns" in classrooms and other settings. As this literature shows, most whites are unaware that their behavior reflects a privileged attitude. Not all of the activists in this study used the term *privilege,* but most had a lot to say about the necessity of openly confronting the prejudices and behaviors that whites can bring into multiracial efforts even as they work for racial justice.[11]

"I CHECK MYSELF"

Phyllis Hart directs the Achievement Council in Los Angeles, where she works with public schools and school districts to address racial equity, and also lobbies for policy change at district and state levels. Phyllis stresses the importance of building the council as a multiracial group because "we believe in practicing what we preach." The group is about a third white, a third black, and almost a third Latino, with one or two Asian American staff members. Phyllis has become alert to a number of ways that whites can dominate multiracial settings in their work, even if unintentionally. She now "checks herself" and intervenes to counter these dynamics:

> People of color have said that when they're in rooms with white people, white people can dominate the conversation. They will talk over the person of color. The person of color could have said something, but no one acknowledged it until a white person says it. Then it becomes acknowledged, then it becomes important, and people write it down. It's the white people who write about the work, and people of color don't get the chance to get published. I've become more aware of that. I will check myself.

Phyllis tries to be pro-active about equalizing dynamics:

> Sometimes in discussions I have maybe spoken up two or three times, and then I'm aware that some other people haven't said anything. Sometimes there's someone in charge of the meeting where people of color are being looked over. In these situations I will try to change the dynamics in the room. I will either quiet myself, or if I've heard

somebody else mention it, I will say, "You know what so-and-so said was really important. I'd just like to add on to that." When you're conscious of it, then you try to bring that into the room.

Although Phyllis "checks herself" and other whites, she does not in the end shy away from what she thinks is right. Being aware of the problem of white domination does not mean falsely agreeing with people of color or refusing to confront them on differences;

I now know that not every African American person in the system is about advocacy for African American students. I know now that institutional racism is promoted by people in the system whether you're black, brown, Asian, or white. You get caught up in perpetuating policies and practices that impact those populations. We all need to examine ourselves. And I have pushed back on African American leaders who are not doing right by black kids.

"CRACKS IN THE SYSTEM OF RACIAL IDEOLOGY"

Laurie Olsen, the executive director of California Tomorrow, also consciously builds multiracial teams to do trainings with educators on racial equity issues. Laurie is very aware that individuals are perceived as representing their racial groups and that "you're never just two people going about life." She has learned through painful experience that even whites' well-meaning and apparently nonracial practices can replicate historical patterns of domination. She recounts a case in which two African American women objected that African Americans' experience was being marginalized in a group discussion.

The women said, "We're not going to participate in something else that is going to marginalize us again." I tried to step in and say, "Let's create a fishbowl so people can hear what's going on and have a few people that feel strongly about this be in the fishbowl." The two African American women that had raised the original objection just got even more furious. "A white person putting us into the center where we're on display? Forget it! We're not going to be your specimens again."

Fortunately, the discussion group stayed together to work through the crisis even if they were never able to reach complete agreement:

There were some things about what happened that we never quite agreed about because it took on all of the weight and all of the emotion of the history. It was bigger than that moment; it was far beyond that moment. We have different histories. In that sense, we did not ever come to a real shared analysis of the moment. What we came to was a really deep understanding of each other's experience of the moment. That allowed us to keep working together.

As a result of that experience, Laurie has become more conscious and intentional about considering the racialized aspects of seemingly color-blind practice:

> You never pick the one black person in the room, put them on display in the middle in a kind of get-you situation where everybody is examining and analyzing that person's behavior.... Even if it's like a casual thing of asking people to come up and say blabbity-blah, I never do that without really asking permission first separately. There is a whole history of African American people being studied by white communities and where that has led. You do not in any way replicate those patterns.

Laurie finds that open conversations about race in multiracial settings are crucially important but can be frightening to many whites, including her. Sometimes a white person makes a mistake, like in the fishbowl example, and a person of color expresses anger. Laurie ties the fear of black anger she sees in herself to the history of racism:

> This is really personal, so I'll just say it and admit it. For me, an angry, large, African American person can be terrifying. If I'm in a situation where I'm working with a school or facilitating a group and a large African American—and it could be male or female; actually gender is not an issue in this—starts to express some real anger about something going on, I go to a place in myself of absolute fear. Of just fear. That's what I'm grappling with internally in that moment. What gets tapped is that deep white fear which frankly I connect to fear of slave revolt. On a very visceral level it's like my life is in danger; my way of life is in danger. It just goes to some really primal place. It's bizarre but it's there.

Laurie has come to understand these moments of fear as representing "cracks" in the racial system:

> This is a little metaphorical, but I think racial ideology for white people, or at least for me, is like this system. When there are cracks in it, it's like the whole thing gets off kilter. It feels like that, too. It's like, "Oh, my God!" Your stomach gets sick. It's one of those moments

where all of the weight and depth of white ideology in you just cannot be maintained. There's something major at your core that is being thrown off kilter. It makes you realize how much in that system you are. I came to recognize that feeling, and I actually locate it physically in me.

Rather than run from this fear, Laurie wants to learn from it:

When I feel that happening, it's like giving birth. You have to embrace the discomfort and the pain. You have to say, "Yes, this is what it's going to take for me to be in this work." Rather than get defensive or resistant or try to gloss it over, you have to open up for it. . . . I feel like one of the things white people have to learn is how to move through those moments in a way that doesn't send you fleeing from the fight.

By being open and honest about her feelings at the moment, Laurie can appeal to the group to help take responsibility for moving forward through the crisis:

That moment happens to me many, many times when I'm working with groups, and the race issue comes up. I realize I have to say, "Okay, everything else needs to stop. I need to create room for this. I need to create space for what this person is raising or what I'm feeling."

Although whites can find being challenged on their behavior to be uncomfortable, if not deeply threatening, Laurie stresses the opportunity for meaning and excitement in people's lives that collaboration across racial lines brings:

It's a lot easier for people to give up on each other or for people to feel kind of hopeless about trying to break through the barriers in trying to take on antiracist work together because it's hard to do. It's scary to do. People have had a lot of bad experiences and a sense of hopelessness about it. I try to help people get in touch with that part of themselves that wants it, that sees it as important work, and that recognizes that it's really the work that is part of giving birth to a different kind of society.

"BE IN A CONSTANT MODE OF REFLECTION"

Alex Caputo-Pearl is a teacher activist in Los Angeles. He teaches at predominantly black Crenshaw High School and helped found a teacher-parent-student activist organization called the Coalition for Educational Justice (CEJ), which works to address racial justice in education. Like Rachel, he moved to the school's neighborhood as part of an effort to build long-term relationships in the community. Alex strives to build the multiracial organizations that he believes are necessary to create educational justice, as well as prefigure the future society. As the quotation from Alex at the beginning of this chapter indicates, he finds this to be a trial-and-error and a depend-on-each-other-throughout experience.

Alex grapples with the kind of white domination that emerges when white teachers like him have more education and knowledge of policy issues than most of the parents and students of color in their activist group. If these differences are not recognized and positive action to address them is not taken, the result is the replication of racial hierarchies within the group. Alex is critical of a color-blind organizational style that claims to be democratic but in reality is far from it:

> Some sectors of the antiglobalization movement that are more heavily white can have this problem. I'm not saying all, but I've noticed that among some sectors there can be this attitude that we're totally and fully democratic. That means anybody can talk whenever they want, and no one is going to get challenged. Who are the ones speaking? It's white people. It's men. It's not democratic. It's a reflection of the total lack of democracy in the development of all political organizations within the U.S.

Alex believes that multiracial groups need strong norms to equalize participation in part because many white males are used to leading and will perhaps unconsciously dominate discussions:

> At CEJ's general membership meetings, we often have a teacher and a student as cochairs or a student and a parent as cochairs. At the beginning of every general meeting they say, "We're the chairs today. We are going to make our own decisions about who we're calling on, who we're asking to give it a rest, if you're talking too much. We are going to give priority to women and people who speak a language other than English to make sure that historically marginalized groups are represented very well in this discussion."

Some white people may be offended by these practices, but Alex believes they are essential:

> Occasionally there will be problems with that. Sometimes people get angry and have left the organization because they felt like white people were being discriminated against. But we have felt the benefits far

outweigh the costs. That approach helps both in recruiting new people and in strengthening the existing people that we have in the group to really give input.

While group norms remain important, Alex also emphasizes the need for white activists to be in constant self-reflection on their roles and behavior. If they are willing to be reflective and participate in an organization with positive norms for equal participation, then they can play a critical role:

> Skilled white organizers in a multiracial context can also have a role helping to give legitimacy to an antiracist critique of society. Some people will say, "Okay, this is a little bit different. It's a white person that's saying that racial oppression against blacks and Latinos is happening in these different ways." All of that is only really possible and happens most effectively in multiracial settings.

"NORMALIZING" DIVERSE RELATIONSHIPS AND COMMUNITY

Education activist Christine Clark has worked for many years in preservice teacher education and as a leader in the National Association for Multicultural Education (NAME). Christine agrees that white privilege and racialized structures infect racial justice organizations and must be addressed. However, she stresses that it is important for multiracial groups to allow for mistakes. Christine has found NAME to be a multiracial community in which people can address racial dynamics openly, make mistakes, and learn from them in a supportive way:

> I would say NAME is probably the most enduring support in my life. It's a place where you can grow up. I know that I made a lot of mistakes as a member of that organization in terms of things that I've done or said or how I've behaved that I'm not proud of. Yet I feel like people who have known me for fifteen years in that organization have allowed me to grow and develop and mature. I think that I enjoy a fair degree of respect for my work both in the organization and as an academic. It's like the family I get to go home to.

In fact, as people worked together and formed friendships, they began to normalize diverse relationships and community:

> Early on, one of the things that I loved most about NAME was that, when we got together, it was one of the few places where you would

have profoundly diverse groups hanging out together. We would go to restaurants, and it would just be different. I never really thought about it as being so strange until I realized other people reacted to us like we must be a part of some religious cult. The only other time you see that diverse a group is Jehovah's Witnesses. Literally! That's not to say we don't have intragroup politics because we certainly do. But we have begun the practice of normalizing racially and ethnically diverse relationships and community building in ways that allow informal interaction that's organic and natural and not forced and trite.

Christine continues to be self-reflective but suggests that whites have to accept who they are and be authentic in this work:

As you get older, you start to figure out where you are and who you are with more confidence. I feel like I'm moving into that. I'm starting to feel less anxiety about not being able to be all things to all people and just starting to just say, "Well, I am who I am. I understand what I understand, and I make mistakes where I make mistakes." At some point, people are just going to have to accept that. I think that's happened to me all my life. I know people have accepted me for where I am and who I am all my life. But I just never really thought about it that way because I was always trying to do better, constantly analyze and reflect and connect. Now I just am, and I allow the chips to fall where they may.

Indeed, some racial justice activists can talk the right talk but not know how to relate to people in an authentic, human way:

There are people who I can tell have no sociopolitical consciousness, really. They don't have a broad, grandiose analysis of things. Yet the way that they're able to interact with people on a daily basis, they always get it right. They always honor who people are. They always treat people with dignity and respect. They're always kind. They're always understanding. I admire that because I find that people who often get the larger issues fail at that miserably.

In the end, true collaborative relationships have to be based upon mutuality and striving for human connection together:

I use Freire's language of engaging in struggle to become more fully human. Connected to that is a desire not to lose dignity with others and not take dignity from others in terms of how I interact. I feel like I fail at that every day but that I get up and keep trying. I want to get to a place where the way that I interact with people is a living example of my sociopolitical belief system. That means to try to approach things with an appreciation for where people are and to engage them in a way that will help bring more justice into the world and more understanding, more collaboration, more partnership, and more humanity as opposed to more suffering, more anger, and more resentment.

In sum, white activists appreciate the need to challenge behavior that leads to white domination in multiracial efforts. Moreover, they suggest that positive action should be taken to promote more equal participation, for example, by whites taking responsibility for their own behavior and by setting group norms that encourage the voices of people historically marginalized. Nevertheless, the weight of institutions constantly infects these dynamics by striking fear in the hearts of white activists when racial conflict flares. Rather than fleeing, however, if activists appreciate these moments as "cracks" in the racial system and hang together, they can become profound learning experiences that advance collaboration and lead to authentic human connections across lines of race.[12]

Leadership and Power

I have so far discussed efforts to combat white domination in multiracial efforts at the interpersonal level. This section focuses more on institutional arrangements. If whites as a group have dominated leadership positions in society at large and if they continue to dominate in decision-making arenas that affect communities of color, how do multiracial efforts avoid replicating those power relationships within racial justice efforts? How can multiracial efforts ensure that they will closely reflect the interests of communities of color?

"THOSE MOST AFFECTED SHOULD LEAD"

The Black Power movement of the sixties offered an answer to these questions that continues to resonate with some white activists today. I am referring to the call for self-determination for people of color. In the view of Black Power advocates, true liberation from racism and colonialism would come only when oppressed peoples had the right to decide their own fate and take control of their own institutions. This position sometimes led to separatism, as groups like SNCC transformed themselves from multiracial to all-black organizations. Within the broader movement or within multiracial organizations, self-determination meant that people of color should lead the fight for racial justice. The role of white activists, then, was to support the leadership that arose from communities of color. That principle, as well as the institutional arrangements that follow from it, would ensure that racial justice efforts would remain aligned with the interests of those most affected by racism.[13]

Many white activists today continue to appreciate the importance of self-determination even if they do not fully embrace the way sixties' radicals implemented it. Cathy Rion is a young activist who sits on the board of Californians for Justice, a youth organizing group for whom she previously worked as an organizer. Cathy is also a member of the Heads Up collective in the Bay Area, a small group of white activists who have a dual mission. They support the work of organizations of people of color, and they cultivate an antiracist and anti-imperialist understanding in predominantly white movements.

Cathy stresses that people of color should lead racial justice efforts because those most affected understand the issues best:

> When you're talking about problems that are driven by racism or have a racist component, which most societal problems in this country do, then the people who would be most effective at leading social change efforts are people who are most affected by problems. If you're talking about something that's racist or a problem whose basis is racism, then folks of color are going to be the ones who get it and have the best understanding of how it works and how it impacts their lives and therefore most effective at figuring out the strategy to change that.

People of color should lead for another reason, too, in order to combat the tendency for whites to dominate:

> As middle-class and upper-middle-class white folks, we're trained that we know what's best. We are experts. We're trained not to listen to people of color, particularly if they're not educated or don't use a particular language. There's all this stuff that we grow up breathing and learning. We have to make a real effort to unlearn these things. We can inadvertently push things in the wrong direction or just try to take control of something.

Cathy feels that many white activists in predominantly white organizations focus too much on trying to diversify their organization by getting people of color to join them. Rather, she feels that white activists should be asking themselves what strategies people of color are pursuing and seeing how they can support those struggles. For example, Cathy's Heads Up collective has worked to support the Deporten la Migra coalition in its efforts to counter repressive treatment of undocumented immigrants.

However, at Californians for Justice (CFJ) things are different for Cathy. In this case she is a member of an organization that is composed predominantly of people of color. CFJ's adult organizers are mainly people of color, and the group's youth leaders come almost entirely from communities of color. As a former organizer and current member of the board of trustees, Cathy is part of CFJ's leadership team:

> Within the context of CFJ, at this point I don't think a whole lot about what it means to be a white person. I'm constantly checking myself in terms of my participation and not taking up too much space. But it's also one of collaboration where I'm part of the team. I happen to be white, which means I need to be careful about how I tread. But I'm very much a part of the team at CFJ.

How does being a collaborative member of the leadership team square with following the leadership of people of color? Since the vast majority of CFJ are people of color, Cathy feels there is no question of white domination. In fact, creating an authentic leadership role for white people is vitally important to Cathy:

> I really believe in multiracial movements that include white folks. We were just talking about this in Heads Up. There's a challenge. There's this tension between taking leadership from folks of color and ourselves taking leadership and initiative. Nobody wants to just be following somebody else's beck and call. It's not going to be effective. It's not going to be fun, and it's not going to build movements.

To take on an authentic leadership role, whites need to participate in the kind of open process of discussion of racial dynamics within organizations discussed in the preceding section:

> Groups need to create a culture where I make it clear that I'm happy to receive feedback and that I'll receive it in a humble way and not freak out about it and not make it a huge, huge, big hullabaloo, which often happens. It's being like, okay, yes, let's flag that; that was not okay. Let's check in later and move on. If you're in a meeting, not letting it highjack the meeting into this big process thing.

However, Cathy also worries about making the opposite error of white activists' losing a sense of their own integrity. They can be so afraid "not to make the same mistake once" that they become paralyzed:

> White folks can get really freaked out when we mess up. As I heard cultural diversity trainer Laurene Finley say, white people can be so careful that they don't make the same mistake once [laughs]. It's true. I can definitely fall into a tendency to tip-toe around because I'm too afraid to mess up. That doesn't do a service, you know.

In Cathy's hands, the principle of following the leadership of people of color does not appear to constitute an absolute mandate. Rather, it represents an essential starting point to get to more equal collaboration; it is a dynamic arrangement that has to be continually monitored and negotiated. In the end, the principle of leadership by people of color serves as a critical counterweight to the pressures of reproducing societal racism within multiracial efforts.

"I'M VERY SELF-CONSCIOUS NOT TO BECOME *THE* LEADER"

Other activists in the study share Cathy's concern about white domination. Even if they do not articulate the same principle, they are searching for ways to balance leadership. Bob Peterson thinks that people of color have a special leadership role to play and that sometimes whites need to defer to people of color in leadership. Bob is a teacher and political activist. He teaches at La Escuela Fratney School, a two-way bilingual public school in Milwaukee with an explicit antiracist curriculum. He is one of the founding editors of *Rethinking Schools* and a cofounder of the National Coalition of Education Activists (NCEA). He is coauthor of *Rethinking Columbus,* an antiracist curriculum guide for teaching about the impact of the arrival of Europeans in the Americas that has sold more than a quarter of a million copies.[14]

Bob is a socialist who believes that racial divisions have led to the failure of many progressive efforts. Indeed, people of color have often been marginalized by these movements. Consequently, he believes that people of color must play a strong leadership role in any multiracial effort:

> In a broader sense, I definitely see the need for African Americans in particular and people of color in general to be in leadership in social movements in this country. If it's not there in a social movement, at least over time, those social movements and organizations are ultimately destined to fail.

However, because Bob sees the larger struggle for a just society as a common one for all, he feels whites should be able to lead in this effort as full-fledged collaborators:

> I have a strong class perspective. I see the struggle as a revolutionary struggle ultimately against a capitalist class which is predominantly male and white. But has its black female figures up there, too. Ultimately it is the same struggle. Within that struggle, there are some very sharp differences. But ultimately the structure of society has to be fundamentally changed. I'm a collaborator in that effort as much as anybody else.

Bob does not see himself as a supporter of someone else's struggle:

> People use the word *ally* sometimes. I don't like that term because I think some of the people that use that term use it in such a way that one can never as a white person offer leadership in a multiracial situation. We're always secondary. I think that sometimes we can offer leadership. Sometimes we don't offer good leadership, but that depends on the situation and the people.

In practice, this means that collaborations must work intentionally to have coleadership that involves both whites and people of color, as Bob did with his colleagues in NCEA. Racially balanced leadership, however necessary, may not be sufficient if issues of race remain hidden. Bob believes race should be placed squarely on the table. In fact, he argues that the NCEA was able to transform itself from a predominantly white group to a multiracial one because it addressed racial dynamics and consciously worked to balance its leadership:

> We learned you have to put the issue of race on the table both in terms of your political programming but also in terms of your own internal dynamics.... Our perspective was that the only way to build a multiracial organization was to put race on the table. It was to organize workshops around racism led by white, black, and Latino people who spend their lives doing antiracist training, you know, make sure that's always part of our workshops and conferences.

Racial dynamics were conditioned by the fact that most of the whites in NCEA were college-educated teachers, while the people of color were parents and community activists typically with less formal education:

> Part of the problem was the people who started the organization were teachers who were fairly sophisticated in terms of everything. We

probably had email before other people, okay. Then other people came along and joined the ranks, people who are community and parent activists, who weren't as sophisticated, not as middle class as teachers. There were different types of issues, informal leadership versus formal leadership and whether that informal leadership was on the basis of race. People weren't saying you white people are caucusing to dominate, but it was happening more informally.

To help address the imbalance and give people of color a chance to talk among themselves and assert their views more strongly, NCEA used racial caucuses. Whites were uncomfortable at first:

> The first time we did that, the white people just sat around and looked at each other. It's a white antiracist caucus obviously; it's not a white power caucus. But those are wonderful issues to talk about because you educate people in the process, particularly white people being educated by people of color who are fairly sophisticated, although not the same form of sophistication perhaps as the more polished teachers.

Although the group's understanding of race grew through these processes, NCEA continued to struggle with internal dynamics as members' outside experiences reinforced racism and mistrust:

> Some of the parents would come and do a Mau Mau kind of thing about teachers, saying, "All teachers are for shit because my kid's teacher is a racist pig." I mean really extreme. Some of the teachers would become defensive and say, "That's not true. I'm not a racist pig." So we tried to guide conversations to issues of institutional racism. We challenged individual racism for sure. But we said, "Okay, so you have some racist teachers. What's the institution doing about it? Is there antiracist training? Are people being fired? Are the textbooks helping or pushing people?" Those are issues as opposed to just throwing up your hands and being pissed off at a teacher.

Although Bob believes in the ideal of truly collaborative multiracial leadership, he also recognizes that there are times when whites should defer to people of color to lead. For example, Bob declined an opportunity to become principal of the Fratney School because he thought it important that a person of color be in that position:

> In this school I'm very self-conscious not to become *the* leader—in the area of becoming a principal. I don't think a school which is 13 percent white needs a white person running it. So I've supported other

people. Paula, a Latina, is going to become principal here. There are other reasons to not become a principal, too. It's a thankless job. But as you get closer to retirement, you also realize it means you really boost your retirement a lot. But I'm not doing it, and that has a lot to do with race.[15]

Again, Bob points to a required balance. He seeks out the advice of people of color he respects and defers to people of color sometimes in leadership, but he does not relinquish his own integrity as an activist and a leader.

"FACILITATION AND COLLABORATION ARE NEXT GENERATION CONCEPTS"

If Bob Peterson speaks of the need for coleadership between whites and people of color, the young activist Michael Siegel stresses the need for a new model of leadership that is collaborative and empowering of others. Michael is executive director of Oakland Leaf, a community-based nonprofit that blends the arts with social consciousness in its work with youth. Michael grew up in a left-wing family that was part of a multiracial activist community in Oakland. A former teacher, Michael cofounded Leaf and helps lead its summer peace camp. Leaf offers a variety of programming geared to empowering young people as social justice activists and leaders of their community.

Michael helped build Leaf intentionally as a multiracial organization. He feels that is critical to Leaf's ability to do its work:

I think the more diverse Oakland Leaf becomes, the stronger we become. A lot of that has to do with the fact that the more connected and in tune with the community we are, the better we are able to design great programs to attract high-quality people and to develop a clear message and vision.

However, Leaf also serves as an experiment in realizing the multicultural vision Michael and his colleagues have for the United States:

One perspective I have is as a homeboy from Oakland, growing up among so many people of diverse backgrounds and seeing how much potential we have. A lot of petty things divide people—divide me from other people and divide us as a community. One vision I have is of Oakland being this place of immense resources, immense diversity, and feeling like this city can be a model for the world in terms of people working across racial and class boundaries as a community. In some ways, Oakland Leaf is our step forward in terms of promoting this next level toward a society of collaboration, of community empowerment, of looking at assets versus looking at deficits, of bringing people together.

Meanwhile, pressure from the dominant society tends to reproduce racial hierarchies within the organization. Michael recounts a case in which a newspaper reporter featured him in a story while ignoring one of the group's partner organizations, which was led by a person of color. Reflecting on experiences like that, Michael says other whites are more comfortable with him as a leader:

I do see it in racial terms because I feel that the reason I am so comfortable speaking out is because I've been encouraged to by all sorts of people in my past. I think one reason that people want me to speak out is because I'm a well-off, well-dressed, maybe a good-looking white guy that people are comfortable with.

Michael thinks a lot about his role as a white leader in racial justice efforts. Like Bob Peterson, he is looking for a racial balance but is not always sure what that balance should be.

To resolve this dilemma, Michael looks to collaborative and especially facilitative leadership. In other words, white leaders—and for that matter any leader today—should be focused on the development and empowerment of others as leaders. That is precisely the mission of Oakland Leaf. For Michael, facilitative leadership provides a route to true collaboration in multiracial efforts:

I feel like I'm courageous and someone who takes risks that other people might not be willing to take. I'm willing to work hard. I feel like I have a lot of skills that are useful to movements and organizations. Given my skills and my personality and my spirit, I'm willing to take leadership positions. I'm slowly learning that a lot of leadership is building teams and facilitating the voice of others. That is how I can work with the people around me so that we can take leadership together and not try to put myself at the head of anything.

Oakland Leaf works hard to build leadership among its multiracial staff. It is dedicated to empowering young people as community leaders, not just to providing them with an arts or education experience. Michael talks about Myles Horton, the founder of the Highlander Folk School, as his hero precisely because he promoted the leadership of others:

As a white man, he helped create a venue for education organizing and strategizing on issues of social justice and economic justice. That was heroic work. For example, he helped create a venue for the literacy campaigns that happened in the South. People he worked with helped design these campaigns, but he didn't try to take ownership of these campaigns.

His most important work was to help other people take leadership for this work and develop their own organizational capacity. His vision was of himself as a facilitator and not as a leader. To the end he denied his role as a leader. I think that is essential for the type of social change that needs to happen in the future.

Michael feels that he is part of a younger generation searching for and experimenting with new models for multiracial organizations and racial justice work. He says, "In this context, these words like 'facilitation' and 'collaboration' are really the next-generation terms and concepts for movements of the twenty-first century."

"RIGHT RELATIONSHIPS"

So far, in this section we have seen examples of activists influenced, directly or indirectly, by currents of the socialist and solidarity movements, which reach back to the sixties. However, the views of these activists are broadly shared by others in the study, even those who appear more conservative. Kathy Dudley is an evangelical Christian who moved to a predominantly black west Dallas neighborhood in the early eighties and founded Voice of Hope Ministries. As discussed in chapter four, black pastors were initially suspicious of her, but she worked hard at partnering with them. Kathy later founded the Dallas Leadership Foundation (DLF) as a faith-based, multiracial network to support community development efforts in the black community. She constantly looks to the Bible to help guide her understanding. However, her understandings are also profoundly shaped by her longtime work with black pastors and church communities in Dallas and by the model of black Christian community development advanced by John Perkins.

Inspired by biblical injunctions to form "right relationships" with fellow human beings as models of a right relationship with God, Kathy has come to a very complex understanding of how to build multiracial relationships. She stresses honesty and accountability, among other things:

We had what I felt were biblical guidelines to guide us in building relationships with honesty, dealing with problems, being fair and honest, having really good administration, and making sure that every time a vision would emerge, that it came through a whole vision-casting process. That vision was mutually owned, and we worked out the roles and the responsibilities. The role we played in DLF was to hold everyone accountable and create systems of communication, information sharing, and rejoicing in celebration so that everybody felt that they genuinely were part of the issue.

Kathy finds herself having to combat a "white savior" mentality that prevents mutuality in cross-racial relationships. One way to combat that kind of paternalism is to create venues where whites meet on more equal terms with strong African American leaders. She took that approach with herself:

Moving from Voice of Hope to Dallas Leadership Foundation—that was a major shift for me. I decided to go to wealthy, resourced, educated black people in the city, people who didn't need me, and find out what role I was supposed to play. If we only operate out of that sense of need, to some degree we end up operating out of a sense of superiority, subconsciously.

Responding to the concerns of black leaders, Kathy established the Dallas Leadership Foundation, which, for one thing, creates venues in which white business people form partnerships with black business leaders. That requires open discussion about race at both interpersonal and systemic levels:

When we feel those tensions, we tend to want to run and hide because we don't know how to deal with them. We're not really taught how to deal with a lot of this. As a result we often get divided along racial lines. Whenever I feel that that's happening or could happen, I just bring it up and say, "Let's talk about this. Is this race? Is this culture? What is this?" I think that's helped. It's a discipline. It's not always easy, but I think it's important.

People find it particularly difficult to be honest on issues of race, but Kathy believes that forthright conversations—however painful—are necessary for racial healing:

More than anything else, no matter what our cultural tendencies are, if we're more reserved or not, deep down we want people to be real. We want to know that what we get when we're with them is honesty. We don't have to guess or try to figure it out or manipulate or do any of the other things that we tend to do because we don't really want to be honest. We don't really want to face the pain that is sometimes caused by honesty. But it's also the only way you get to healing.

Kathy stresses mutuality in relationship and strives for true partnership that draws on everyone's talents:

> How do you build real relationships? I mean ones that are based on genuinely assessing all the opportunities and histories and cultures and gifts and knowledge that we all have so that real transformational change can take place. This kind of relationship brings real hope. This way real health can be realized spiritually, as well as physically.

However, even though Kathy stresses mutuality, she has also come to appreciate the need for people of color to be leaders in this process:

> I consider myself an equal partner, but we are looking at issues that disproportionately affect the being and the living of a particular group. In my case, I feel called to work primarily as a focus with African Americans. It means that the ones that I need to make space for are African Americans because I believe that whoever's closest to the problem should have the greater authority.

Because Kathy grew up in poverty, she feels she has some authority around that issue and a greater voice compared to people who have never experienced the life of a poor person. She makes the analogy to people of color, particularly African Americans, with whom she mainly works:

> When it comes to being black in America and what that means or being black in the world, I don't have the same authority. I have an authority because I have become a student, because I have been incarnational in that struggle, because I have practiced what I believed. It gives me an authority. But I will never, ever have the same kind of authority as African Americans. I realized this living in west Dallas. No matter what we did, no matter how much we tried to apply the biblical principles, no matter how good we tried to be, we could never be to that black child that was our neighbor what they needed, and that was to see someone that looked like them. That gave more authority.

When Kathy first started to work with black pastors, she worried about her role as a white person. However, she came to see that there were different roles to be played as part of a larger whole:

> Within that context of equality you can accept the parts you can play and the parts you can't play. That's true partnership and true equality. I don't have to be the same. I don't have to be as gifted as you in

everything. I don't have to have the same history. Sameness is not equality. That's the flaw of many of the ideologies that we've seen. We need to value the part that we can be in the whole. When we're really who we were designed to be, and we fit, and we're willing to flow in the context of that connectedness, then we're equal. We are doing what we were called to be and to do.

What does this mean institutionally for building multiracial collaborations? In building DLF, Kathy started with African American churches, like Perry Perkins did, and then invited white churches to join in. In fact, Kathy even speaks of self-determination for African Americans. Like other activists, she talks about finding a balance in roles for whites and blacks:

> How do we as whites really make the best contribution? And not just whites, but people across different racial ethnicities. For my own journey it's one of saying, how do I build upon and how do I add my gift? It might be playing that linking and connecting role, playing that ligament role, but really letting African Americans set the stage for how they feel those need to be and even how they invite the broader society into the journey.

Reaching that balance requires that whites step back and listen. Rather than being concerned only about their own leadership, white activists need to place attention on supporting the building of black leadership:

> At this point in history white people need to be listening a lot more. We need to be looking at how do we, both individually and corporately, help black leaders succeed? I think we should use our influence, our connections, in ways to help to break that barrier that I was talking about earlier. At least for my life, that's a major shift. It doesn't mean that I can't be respected in my gifts. If the Lord tells me that I'm the one to lead, or we agree that I'm the best qualified to be the president of the organization, I ought to be that. That's a justice and a fairness issue again.

This kind of support appears similar to Michael Siegel's notion of facilitative leadership. Indeed, Kathy follows religious conceptions of servant leadership. Yet support for black leadership claims special importance because the dominant society continues to make it harder for people of color to be respected as leaders. In fact, Kathy appreciates the importance of black organization and black power:

It's so much more difficult for an African American leader to go in and see their vision fulfilled because of racism, because of lack of access, because of all these different things.... Why do my ideas have a better chance of getting funded and realized than this brilliant black woman's across the street? There are reasons for that. I think that we should be sensitive to that and not be afraid of black power in a good sense.

Given the difficulties black leaders have in asserting their leadership, Kathy is humbled that many of these leaders have welcomed her guidance and by doing so empowered her:

I think it's being in genuine fellowship, of worshipping, working, living in the black community and church, feeling very accepted, obviously, and empowered. To think that some of the greatest black leaders in the nation in my opinion, in Dallas, empowered me publicly and partnered with me to do DLF is very humbling.

In the end Kathy finds the process of forming "right relationships" to be an ongoing journey, a road that is built along the way, one that moves back and forth from interpersonal relations to action for systemic change. Kathy worries about how deeply the changes are being made but sees progress in this ongoing journey:

I think DLF is still on that journey, moving toward it. If I look at our almost ten-year history, then I feel like we are definitely on the right road and building the kind of real genuine relationships, both individually and structurally, that can change systems, as well as individuals.

In this section we have seen white activists and their colleagues trying to negotiate a difficult dilemma. On the one hand, those most affected should lead. On the other hand, activists work for a truly multiracial movement as a practical imperative and as a model for the future. At first blush, there seem to be some real differences in how activists negotiate this challenge. Some come to emphasize the need for people of color to lead while others stress equal collaboration. Yet the "followers" like Cathy Rion often end up coleading, perhaps in a facilitative manner. Meanwhile, those like Perry Perkins or Kathy Dudley, who stress the importance of reciprocity, are not blind to the pressures of white domination. They have developed other mechanisms to ensure that the collaborations stay true to the interests of people of color. Perry makes sure that black churches are firmly on board and own the process before inviting whites in. Kathy works to support black leadership, while she offers her own talents and gifts as well. All of the activists appear to be working toward a balance in an ongoing experimental process of building collaboration They both lead and facilitate the leadership of others. What appears to be required is an awareness of the pressures to replicate white domination and an intentional effort to build and ensure a strong voice and leadership by people of color if both their interests and true collaboration are to be achieved.[16]

Conclusion

If racism in the institutions of American society can be perpetuated without overt racist intent, perhaps that same dynamic can occur in racial justice organizations as well. What can we learn from these activists to help us create multiracial relationships and venues that do not unconsciously replicate racialized power relations in the dominant society? Just as racial justice activists call for positive affirmative action in social institutions to overcome the normal workings of institutional racism, they also find that intentional action must be taken within their own organizational settings. As we have seen, activists take action both at interpersonal and institutional levels. In other words, they address white privilege behavior among individuals, but they also work to create organizational processes so that people of color are empowered and are represented in leadership.

Even as activists work around personal behavior, they stress not taking these issues too personally. Mistrust arises from historical oppression. People of color might well be suspicious of white activists and not assume positive intent at the start. In fact, the issue is not really white activists' personal intentions. Rather, whites need to accept that trust will take time to build. They need to prove themselves through actions and by making a long-term commitment to working for racial justice.

Activists find that whites can ignore racial differences, working out of color-blind assumptions. They stress becoming aware of and addressing racial differences openly within multiracial collaborations. However, whites can also make the opposite error of essentializing race. They can become so overly self-aware of racial differences, so worried about dominating people of color, that they fail to deal with people of color as fellow human beings and lose their own sense of themselves. They can become afraid "to make the same mistake once." Activists have to appreciate the importance of racial differences while building multifaceted relationships. Divided often by race, whites are united with people of color as activists, as people of faith, as Americans, and, perhaps most profoundly, as fellow human beings.

I thought I might find very different ways of addressing these dilemmas, given that the activists in the study work in diverse institutional settings and out of a variety of political traditions. There certainly were some differences in emphasis. Some of the interviewees push for more or earlier discussions of race within their organizations, and others push for less or later discussion. However, all of them felt it was critically important to openly confront racial differences and address white behavior when it serves to perpetuate white domination and silence the voices of people of color. Some stress the importance of following the leadership of people of color, and others emphasize equal partnership. Still, every one of them appreciated both that people of color have a special role to play in leadership and that whites have important talents and resources to contribute as well.

I also thought I might find differences among the activists in relationship building with African Americans and Latinos. Yet they spoke similarly about both groups and had little to say about the differences. These differences may, indeed, be important as was hinted at in Katherine Carter's views. Indeed, four of the activists said that they find greater mistrust on the part of African Americans. However, so few activists had extensive experience with and reflections on working with both groups that I cannot really address this issue.

The interviewees pursue their efforts at multiracial collaboration "under the weight of history." Indeed, when tensions flare, as they inevitably do at times, these activists have learned not to flee the scene. Rather, they have come to see these moments as "cracks" in the racial system, as Laurie Olsen aptly put it.

These pressures, however, are not new. In a study of racial dynamics within the civil rights movement of the sixties, Gary Marx and Michael Useem identified a number of structural causes for the tensions activists continue to face today, many of which are highlighted in this chapter. Moreover, they showed that other cases of what they called majority involvement in minority movements—the U.S. abolition movement of the nineteenth century and the untouchable movement in India in the twentieth century, for example—suffered from similar dynamics. Marx and Useem had little to say about how such tensions might be addressed and argued instead that these tensions often destroyed collaborations when movements were at their height or when the dominant society proved resistant to further change.[17]

The activists in this study are, by contrast, firmly committed to struggling through these dilemmas in pursuit of a multiracial vision and practice. There has not been much research on how to address these dynamics in the contemporary period. Most of this literature has focused on interpersonal dynamics rather than institutional processes. The literature on white privilege talks about the need for whites to examine their assumptions and behaviors, which aligns well with some of the findings reported in this chapter. There is less research on the dynamics and tensions created in organizations geared to action on racial justice. However, what little research there is echoes some of my findings. For example, Eileen O'Brien's study of white antiracist activists discusses the People's Institute for Survival and Beyond, which teaches white activists to be accountable to people of color through the building of authentic relationships. The institute articulates the need for whites to follow the leadership of people of color, yet the group itself is multiracial and has white leaders.[18] Meanwhile, several analysts of community organizations have emphasized the need to address racial issues openly as crucial to forming closer ties across race, as well as to ensuring that the organization stays true to the cause of racial justice.[19]

Since the debates over Black Power in the sixties, almost no research has focused on the issue of who should lead racial justice efforts. In a rare exception, Becky Thompson has examined interracial dynamics within nonprofits in the contemporary period from the point of view of the white activists she interviewed. She found some dynamics similar to those discussed in this chapter. Some white activists felt that people of color should be at the head of these nonprofits while others felt that whites could lead if they were the best qualified. All wanted arrangements that ensured strong leadership roles for people of color, and many pursued a shared leadership model.[20]

The activists in this study are committed to building multiracial venues despite, or perhaps because of, the tensions and difficulties they face in doing so. These locations—schools, community organizations, and advocacy groups—are contexts in which whites can build the personal friendships and public relationships that advance their immediate goals. However, they appear dedicated to these experiments even more because they represent the crucibles in which to forge in the present models for a racially just society of the future.

White racial justice activists seem to be struggling for a new model of leadership. They seek an approach that is both collaborative and facilitative of the development of the leadership of others, especially people of color. When white leaders of organizations see their job as building the capacity of others, they can work toward resolving the tension over their roles as whites in racial justice efforts. In the next chapter we take a close look at the struggles of white activists to define their identity as racial justice activists.

CHAPTER SEVEN

"Where Do I Fit?"

Building New Identities in Multiracial Communities

The first word that comes to my mind is "contradictions." It's between principles and living in the real world because we have not walked away from our class and race. We've stayed in this neighborhood, but we have lived a very different kind of life than any of our family or friends. The principles we try to follow are about justice, equity, and love and trying to figure out how to do that.

—Randy Johnston

I also feel very much in the middle—like I don't fit in. The white people that I grew up with don't understand me. I can't have conversations about this stuff with them. I can have the conversations with black people, but they don't necessarily understand me or get me, either. So I'm just stuck in the middle. I do think about the fact that I don't fit in here, I don't fit in there, and wonder where do I fit?

—Janet Morrison

WHITE ACTIVISTS ARE working for a better world, one free of racism and based upon the values of human brother- and sisterhood, yet they are living in the world as it is. All activists who dream of the world as it should be find themselves in tension with dominant societal values to some extent, but white racial justice activists seem to face a particular tension. In a sense, they live between two worlds; they are "stuck in the middle." They have made a break with the dominant white society by taking up the cause of racial justice. This fact places them in tension with many other white people, often including their family, neighbors, and old friends. Their values are more likely to be similar to those of communities of color, with whom they might share the political and moral project of building a racially just society. Yet they are not members of communities of color. In other words, they claim a problematic identity.

We can understand this dilemma as the process of negotiating the tension between social and political identities. Socially, or culturally if you will, racial divisions are very strong because they have been deepened for many years by legal and then social codes enforcing segregation. While much has been written about how whites lack a clear sense of what constitutes a white identity, we also know that the color line has been perhaps the central social boundary in U.S. history. At the same time, political views tend to line up with these socially constructed racial lines. By wide margins, African Americans are more supportive of government efforts to make economic distribution more equitable and provide social welfare services, for example, as well as to eliminate racial inequality. The activists in this study find themselves politically more aligned with people of color yet socially still white. Activists of color do not face this problem. Certainly, not all people of color are racial justice activists, but those who are tend to be celebrated in communities of color as leaders and "race champions."[1]

White racial justice activists are typically not celebrated in white communities. In fact, white activists report ongoing tensions with mainstream white America. In the last chapter they also reported continuing mistrust from communities of color. In a society that remains racially polarized, many find themselves "stuck in the middle."

I found that many white activists look to their multiracial activist networks in order to address this dilemma. These networks provide support for activists and a sense of belonging. They constitute a place to which to bring other whites, lessening isolation as they do so. Meanwhile, white activists can form closer social ties with people of color in these groups and communities as well. In other words, rather than being permanently "stuck," the activists try to forge new social and political identities in multiracial community. However, this is not an easy road to follow and they experience many bumps and bruises along the way—both from white communities and from communities of color.

Tension with White Communities

In chapter five we examined how activists influence other whites toward racial justice. In that chapter the activists in this study discussed a number of the difficulties and challenges they face in searching for effective strategies. In this section I focus on the activists' personal negotiation of their place vis-à-vis white communities. Most of the interviewees reported tensions and conflicts with their family and friends in their quest to build a different kind of life.[2]

"I'VE CROSSED A LINE"

Randy Johnston describes himself as "a white middle-class guy who's got an unusual relationship with black activists. And not just a relationship, but I move with it." Randy grew up in a family that was part of North Carolina's elite. He developed a commitment to racial justice in college and later moved to Greensboro to run a nonprofit social service agency. There he met black activists in the Beloved Community Center and began a long effort to transform his agency into an organization that empowered low-income African Americans. Randy also works with the Greensboro Truth and Reconciliation Commission, where he tries to get the city's white community to take responsibility for a history of racism that led to the killings of five anti-Klan demonstrators in 1979. More generally, Randy sees himself as trying to influence white liberals to support and ally with black activists in the community.

As Randy said in the quotation at the beginning of this chapter, he has chosen not to abandon the world of elite white North Carolina. He lives on Madison Street in a historically affluent white neighborhood. From this "inside" position, he feels he can influence other whites:

> I work with my people, the people who are running things, to get them to understand that the way to a healthier personal place and a healthier community is through being engaged with and learning from the people who are engaging you about yourself, about your behavior, and about how you think. That's the transformational part. If you're inside the machine, it's hard to really understand where you need to change. Those things need to be initiated from the people who are marginalized by all this. Those folks need to come at it. Then they need people like me who are on the inside to try to help people see it and understand it and transform both the systems and individuals.

Randy works to influence other whites in the context of highly charged race relations. The 1979 killings of anti-Klan demonstrators continue to polarize the city. The Truth and Reconciliation Commission, which was meant to help heal those wounds, has worked to engage the white community but has faced its share of hostility from white politicians and community leaders:

> People take it very personally. I worked with a lot of people in Greensboro before I came here. I had very good relationships with most of the influential, progressive people in Greensboro when I arrived. I kept those for a while. But over the years I really challenged them on a lot of things and was on the other side of a lot of issues. And it gets real personal.

Consequently, Randy feels he's paid a price for his stand for racial justice:

> The price we've paid has involved relationships with friends and family. It's involved relationships with the power structure here, which really affected our ability to operate and raise money as a nonprofit. It's affected a lot of things. It's just put me in a very different place in all my social and political relationships than I would be had I not chosen this path. There's a whole bunch of upside, too, and I'm not whining about it. Probably the most painful part of it is the relationships, the strained relationships with friends and family.

Randy faces sometimes painful tension with the members of his family who are products of the Old South. Randy says he loves his grandfather to death, but the man tells racist jokes:

> When I worked for black state representative Mickey Michaux, my mother said, "For God's sakes, don't tell your grandfather that you're working for a black." So, of course, I wrote him a letter and told him. He wrote me back a really nice letter, which I can't find. It kills me that I can't find it. He said it was nice, about the relationship between black people and white people and how he's always known that he'd done the best he could, but things weren't the way they should be. And he was proud of me. But at the end of it he said, "P.S. Did you hear the one about the 'n-gger' who did...?" He put the beginning of a "n-gger joke" at the end of this really moving letter. I've grown up with that. I loved him to death. But it's a—[pause]. I can't find that letter. I always think it's going to turn up, but I'm beginning to think it isn't.

Unlike his grandfather, Randy describes his dad as a liberal, like most of his white friends. However, he says, "They're the people here that I fight the most." If someone makes a blatant racist remark,

> You engage it. But at least you know where they are, and they know where they are [laughter]. The harder thing is the people who don't think that way. They won't say those things. They won't use the "n" word. They never do any of that kind of stuff. Liberal paternalism is just so rampant, and it's just about impossible for people who are acting it out to see. When you start pushing them to see it, they get really angry and upset at you.

As an example, Randy talks about challenging the comfort level of progressive whites who keep a distance from the black community:

> Theirs is kind of a false progressivism because it's very white. Progressives who are inside political systems and institutions can't really be honest progressives without finding a way to get into a relationship with people of color, people who are marginalized. They're just way too comfortable in their white political world, claiming to be working on behalf of all these people that they don't know. But I don't know how you frame this in a way that doesn't get people to shut down or feel like you're pointing fingers and condemning them. It's hard because these are people who are usually already doing liberal things. To raise the idea that if they don't go right at this hard issue, they're doing some harm along with their good, is a very hard discussion to get people to have in a healthy way.

In the early days of his activism, Randy says, he challenged his friends sometimes in ways that were not very productive. That may have led in at least one case to a broken friendship:

> There's one relationship in particular that I damaged severely through this work, and that I really regret. We're both working to repair it. It was a friend that I had done a lot of political work with. I went at him one time over something, and it just broke the relationship. Our wives were friends, and our kids were friends. We share a lot of the same friends. So it's just been a very hard, awkward thing that we're working on. I wish I had that back.

Conflict with friends is painful. Randy feels he had to get past his "angry man" routine so that he could focus more on how to move people forward:

A distance develops with the people of your class and race, family, and friends. There is a certain amount of loneliness and pain because people do take what you're raising very personally. You have to go through that. I think we're getting to a place where we're dealing with all that in a better way. A lot of it was I just had to get past the self-righteousness. The other part of that is kind of an anger. I had to get past my angry man routine and just meet people where they are and work with them. It doesn't do any good to denounce folks.

Nevertheless, racial polarization in Greensboro often causes a line to be drawn. Randy is clear that he stands with the black community for racial justice. To many white people, that means he crossed a line:

There's no question that I crossed a line. I didn't know it when I was crossing it. I didn't realize it until I looked back and was on the other side and couldn't go back. You talk about my identity, how I see myself. On the community issues most of the establishment folks would put me squarely with [black activist] Nelson Johnson and them. They just know that's my starting point. So that's my identity to them. Because of the unique nature of Greensboro with the Klan and Nazis and all that stuff that happened, the line is probably a little bit more pronounced than it would be somewhere else. But I'm definitely across it.

Randy's stance affects his immediate family, too:

There have been times over the years where my wife, Grace, just felt very lonely because of my work and her support for my work. The way she grew and evolved with me was through her work in the schools. She was able to see domination and the systemic stuff, and she became engaged in school issues. She's been my primary source of support through all this. But then there have been times when she would feel very lonely, and she's gotten frustrated with me. She would say to me, "You have Nelson and Z. I don't have people like that I can talk to about this. None of my friends have a clue about any of this."

As Randy's wife suggests, support from other activists in the Beloved Community, both white and black, has been crucial to Randy. Indeed, he now identifies strongly with a multiracial activist community. Nevertheless, he continues to have one foot firmly planted in the broader white community. In the end, Randy says he feels a dual identity:

I feel very much a part of a community that includes a lot of activist black people. That's part of my identity. But another part of my identity is that I live on Madison Avenue. I go to the Carolina/Duke basketball game. That's a hard ticket to get, but I have a way of getting them [laughter]. Nelson called me today and asked me if I could go to a meeting. I called him back. I said, "Man, I can't do that. I'm going to the Duke game." He said, "Going to the Duke game? Oh, he's working like a white boy does." It's both those things.

Randy keeps working to build that multiracial community and to move his friends and his community into relationship with activists and communities of color, but he sees it as a long-term process:

My biggest accomplishment is being in my late forties and still having the energy to keep at this, to keep growing and learning and understanding and pushing....Transformation is what I think we're all struggling for. It's the whole community that needs transformation. God knows, a lot of what we're about trying to say is that middle-class and upper-class white people can't get there by themselves.

And neither can Randy.

"JESUS MARGINALIZES ME"

Presbyterian minister Z. Holler is one of Randy's activist friends, and Z. also finds himself straddling two communities, his white Presbyterian congregation on the one hand and the multiracial, predominantly black Beloved Community group on the other. In chapter four Z. told a story about his mother's yard sales, a symbol of the sharp and deep racial divisions in Greensboro. He has dedicated his life to overcoming that boundary by bringing whites and blacks together. A veteran of the civil rights movement, Z., now retired, has been particularly active in the Truth and Reconciliation Commission. He remains closely connected to his old friends but nevertheless feels "we're not coming from the same place at this point." Indeed, Z. finds himself on the margins of white culture:

We were going around in a circle the other night in this class, saying who we are. My wife Charlene's comment to start with was, "Well, we've been marginal." Like my mother's sales there at the railroad track, you're on the edge. I can't identify much with the public expressions of our consumer society, like sitting watching CNN News. All of the commercials really make me angry.

Nonetheless, Z. has come to accept that marginal position vis-à-vis mainstream America. This acceptance comes in part from his religious tradition:

> Jesus marginalizes me. I can't really fully embrace the culture of which I'm a part, the white thing. Certainly the capitalist, consumerist, comfortable way that I fell into and I was born into. It's deeply flawed. It's deeply wrong, and it has cost other groups terribly—the poor, the black, the rest of the world. I've been working some with Indians, Native Americans. Reading Howard Zinn's *People's History* was an eye-opener to me. Growing up antilabor and realizing what a trouble it's been for people to really be a part of that thing. Not just blacks. When I try to tell folks about it, my friends, my colleagues, they think I'm crazy. Or they sometimes give me that impression.

His style is perhaps a little less confrontational than Randy's. How he responds to racist remarks "depends on the context":

> I'm not disposed to try to embarrass people. After the racist remark, I work around to where we're sitting beside each other. I say something like, "Tell me about that. Help me understand. You know what I'm doing. I'm working antiracist." Then you get something going with people. My friends pretty much know where I am so they don't fire off racist volleys. They might counter or contradict what I'm saying. They might say, "Oh, come on. You don't believe that" [laughs].

However, some tension and feelings of isolation can't be avoided. For example, Z. has been asked to preach less in his old congregation.

Like Randy Johnston, Z. has gotten support from his wife, but she has suffered because of his activism as well:

> I don't have the freedom to just go ahead and be one of the crew and enjoy being in the social world and all that stuff. With good conscience, it's hard for me to embrace a whole lot of this stuff that goes on. It's hard for Charlene to understand it.
>
> To be suddenly married to an activist, that's a bad word. You talk about activist, that's a bad word in these parts. I'm not exactly an activist, but I am said to be one. So this work that I've been much involved in has been costly to her. We could be palling around and have a lot more time for developing our social relationships with folks like us. But my work takes time and energy. It's not easy for her. And she's worked with that marvelously well. But it causes tension, and we have to deal with the tension.

Over time, Z. has become closer to the black community socially, as well as politically. He finds himself more comfortable in Reverend Nelson Johnson's social justice and activist-oriented Faith Community Church than the Presbyterian congregation he used to pastor. He describes Faith Church as "nearer [to] being our spiritual home, our community of faith, than the Presbyterian Church of the Covenant." Yet he struggles with cultural differences around worship styles in the black church:

> We do everything differently. I am not comfortable in worship in the black style in Nelson's church. I'm a Presbyterian, a Calvinist, for heaven's sake! [Laughs] Drama is not what we're into. It's not jumping up and down. It's not repetitious "hallelujah," all of those things. Well, that's my conditioning. It's their faith. That's the way they think of God. God is mighty. God is good. Repeated, repeated, repeated and with this Pentecostal approach. Well, it's uncomfortable for me.

A commitment to reach across racial lines and work together brings a real measure of acceptance:

> I go and I preach there. They allow me to do that and respond rather well. They seem to accept me for what I'm trying to do. I think it would be equally hard for them to spend any time much in Presbyterian worship services. That's even hard for me now that I'm initiated to the possibilities of passion and so on.

However, the tensions don't disappear. It's a difficult process:

> Our continuing struggle is that we come from different cultures. That's the problem about racism. You're raised in the culture of a racist white society versus being raised in the victimized poor black society. They let me know I'm a cracker every once in a while [laughs]. Well, that's not a nicer word than "n-gger." It's the cultural counterpart. It's hard to overcome that stuff. You have to set it aside and say, "We're going to understand each other. We love each other. We're not going to let that throw us." But that's not easy.

Meanwhile, despite his growing embrace of the new multiracial Beloved Community, Z. talks of his love for the congregation he used to pastor and says that he continues to receive love and support back from them. He is searching for a way to bring his community forward with him to join in building a Beloved Community. He wants to embrace his heritage as a foundation for becoming something better:

God intends that we be free to be what we're created to be, the best that we can be. In the case of a white person, you're white. That means a whole cultural heritage that we need to take hold of in a way that can turn it to the good of the human race. The blacks have really worked at that with black theology and the African heritage, that sort of village model I'm thinking about. Okay, so you are what you are. And that's the way you can move toward being something more than what you've been.

"I DON'T TAKE IT PERSONALLY . . . YET IT'S VERY PERSONAL"

As an activist in New Orleans, Doug Anderson struggles with many of the same tensions as Randy Johnston and Z. Holler. A trainer and community organizer with the People's Institute for Survival and Beyond, Doug grew up in a working-class family in a suburb outside of St. Paul, Minnesota. His parents held moderate racial views, but Doug's uncle was a white supremacist, and there was much overt racism in his community. Like Z. and Randy, Doug feels it is important for white activists to accept their heritage and their connection to the white community. In part, connections are necessary to influence other whites toward racial justice, but Doug also feels that rejecting the white community would represent a denial of self, of who he is. In his view, denial of the past does not provide a firm foundation for moving forward.

Doug joined European Dissent, an organization of white antiracists, and has focused in part on "reflecting and understanding my personal background." He is critical of white activists who reject their past and attempt to join communities of color:

> People of color that I work with say, "Once you get an awareness of this, you just want to come and hang out in our community. Go take care of your own people. See white people as your own. Don't kick your family to the curb. What does that say about your personal values system that you're able to reject and dismiss the woman that gave you birth because of what her values are? She gave birth to you. Yet you can't work with your own family because you're so radical, so you want to come and hang out in our community?"

In fact, Doug focuses to a great extent on building an antiracist movement among whites. In European Dissent,

> We're trying to create a culture where we value and understand that, as white people, we have a cultural commonality and that there could

be a sense of a white antiracist culture. If we come together as white people in the name of change, we could have a powerful voice. Racism and race is a very real thing, so it's okay for people to caucus and to be a part of racial communities. That's not a bad thing. We don't have to be color-blind in this society. We can start by being able to sit in a room with white people together and say, "What can we do as a group of white people speaking out against how the city is being rebuilt in New Orleans?"

Indeed, Doug insists that being pro-black does not mean being antiwhite:

Imagine the power that we could have if we all stood up. It doesn't have to just be communities of color that speak out, although usually it is. How do we begin to make it a normal thing to stand up as white people and say that this is wrong? Being pro-black or pro-Latino or pro-any other ethnic identification that people of color use, being pro-black does not have to mean antiwhite. The more we can respect and understand that, the more we can be effective in change work.

Although Doug works specifically with whites, he also strives to create multiracial relationships in the People's Institute and in his other work. Yet it is not easy to cross over the historic color line, and tension occurs with people of color, too:

When I stand up at a meeting and make a comment, and people of color don't know me, people are like, "Oh, no. There goes another white man spouting off. There he goes at the mic again. White people always have the mic. They're always the one speaking up."

Doug tries not to take it personally:

It can be hurtful to constantly be reminded that, when I walk into a room, people of color are going to view me as a white person. We want to get past that, and we want to be seen for all of our gifts and for who we are. It's just not a comfortable thing to always be reminded of race. But it's a reality of the culture and the society that we live in. The more we can keep that in mind, the more effective we can be. I don't mean effective as community organizers, I mean effective as functioning members of a human family.

Yet, for Doug, a painful aspect remains:

I understand that, as a white person functioning in this society, my actions are going to be perceived by people of color as racist no matter what my intentions are. So I'm at the point where I don't take it personally anymore. But yet, I still know that it's very personal—if that makes sense.

While Doug continues to struggle with his personal role, his work to build relationships across race offers him hope for true human connection:

> I feel like I have gained vast life experiences and perspectives that give me a way to see a connection with the whole human family. I can understand why an African American friend in Atlanta has now changed his name to Sayoun to connect with his roots. It's important for him that he live out African rituals and connect with where his people came from. I can understand and respect that. I can refer to him as he likes to be called, as Brother Sayoun, and feel a genuine connection with him and a brotherhood of man.

Affiliation with Communities of Color

Although white activists mention tension with whites, many also comment on their affinity with people of color.[3] To some extent this is a moral and political affinity because both white activists and communities of color place a high value on racial justice. However, because many activists spend much of their lives working in and with communities of color, they also develop a growing social identity as well, which nonetheless appears to have its limits. In chapter six, we looked at how activists attempt to build collaborative relationships and discussed some of the tensions and limits of those efforts. I now explore more directly the personal dilemmas activists face. No matter how closely they connect with communities of color, they cannot "be black." Once again, it appears that striving to forge a multiracial community represents the best hope for white activists to create a home for themselves.

"I PUT ON NO PRETENSE TO BE BLACK"

Industrial Areas Foundation (IAF) organizer Perry Perkins has spent much of his life building multiracial community organizing groups in Texas and Louisiana, bringing together people of various races and faiths. For many years he has worked closely with African American pastors and congregational leaders, immersed in black church life. Since the African American Church plays a central role in the African American community, Perry feels strongly connected to and accepted by black communities because of his engagement with the church. Politically, Perry has stood with the black community in many struggles.

The combination of Perry's political stand and his understanding of black church culture has led to a high degree of acceptance:

> I know I can go into the black church culture and very quickly communicate to people that I understand the culture and that I have some literacy and some experience and respect for that culture that allows me to be involved in that culture. There is a notion of being accepted in because you've earned your stripes.

In the context of racial polarization, Perry's close identification with African Americans stands out and is noticed by black pastors, leading some to joke that he is not really white:

> There is a notion in the black community that when you have committed yourself to the black community in that kind of way, where you are accepted in, people begin to question your racial origins. This is very true in the South. They joke about it. I've had pastors introduce me and say, "Look, I know he looks white on the outside, but I don't think he is." You can play with it. But white people can get kind of confused and think they're black. That's bullshit. I put on no pretense to be black. I am a white guy.

Although Perry wants to remain very clear that he is white, he does experience a strong social and cultural connection with African Americans. He very much enjoys black church culture and appreciates the opportunity to become multicultural:

> You really become multicultural in a sense that you've really been opened up to a whole world. Peter Paris, in his book *The Social Teaching of the Black Churches,* talks about the black church as a surrogate world. Because blacks were powerless, they had no franchise and no way to impact public life, so they created a surrogate world where there was public life. That's been the main place of black culture, music, and all kinds of artistic expression. Black politics and intellectual development are all in some way connected to the African American Church. Being accepted in and developing some understanding and appreciation of that community, its theology, and its culture is very rich. I think it improves your life and your enjoyment of life.

In the context of his organizing work in Louisiana, Perry wants to stand in both the white and the black world so he can bring them together. Speaking of his work in the black church, Perry says he has a "deep respect for that culture and that community, which then allows me to operate in both worlds and then to invite people in both worlds to come together. I mean in many ways that's what the organizing is about."

"I FELL IN LOVE WITH THE AFRICAN AMERICAN COMMUNITY"

Kathy Dudley, like Perry, finds an affinity in communities of color. Kathy moved her family to predominantly black west Dallas in the early eighties and spent many years working with black pastors in the Voice of Hope ministry she founded with them. Kathy, an evangelical Christian, says, "I fell in love with the African American community through that journey." Kathy even says that, in many ways, she feels more African American than white. However, like Perry, she wants to connect closely with the black community, not "become" black. She says it remains important for her to stay connected to her past:

> We probably culturally are a blend because in many ways I feel more African American than white. But we've made the commitment to stay connected to our roots. Periodically I'll just go back to Virginia, and I'll just hang out where I grew up and be with my family. I don't ever want to hate that. I can hate certain things we did that I think are wrong but not the core or essence of who we are.

Not everything was smooth going in terms of her family's acceptance in communities of color. Kathy has faced her share of mistrust and hostility from some African Americans in west Dallas. Her kids experienced rejection and even violence at times, too:

> My oldest son, when he was in public school in Dallas, in a majority Latino school, as a matter of fact, was beaten up by about a dozen Latino gang members. He was really hurt bad. Scars on the inside more than on the outside. It was not an easy thing. I'm not in any way saying it was.

Despite the pain, or perhaps because of it, Kathy feels her sons are now stronger:

> Am I glad, and are they glad, now that they are grown? Yes. We feel that hopefully they have a better understanding of life than they would have ever gotten had they not made the choices....My sons

experienced learning and life at a different level. That has impacted the way they view race, the way they view women, the way they view the world in general at twenty-seven and twenty-nine. Totally different had they not gone through the pain, had they not been rejected.

Although Kathy understands the historical roots of black rejection, she feels the need to challenge it:

It's always digging down deeper for what is true and what is honest and what is fair and what is pure, if you would. We try to live by those principles. If truth is not there, in rejection of African Americans toward my kids or us because we're white, that has to be spoken to just as prophetically as speaking the truth to whites if privilege is being enforced or unfairly taken advantage of in different ways.

Although her children experienced some tension with children of color, by and large they were growing up immersed in and part of black culture. Kathy says that at one point, in fact, her children were starting to hate white people. Consequently, she took them out of the neighborhood schools and sent them for a year to a predominantly white, Christian school so they could learn "that white people aren't all bad either." Kathy wanted her children to be connected to their white tradition:

There are lots of choices around race issues. You have to decide what's right and wrong. There's history that is bad and good. We all have to accept that. But to deny who you are is not healthy, either.

Issues of identity cannot be easily solved; rather, they represent an ongoing journey:

There's pressure when you're white in this kind of work to become "them" in order to be affirmed. Maybe that's true in any cross-cultural work. There are huge issues of identity and belonging. Where do you belong? Where do my children belong? How do they find belonging? We have to work through those things. My youngest son married an African American. We have a half–African American grandbaby that we just adore. There are all the issues of identity that he will have to struggle with. But I think it will be easier because we didn't feel like we had to become somebody different than ourselves to affirm someone who is different.

Although Kathy speaks of "who you are" in racial terms, she also wants to get beyond race as the sole basis of belonging. Kathy founded the Dallas

Leadership Foundation in order to bring Christians together across racial lines to support community development and racial justice. Although the foundation undertakes community and economic development projects, her deeper goal is to change human relationships. That's a process her family models as it undergoes its own journey:

> I think that's helped me to remain feeling good about being a white person. I am a white person who at the same time is probably very African American on the inside, culturally, because I've assimilated so much of that. But I'm very comfortable. This is the beauty that I see in my kids now and my husband as well. No matter where we are, we're very comfortable cross-culturally because the issue has never really been as much race as it has been truth.

"TENURE IN THE SHARING OF LIFE"

John Heinemeier has lived a life immersed in the African American community. He has served as pastor of black Lutheran congregations for the past forty years in East Brooklyn, in the South Bronx, in the Roxbury neighborhood of Boston, and in Baltimore. He has helped to build multiracial community organizing groups in the IAF network but sees his main work as ministering in the black communities where he has lived and raised his family. John and his wife adopted a black daughter in part to share more deeply in black life. John grew up in a small town in Texas and early on rejected the segregation and close-mindedness of the Lutheran tradition in which he was raised. For John, his commitment to racial justice lies in his tenure in sharing life with communities of color:

> I think the intention to have tenure in cross-cultural situations is where it starts. You want to be here and want to stay over the long haul. Almost all of my ministry has been in lower-income African American and to some extent Latino communities. That has been very purposeful and very deliberate. It starts there. I would say that almost in a classical pastoral pattern my ministry has been a combination of seeking justice on one side and consolation on the other.

Through that sharing of life, John has created his own life and found himself:

> It's a question of tenure. That is the way in which I have both been called to do this and then have done it. I have been a part of cross-cultural life and work for forty years. That has been probably the most significant

factor: that it has been long lasting, that it has been for the duration, that it has not been interrupted, that it is still constant and true, and that it is not under a sense of obligation or sacrifice. It is who I am.

Through tenure, John feels very accepted by and connected to black communities:

> You talk about paying dues. There are dues to be paid in this work that is constant, and it's based on tenure. Not just tenure, but it can't be apart from tenure. You really convince by example and by sticking around and by what you do. You're there for real and not just episodically. It's when that hurdle is crossed with at least many that the real coming together happens. It doesn't happen right away.

John is close to his own black congregation and turns to its members when he needs support:

> The surest and most dependable antidote that I have had over the years for despondency, discouragement, and being low is to go into the local community and just talk with people. Those local communities have almost all been almost totally nonwhite. To experience both what I have to give in that conversation but even more in their acceptance of me to be affirmed and to be loved. To love and to be loved with local people across racial lines has always been an antidote to despondency for me.

John does not want to take this support for granted, and he worries that the need to be affirmed by local people is not all noble. Nonetheless, he considers the acceptance he receives a powerful gift:

> I get support from the people in a *very* fundamental way. I think this goes back to the beginnings. I always marvel at that. It is what I would call in theological terms gracious. It is always a gift to me.
>
> It is a gift that they would accept me, would integrate me, my wife, and my family into their life and into their community to work. It's dear to them. That has been an astounding affirmation to me. It is where I go when I get down. I go to the people. I don't go to the church. Sure enough I don't go to the bishop. I'll go to the people here in this community and be affirmed—in very simple human ways of mutual acceptance, being with each other. That has been a priceless support to me, has been the people.

John has a highly developed sense of caring because of his long immersion in the black community. Consequently, he feels that he and people of color approach racial justice in a similar way. In other words, he doesn't come "from the outside" developing a commitment to racial justice. Rather, he starts from membership in the community, the sharing of life, calling his approach "organic":

> When it comes to racial justice, distinct probably from some, I have not been nearly as much of an ideologue as perhaps other white folks who've been involved in racial justice. It has been more as part of a community rather than cause oriented. It has been sharing the life of a community and shoulder to shoulder, as opposed to coming in ideologically and as a flaming advocate. It has been far more in concert with folks. It's been far more out of that sharing of life that I've been driven....I use the word "organic," coming out of where I was, immersed in the black community.

At the same time, John recognizes the limits of his membership in the African American community. He is more accepted within his congregation than out in the public world of the black community:

> It's always been remarkable to me that, especially after a tryout period, how little I am challenged on racial grounds among the people I work with, members of the congregation, with people that know me and that I know. Most of that challenge comes from outside the congregation. There it happens all the time. You have to be much more guarded and strategic. That has been a constant all these years. And in some cases it's really kind of painful. But it's so expected and so predictable. It's just kind of part of the territory.

Like Doug Anderson, John puts this mistrust and even rejection in historical context, but it is painful nonetheless:

> This happened in Roxbury among young black men on the streets. This may seem like a small thing, but it was there. It was by no means all of the young blacks, but it ended up often enough to become a bit of a pattern. In approaching them, oftentimes, to have people spitting on the street as they approached you. Well, not all of that was extra saliva in the mouth. At least I interpreted it that way. I may have been wrong, but it happened so often. Those things jar you for a bit, and then you understand it. That's part of the history of this country and part of the racial disaster that we've created in these United States.

John recounts a truly disastrous event when he "put on his black hat" and tried to speak for black pastors in the Black Ministerial Alliance (BMA) in Boston. He was not only a member of the alliance but also sat on its leadership team. Nevertheless, he confronted the limits of his role at a meeting with white and black pastors. The BMA ministers had come to discuss joining the Greater Boston Interfaith Organization (GBIO), a multiracial and multifaith community organizing group affiliated with the IAF. John went too far by raising what he thought were the concerns on the minds of the black pastors:

> And man, did I catch it that day from black pastors! My colleagues in BMA ran me over the coals. Not mercilessly. They still were collegial. They just said, "John, how *dare* you?" Publicly, at the meeting. "How *dare* you think you can talk for black clergy and present these hypothetical objections to joining GBIO? How *dare* you think you have the right to do that?"

Despite his close ties, John recognizes the limits. He will never "be black":

> At the end of the day we live in different places. That is just the way it is. I will never be black. No matter how much I would like to think that those barriers can all be transcended, the truth be told, I think there's almost always some distance remaining. It's just almost biological. It's certainly historical. There is such damage in relationships, such inequality, and such a stacked deck. Even somebody who's been around as long as I have been in the black community, forty years, would be foolish indeed to think that that distance is not still there. That's the way it is, man.

While pastoring black congregations has been John's priority, he has also worked to build multiracial and multifaith organizations like GBIO. In the end, John says he identifies with this kind of multiracial group, that is, with people who share his values:

> I identify more with people who have similar values. That's white and black. I have almost as little tolerance for black middle-class suburbanites as I have for white middle-class suburbanites in terms of values. I wouldn't make that so racial. I would make it more what you stand for.

These multiracial communities provide John with important support and a sense of belonging. John speaks of the "juice" he gets from IAF organizers, as well as how he has "meshed" so closely with African American pastor and IAF leader Johnny Ray Youngblood. Indeed, John describes his ultimate project as racial reconciliation, not justice. Justice is necessary, but true multiracial community based upon reconciliation is the goal:

Power-oriented and power-delivered justice work is not very satisfactory if it can't have some reconciliatory goal. Just to bludgeon someone to get your way and to work on something cruelly justice oriented is limited. At its best organizing is working at redemption, it's working at what King called the Beloved Community, and it's working toward reconciliation. That's the ultimate goal, even beyond justice. That can never be accomplished without justice, but justice itself is not the ultimate goal. It is reconciliation.

Indeed, it would be fair to say that John tries to embody in his own person God's project of racial reconciliation. Despite the historic obstacles, he remains hopeful about the possibility of creating a truly human, multiracial community in part because of the affirmation he has received from African Americans:

> The question is, with that being said, can we still work together? Can we still meet as human beings? And the answer to that is yes. It's like in the biblical story. Remember the story of Joseph being sold by his brothers into Egypt as a slave? He was the one who had to forgive them. In other words, the impetus for some kind of grace had to come from the offended party. That is the way it is still today.

John feels privileged to receive that kind of acceptance:

> The sad reality is that the black community will have to be more generous than the white. To their credit, many are. You'd think it would be the other way, that the offender would make the overtures toward reconciliation. I find more of it coming from the black community, at least in my life and work. And that is a position of great privilege, to be in that situation and to be a recipient of reconciliation from the offended party. Man, that's rich. That's been constant. That is not to be trivialized. That is not to be domesticated. That basic acceptance has come from the offended party. I treasure that. I really do.

"I IDENTIFY WITH PEOPLE WHO DO THIS WORK"

Educator Christine Clark at the University of Maryland reflects the complex stance across the color line that many white activists maintain. She has had her share of tension with other whites. Indeed, at a young age she was beaten up by whites who called her a "n-gger lover." Christine takes some of this in her stride:

I heard Geneva Gay, a black woman professor from the University of Washington, make this joke. She said, "I don't understand why my students choose to do this work for a living and then wonder why they're not well liked." I think that there's some real interesting and provocative truth in that. You don't choose to be a social justice change advocate because you expect people to run from their homes and throw their arms around you and embrace you.

Christine married an African American man, and this relationship gives her a deeper connection to the black community:

I identify with black men in a way that may not make sense to them, but it makes sense to me because the man who I love is black. That influences how I interact with black men. I think when you love somebody as the primary person in your life and other people share that attribute with them, then that carries over.

People notice it because they say, "Oh, I heard you have a thing for black men." I say, "Oh, that's ridiculous." But, of course, I'm going to have an affinity for black men because the man who is in my life in the most important way is a black man. I hang out with all his friends, who are black men. That becomes a community for me.

Christine wants to make it clear that she is not abandoning her whiteness; indeed, she recognizes the limits of her membership in the black community:

I don't want to say that I run from my racial identity or that I try to claim one inauthentically. You know, because I'm married to him, that gives me some kind of entrée because I don't think it does. But I do think that I identify with black people on some level or I wouldn't end up in a largely black group when I go to NAME. So there's something going on.[4]

Moreover, the black community is diverse, and Christine struggles with connecting to black Christian conservatives:

I have a real problem with socially conservative Southern black Christians. It has influenced and maybe fed racism in me because I could easily say I can't stand Southern black Christians. They drive me crazy. I find them insular. I could say that I find them simple, all these things that reinforce stereotypes. There's something about the fundamentalism that drives me nuts because it feels like unchecked colonization. It feels like white supremacy that's been accepted on some level. It's very homophobic, and I'm hostile to that even though I understand it. It pushes my buttons.

Christine's sense of identity and community is multiple and overlapping:

I look at it through a lot of different lenses, depending on where I am and what the situation is...I find affinity with white women who share certain attributes, like educational attainment, like the discourse style, linguistic skill sets. I also find affinity with people who are very much like the folks that my husband grew up with because I've known them for twenty years. So I can sit down with a group of older black men who want to tell dirty jokes, and that feels like hanging out with my father-in-law. Or people who tell stories about growing up in a particular kind of discourse style. That also feels like my husband hanging out with his best friends. Interestingly, that's never been a group that's denied access to girls. His friends never had the gender segregation that I experienced growing up. When I hang out with his friends, I never feel like I shouldn't be there because I'm a girl, which is real interesting.

In the end, however, her primary network is multiracial and activist oriented and, like John Heinemeier and others, is carried out with those who share her values:

I identify with people who do this work. That's my primary family in many ways, people who do this work. If I have a conversation with somebody and we connect on the work, the values around the work, that's the easiest.

Like other activists in the study, Christine wants not only to claim her white identity but also to reshape a new identity around racial justice. She points to the need to construct a new antiracist identity particularly but not exclusively for whites:

I want to bring people into the fold. I want to give them the opportunity to understand that becoming a white antiracist or an antiracist even if you take white out of the equation is as great an identity as the identities that we hold out, like doctor, lawyer, antiracist. They should all be on the same level. Part of the way racism persists is that we don't really give people from dominant groups the opportunity to embrace a positive role. We subsume the roles that they've played in the past. We hide them. We don't talk about John Brown in a positive way. Most people don't even know he was white.

Working to build a multiracial community around racial justice values is continually challenging, but Christine finds that it gives her an opportunity to "feel like I'm making a contribution to something that's bigger than me, a contribution to humanity." Because of that, she's willing "to hang on for the ride."[5]

Variations in Belonging

The large majority of the activists in the study reported tension with other whites and both association with and limits to their relationship with communities of color. Nevertheless, there is some variation in their answer to the question raised by Janet Morrison at the beginning of this chapter, that is, "Where do I fit in?" The history of race relations in any local context may matter. For example, activists in Greensboro may find themselves "stuck in the middle" of a particularly contentious racial divide. Perhaps the San Francisco Bay Area, while not immune from racial conflict, includes a much broader social justice–oriented culture where activists find it easier to find an alternative, multiracial activist community.

Meanwhile, activists in any local context may find more tension with whites at certain times, typically when the community becomes racially polarized. Carol Brook says many whites she knows are supportive of her work today as a federal defender in Chicago. However, speaking of African American mayor Harold Washington during a racially polarized time in the eighties, she says, "People didn't like it when I worked for Harold.... That whole working for Harold experience was a real in-your-face racist experience." She recounts this story at court when Washington's death was announced:

> I must have found out at lunch. I was broken hearted. Broken hearted. I don't know what I was thinking, but I thought the jurors might want to end early so we could all go to city hall to pay our respects. I asked the judge if he would consider ending court early so that everybody could go. There was dead silence in the courtroom because it didn't occur to a single person other than me that we would even care about doing this. And this was the mayor of the city of Chicago.

Variation may also come from differences in family background. Some activists' families are fairly supportive, while others are less so. Michael Siegel is rather exceptional in that he grew up with parents who were political radicals, surrounded by their multiracial group of activist friends.[6] Rather than creating tension with family, this heritage has given Michael "a lot to live up to." He takes responsibility for the complex history bequeathed by his background:

> I'm very conscious of my whiteness. I consider myself a progressive Euro-American. I have communist traditions, and also, for better or for worse, I have pioneering Christian ancestors who took land from Native peoples and other people to secure their wealth. I have a very contradictory ancestry. My Jewish ancestors were very poor. My WASP ancestors were very rich. I am a person who believes in reparations. I believe that I have a responsibility for the role my community has played in oppressing other people. When I say community, I mean my white community.

Yet his relationships with whites are not entirely free from tension:

> I'm comfortable around WASP-y Americans and maybe more conservative Americans. As an educated white person, I can enter any environment. Maybe once I speak my truth, I will be alienated from certain individuals who are white, but I have the ability to represent the interests of people of color and people from low-income backgrounds in almost any environment.

Michael spends most of his time working and relating to a multiracial group of young people in the Bay Area. He speaks about his comfort in this diverse community:

> Truthfully in my heart, I feel very comfortable around people from every background. I would not want race to be an obstacle or barrier to any relationship. I feel that I benefit from having as diverse a community of friends and loved ones as possible.

Finally, some of the activists care more than others whether they get support from family and friends or whether there is tension. The parents of juvenile justice activist Mark Soler were progressive, but they passed away when he was young. Some members of his extended family disapprove of his work:

> I have relatives who think I'm crazy for doing this work generally and especially for trying to help black boys. Not immediate family, but

not that far away. In my wife's family people think I'm nuts. I have friends who I know socially in other ways who think this is crazy stuff to do and a waste of time. They say, "If you have such a good education, why aren't you making a lot of money in a law firm?" That's a condition of public interest law although I think it's focused more on racial justice work.

Mark says he doesn't care that much though about their disapproval. Referring to his work on racial disparities in juvenile sentencing, Mark says this:

> When I talk about getting this report on the front page of the *New York Times,* I think that is one of the greatest things that I ever did. And yet when I tell my wife's father and stepmother about it, they think, "But you're helping black kids who committed crimes." Maybe they like me very much, but they're thinking, "Too bad Mark doesn't have a good job." You know? So there's that. And the truth is I don't really care very much about that.

Nevertheless, it would be fair to say that even activists like Mark, who are bothered less by family disapproval, still feel some pain at the conflict between their lives as racial justice activists and their family's more mainstream attitudes.

Variation occurs, too, in the activists' experiences with communities of color. Some of the activists have intimate relationships with people of color and so get even closer to social identification. Some activists are younger and feel more in doubt about their identity and role, while the more experienced activists seem to have achieved a greater acceptance of self. Some of the white activists live and work in communities of color; others find their sense of belonging in narrower, multiracial groups outside of community settings. Finally, some activists find more of a community of support in activist networks, while others continue to struggle with greater isolation.[7]

However, the basic dilemma remains. For these activists as a group, the threat of isolation is both an obstacle to pursuing their work and an emotional drain. Most of them need the support of some kind of community and a place to fit in. In the end, the very large majority say they identify with a community of multiracial activists, however nascent. While many report receiving support from family and old friends, the large majority turn to these emergent multiracial communities for a sense of belonging on the basis of shared values.[8]

Conclusion

Much has been written about the struggles with marginalization faced by people of color who enter largely white environments like elite colleges and corporate law firms. They, too, are often stuck between two worlds, experiencing a particularly extreme example of the kind of "twoness" W.E.B. Du Bois identified nearly a hundred years ago. Du Bois suggested that all African Americans face unreconciled strivings between their identity as both Negro and American in a white-dominated America.[9] By contrast, we have paid almost no attention to the identity struggles of the white Americans who are committed to racial justice and cross over the color line in the opposite direction.

The character of their struggles, however, is not entirely social. In fact, it is determined by the tension between social and political identity. Cathy Rion captures this social and political divide:

> Socially and culturally I grew up white, and I'm white and middle to upper-middle class. So there's a certain ease and comfort on the one hand with folks who are like me. That's something that is real and on some level I'm okay with. Politically, I feel much more alliance and commonality with folks of color who are doing organizing. I can have a lot more conversation with my ex-roommate, who is a Mexican immigrant and a Justice for Janitors organizer than with somebody who I went to high school with.

White activists fall between their social identity with other whites and their political stance with communities of color. In other words, they share a history and culture with mainstream white Americans, but they have made a political break with its dominant ideology and values. They stand politically with people of color in their antiracist values and in their support for racial justice. Sharing what social movement scholars call "oppositional consciousness," they remain in some tension with mainstream white culture. Yet the power of racial identification maintains some distance between them and communities of color.[10]

In order to resolve this problematic identity, white activists could reject the white community and try to immerse themselves in communities of color. None appear to choose that route—at least none of the activists in this study do. Such a rejection represents a denial of self and forecloses the possibility of moving other whites forward. At the same time, activists face some limits to full immersion in communities of color. They can never "be black." Indeed, to many activists, such an attempt feels like theft.

Rather, activists seem to accept a degree of tension today while working toward building a new community based upon shared values in the moral and political project of racial justice. Such an effort does not necessarily mean that white activists—or their colleagues of color, for that matter—dissolve their old social identities completely. They live in the "world as it is" even as they try to create new relationships. And, in the world as it is, race remains a powerful social marker. Indeed, many activists believe that part of their work requires developing a racial justice–oriented identity for white Americans.[11]

A few activists become loners in a sense, people who do not care so much about belonging. However, the vast majority seek a place in which to belong in activist communities.[12] Penda Hair captures the importance of her network this way:

> Even though I don't see those people every day, spiritually they are with me a lot. When I do see them, it's like getting a meal or something. It refreshes you to go back and do the work. Sometimes the results that we get are bad. You have to have some reason to keep going, and I think that's more faith than tangible results a lot of the time.

Social movement scholars have recognized activist groups as critical places for the construction of new identities. Operating outside of mainstream institutions, they are "free spaces" for the development of new shared understandings. By working together, people create bonds of affection that undergird a shared identity. Multiracial activist groups operate in much the same way. However, they face a particularly daunting challenge. The color line has been so entrenched in American society that efforts to forge a new multiracial and justice-oriented identity get caught in the crosshairs of deeply entrenched divisions.[13]

Progress toward the building of new identities and a sense of belonging in multiracial activist networks is difficult, too, because these networks are small and relatively isolated. There is no visible national movement with which to identify. These groups and networks represent critical sources of support and identity for activists, but they remain limited. To the extent that activists can work toward building a movement, they can construct an identity for white (and other) racial justice activists that, in turn, will find them a recognized and respected place in American society.

Activists can work to move their white social world politically in the direction of communities of color, and they can strive to build a social world, a community, across racial lines with people of color and other whites based upon racial justice values. In fact, in the long run, achieving the vision of a multiracial society based upon justice and cooperative spirit rests in the dissolution of such a sharp political line between whites and people of color. However, that political and moral project, as we have seen throughout this work, requires some progress toward the erosion of the social separation between racial groups as well. In the end, multiracial political solidarity needs to rest upon progress in creating multiracial social solidarity.

CHAPTER EIGHT | **Conclusion**
Winning Hearts and Minds

John Brown worked not simply for black men—he worked with them; and he was
a companion of their daily life, knew their faults and virtues, and felt, as few
white Americans have felt, the bitter tragedy of their lot.

—W.E.B. Du Bois

WITH THESE WORDS, W.E.B. Du Bois opened his biography of John Brown, the white abolitionist who led an armed assault against slavery. Brown had a religiously inspired moral vision of an America freed of the sin of slavery. As Du Bois indicated, Brown identified closely with African Americans, saw their cause as a common one, and deeply believed that he was working in the best interests of both blacks and whites. Brown certainly had fire in his heart. In the words of Reverend Joseph Lowery, referenced in the subtitle of this book, Brown came to deeply embrace the cause of racial justice. So do many white activists who work for racial justice today. How did they come to do so?[1]

———

Nearly half of all African American and Latino students fail to graduate from high school with their classmates. Nearly half! In many urban areas, the proportion is even higher. Yet we know that success in education provides the key to a decent life and to full participation in society, that is, to achieving the American Dream. Indeed, most children of color who fail at school are destined to a life of poverty or economic hardship. Many, especially the young men, will end up in prison. Consequently, educational injustice has emerged as *the* civil rights issue of the day.[2]

We can debate how knowledgeable the average white American is of this situation, but I do not think it will come as a great surprise to many white people. Ever since Jonathan Kozol documented what he called the "savage inequalities" facing children of color in our schools in the early nineties, Americans have heard almost daily reports about the poor state of education in our inner cities and its devastating consequences. Yet knowledge of the facts does not appear to move white Americans to caring and action. Institutional racism of the kind I have just described in education does not require intentional racism on the part of whites. Indeed, few whites support this system of educational injustice because they intend to harm black and Latino children. Rather, white passivity appears to be the main problem. Indeed, even though institutional racism does not necessarily require intentionality for it to be perpetuated, challenging this system does require intentionality and action.[3]

How can white Americans come to care enough about racism that they move from passivity to action for racial justice? I decided to look for clues to answer that question by examining the lives and self-understanding of white people that have made that move and became committed activists for racial justice. In the course of this book, I have drawn in detail from the interviews I conducted to present pieces of answers to that question. In the following section I bring those pieces together to develop a more integrated explanation. In the rest of the chapter I highlight the broader implications of the findings of this project for advancing racial justice in the United States. In the end I explain how whites can come to support racial justice not just because they should do so but also because they fully embrace the cause as their own.

Head, Heart, and Hand

Americans place great faith in education as a force for social change.[4] If whites knew about racism, so this thinking goes, and understood that it continues to exist and oppress people of color, they would come to oppose it. I did find that awareness of racism proves important to the development of commitment on the part of the interviewees, but only partly so. Rather, I found that the activists in this study came to support racial justice through a combination of cognitive and emotional processes at the heart of which lay moral concerns.

Let me briefly recount the findings presented in the earlier chapters. Activists begin their journey to racial justice activism through a direct experience that leads to an awareness of racism, but the real action does not lie in the knowledge gained. What makes this experience a seminal one for them is that through it they recognize a contradiction between the values with which they have grown up and the reality of racial injustice. When they confront this value conflict, activists express anger at racial injustice. They care about racism at first because they believe deeply in the values that are being violated. They express what I call a moral impulse to act.

If we stop here, however, we are left with the do-gooder, the white person who helps people of color but remains at a distance. I find that relationships with people of color begin to undermine that separation. Whites learn more deeply about the reality of racism through these relationships. But more than the head is involved here, too. Personal relationships and stories tug at the heart; that is, they create emotional bonds of caring. Whites become concerned about racism because it affects real people they know. Rather than working *for* people of color, they begin to work *with* them, their commitment nurtured by an ethic of care and a growing sense of shared fate.[5]

As whites take action for racial justice, they build more than individual relationships with people of color. Working collectively in activist groups, they prefigure the kind of human relationships they hope will characterize a future America. In other words, as they attempt to create respectful collaborative relationships, they construct a more concrete sense of the kind of society for which they are working, what I call a moral vision. They find purpose and meaning in a life that works for the kind of society they want for themselves, their children, and all people across racial lines. Some refer to this as a calling, but they all begin to express a direct interest for themselves in a life committed to racial justice activism. Activists come to see that racism harms whites, as well as people of color. It denies whites their full humanity and blocks progress toward a society that would benefit everyone, one that would be in the interest of whites, as well as people of color. Forging community in multiracial groups deepens a sense of shared fate and bonds of caring as it fosters hope for the possibilities of social change. If the moral impulse represents what activists are against, an emerging moral vision represents what they are for, a truly human or beloved community. It provides a foundation for shared identities as multiracial political activists.

Activists develop commitment and deepen their motivations over time, in part through their experiences taking action against racism. Activism provides whites an opportunity to build relationships with people of color, as well as other white activists, and to construct the kind of multiracial community in which they develop and implement a vision of a future society. This is not a linear process but rather a cycle or perhaps a spiral. Indeed, a model of motivation leading to action is too simplistic. Rather, I find that activists develop commitment over time and through activism. Indeed, there may be setbacks or a need for constant vigilance as the pressures of the dominant society constantly push whites back toward a white world and worldview.

For the sake of clarity, I have presented the processes in an ordered form, starting with a moral impulse and leading to a moral vision. To some extent, this order is represented in the activists' lives. However, some activists inherit a sense of a moral vision from their families or their religious traditions and so have elements of a vision at the beginning. For others, relationships come earlier rather than later. Meanwhile, activists continue to express moral outrage even after they deepen their commitment through relationships and construct a moral vision. Each of these processes has its own particular effects on developing commitment. Yet each represents a piece of the larger puzzle of commitment. I have illustrated below how they work together to forge a deep commitment to racial justice on the part of white activists (figure 8.1).

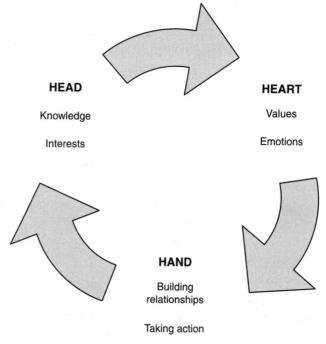

HEAD

Knowledge

Interests

HEART

Values

Emotions

HAND

Building
relationships

Taking action

FIGURE 8.1. Head, Heart, and Hand

It may be useful to summarize the relationship between these processes by visualizing them as a cycle. If we start with the heart, anger at the violation of deeply held values leads some white activists to take action for racial justice and thereby build relationships with people of color. These connections create knowledge about the experiences of people of color and begin to shape a sense of common interests. By working in emergent multiracial communities, white activists develop caring and hope while generating a moral vision of a multiracial society with justice at its center. They continue to experiment with building respectful, collaborative associations in multiracial activist groups, all the while developing a sense of their personal interest in racial justice as they find that activism offers a meaningful life.

Within the context of the interactive approach just elaborated, I found moral concerns to play a key role in the development of commitment and action. This approach lies in stark contrast to most thinking on racial justice, which focuses on the cognitive domain. As noted earlier, we place great emphasis on educating white Americans about racism. Certainly, one must understand that racism is an important problem if one is to take action against it. In that sense I did find the processes of learning about the history and experiences of people of color and of developing a racial justice framework to be important to the activists in this study. Moreover, cognitive knowledge about racism, including research and analysis of how it works, is necessary to know what to do about it. However, by itself, knowledge does not motivate one to take action. It answers the "what" to do but not the "why" to do it.[6]

Motivation comes primarily from a moral source even as its character develops from impulse to care and vision. White activists start with a moral impulse that racism is wrong because certain values they care about are being violated. Through relationships they deepen their commitment as they develop an ethic of caring. The many children of color who drop out of high school are no longer just numbers but rather real people to whom they are connected. Eventually activists make the cause their own through the construction of a moral vision of a just, multiracial, and human community.

The other way in which cognitive processes are typically emphasized is through a focus on the rational calculation of self-interest. If whites can come to see their common material interests with people of color (in better healthcare for example), then they are likely to find common cause with people of color. Or if whites can see that it will cost them less to educate children than to incarcerate them after they drop out of high school and get into trouble, then they will likely support a more just educational system. These are important arguments. Yet I found almost no evidence that rational, interest-based understandings like these motivated the activists in my study.

I do not want to counterpose morality and interests. Rather, what I discovered is that activists find a way to get them to work together and to reinforce each other. In particular, as white activists construct a moral vision of a future society based upon their values, they develop a way to understand white interest in racial justice. As we have seen, these visions encompass material concerns. Activists are working today to address poverty, rebuild communities, and create better educational systems. The future society they envision would offer more equitable social provision for people of color and for most whites as well. Yet it would perhaps more fundamentally be a community based upon what activists see as deeply human values, where people treat each other with respect and caring across lines of race. Out of these values, better material provision can emerge. While interests and morality work together, in the end, activists embed an understanding of white people's interests into their vision of human community, and that is why I argue that moral sources are primary.

Pursuing a moral vision does not mean working altruistically *for* people of color. The activists in this study have developed a clear sense of their own direct stake in racial justice. In order to understand how morality and interests can work together at the individual level, we have to break from the notion that equates moral action with altruism—doing for someone else rather than for yourself. Nathan Teske, in his study of political activists, has criticized the duality of self-interested versus altruistic action. He shows instead that when activists uphold their most deeply held values by working for the common good, they are also benefiting themselves in ways that are quite rational. They construct an identity for themselves as moral persons, which allows them to gain a meaningful life and a place in history.[7]

Teske reconciles morality and self-interest at the individual level, but I also found that activists resolve the dichotomy at the collective level, too, by embedding an understanding of the collective interests of white Americans in a moral vision. The two levels are in fact related. Activists derive meaning in their lives by pursuing that vision. As activist Roxane Auer captured it, "I'm contributing to the world I want to live in." In other words, activists develop a strong and direct interest in living their lives in the present in accordance with the principles on which that beloved community would be founded. Indeed, along with other activists they attempt to work out those principles by implementing them in the present.[8]

It is also a mistake to counterpose cognitive understanding and emotions. Traditionally, we have understood emotionally based activity as nonrational and suspect in politics. Yet there is a large and growing literature in several fields that shows that emotions and cognition are closely connected. Political scientist George Marcus draws upon recent work in neuroscience to show the role of emotion in reasoning. He has argued that emotions are critical to democratic life, and so, in his view, "sentimental citizens" are the only ones capable of making reasoned political judgments and putting them into action. Political theorist Sharon Krause also shows that emotions can enhance, not detract from, democratic deliberation. She begins her critique of the distinction between passions and reason with words that echo the findings of this study: "Our minds are changed when our hearts are engaged."[9]

Emotions play a particularly important role in cognitive processes regarding racial justice precisely because the minds of white Americans need to be changed. As discussed in chapter two, more than a gradual learning process is required. Whites need to break from the dominant color-blind ideology and adopt a racial justice framework. That seems to happen in crystallized moments when a direct experience of racism brings powerful emotions into play. These experiences shock whites out of a complacent belief in the fairness of American society and sear a new racial justice awareness into their consciousness.[10]

In sum, many scholars of race relations and many policymakers have sought to make rational arguments that will convince whites that they have more to gain than lose by working together with people of color. Yet this study suggests that such an approach, however important, is ultimately too narrow. Rather, whites come to find common cause with people of color when their core values are engaged, when they build relationships that lead to caring and a sense of common identity, and when they can embed an understanding of their interests in a vision of a future, racially just society that would benefit all—that is, when the head, heart, and hand are all engaged.[11]

This project is an exploratory study. I have presented rich details from the lives of fifty activists and extensive accounts of how they understand their actions in order to reveal the workings of the processes summarized here. I have suggested that these processes and their interrelationships may be true of white activists more broadly. There may also be other routes to racial justice activism or other important factors that did not feature in the pool of activists I interviewed. Certainly much more research is needed to confirm the findings presented here. I hope that such research will provide a deeper understanding of these processes and the contexts in which they are more likely to occur.

Studies of White Racial Justice Activism in the Contemporary Period

I have found strong support for the theory I have just elaborated in the accounts of the activists I interviewed. Is there support for this theory in the admittedly limited research others have conducted on white activists in the contemporary period? First of all, it is important to recognize that I have examined the development of commitment to activism over time. That has not necessarily been the focus of other research on white activism. Moreover, the model I develop looks at the interactive effects of different processes and examines how they work together. Rarely have others approached commitment this way. Nevertheless, other researchers have identified some of the same factors I have found, thereby lending support to this theory.

Of the factors I identify, the role of relationships with people of color has received the most attention. In writing *A Promise and a Way of Life,* Becky Thompson interviewed thirty-nine white people who have been actively working against racism within a variety of social movements for the past fifty years—the civil rights, feminist, solidarity, and antiprison movements, as well as community-oriented efforts in the nineties. She employs these interviews primarily to construct a nuanced social history of racial dynamics and racial politics within these movements, not to explain the development of activists' commitment. However, along the way she discusses a number of themes raised by the activists about the development of their consciousness and activism.[12]

Thompson finds that relationships with people of color prove very important to white activists. Time and again, activists describe how people of color have taught them about racism, nurtured their commitment to racial justice, and mentored them. She also finds that many started out outraged about racism with a desire to help; through their activism and the influence of activists of color they became more committed to collaborating in pursuit of systemic change. Thompson suggests that friendships and intimate relationships with people of color are particularly important, another theme that resonates with my findings. She argues that through relationships with people of color who have personal experiences with racism whites can make the issue of racism personal to themselves.

Thompson also finds that her activists have developed a strong and direct interest in working for racial justice. Through activism they have built a purposeful life and found a chance to reclaim their humanity in an oppressive world, to save their souls. As the title of her book suggests, racial justice activism becomes "a way of life" for them. Thompson also stresses the importance of building multiracial venues and multiracial community as places where this way of life can be built, nurtured, and sustained. She finds white activists struggling with some of the same issues of place and identity that I find, sometimes feeling isolated and lacking a national movement with which to firmly identify. Thompson also discuss people's spirituality. However, moral concerns and the values that derive from religious faith or democratic traditions do not feature strongly in her account. There is some evidence, however, to suggest that Thompson's activists experienced value conflicts early in their road to activism. Moreover, she stresses that activists live their lives to carry out the principles of a just society; that is the "promise" they make to themselves featured in the title of her book. In the end, then, there are many rich connections between the themes of my study and Thompson's work.

For *Whites Confront Racism,* Eileen O'Brien interviewed thirty antiracist white people, many of whom were activists with either the People's Institute for Survival and Beyond, an antiracist training organization based in New Orleans, or with Anti-racist Action in Columbus, Ohio, which organizes against the Ku Klux Klan. This group encompasses, of course, a narrower range of racial justice activism than that covered by my study. In much of her work, O'Brien examines and compares the different ways activists carry out antiracist practice. However, she also presents her findings on the various influences that have led whites to become activists against racism.[13]

O'Brien finds that many activists have experienced important events in their lives that planted a seed for future activism; these are not dissimilar to the seminal experiences I found. She also finds that some motivation comes from religious and democratic ideals, usually linked to groups or networks to which people belong. Although O'Brien neither stresses value conflicts nor describes the activists' moral visions, her findings bear some similarity to mine along these lines.

What O'Brien does stress, however, is what she calls "approximating experiences," a term she attributes to unpublished work by Tiffany Hogan and Julie Netzer. Since, as I argue as well, whites cannot directly experience racism, O'Brien finds they need ways to approximate that experience. Activists find such approximations in several ways. "Borrowed approximations," the most common type, come from knowing people of color and witnessing their suffering. In other words, relationships with people of color proved powerful in her study as well.

The second kind of approximation, which O'Brien calls "overlapping," comes from reflecting on a white person's own experience of marginalization. She finds that marginalization played a role for women but not men in her study. Indeed, other researchers have indicated that white people, particularly women, can come to empathize with the plight of people of color by drawing some link between their own oppression and that of people of color. Eduardo Bonilla-Silva, for example, surveyed the racial views of a group of white college students. He finds that white female college students from working-class backgrounds are more likely to have progressive racial views. Bonilla-Silva also finds that those who had relationships with people of color were more likely to hold these views as well.[14]

I expected to hear the activists I interviewed recount experiences of marginalization, but only a very few did. Indeed, only a small number of the activists I interviewed expressed empathy—putting themselves in the shoes of people of color. Rather, the common theme was learning to care about racism through personal relationships with people of color. It is certainly possible that both kinds of emotions, empathy and caring, are engaged for many activists, but it seems to me that caring provides a more powerful force for commitment to action.

Recently O'Brien and her colleague Kathleen Korgen have suggested that interracial contact may now be less important as a way to affect white consciousness with regard to racism than in the past. In part, this is because there are more white people who make it their job to teach other whites about racism. However, in part, they argue it has to do with the dynamics of color-blind ideology. Whites can now have a relationship with a person of color without that experience changing their views about people of color in general. I remain unconvinced, however, that things have changed much in that regard. White people have always labeled some African Americans a "good black person," the exception to the rule. I believe relationships will continue to play a very important role in moving whites toward racial justice because they promote caring and a sense of shared fate; as Thompson also notes, they help make the political cause of racism personal to whites. In the later section on multiracial community I indicate the conditions in which interracial contact would more likely have that effect.[15]

In *Whites Confront Racism,* O'Brien recognizes that the shift to a racial justice ideology has emotional, as well as cognitive, components. She treats these elements less as motivating factors and more as issues to be faced in making an antiracist life. Whites experience a lack of support from other whites and a lack of trust by people of color, challenges that I also find. In an article drawing upon the same interview material, O'Brien presents a framework called "mind, heart and action" with some parallels to my own framework. Here, emotional work helps white activists forge an identity and stay committed to the struggle. O'Brien looks at cognition, emotions, and action as a way to describe the dimensions of antiracism, however, and not so much as a way to understand the development of commitment to racial justice.[16]

O'Brien employs racial identity development theory to analyze the ways in which whites struggle to accept themselves as whites in a racist world. Indeed, work in this area provides some parallels to my findings. This research studies the identity changes white people go through as they are confronted with the reality of racism. It does not attempt to explain commitment or action. The model describes how whites are often oblivious to racism at first, then experience inner conflict as they confront its reality for the first time. Some whites retreat in the face of this challenge and hold on to cultural explanations of inequality even more strongly, whereas others begin to move toward an awareness of the extent of racism. The latter may go on to experience many tensions and some inner turmoil about their white identity. Eventually, many whites reach a point where they can redefine the meaning of whiteness for themselves as a positive contributor to racial justice, a stage or status called the autonomous self.[17]

In the face of such heavy attention to issues of white identity, Ruth Frankenberg has called for more emphasis on white people taking action, echoing my finding that commitment develops through activism and relationship with people of color. She interviewed thirty white women in northern Californian to explore the impact of racism on their lives. She also found that interracial relationships, particularly intimate ones, greatly affected their racial awareness.[18]

Cooper Thompson and his colleagues have published a set of short, personal stories by white men who have challenged racism in their lives. Christine Clark and James O'Donnell have also published a set of personal narratives on race and white identity. The stories in both volumes are rich and evocative and variously include discussions of important events in the development of racial justice consciousness and experiences practicing antiracism. The editors do not analyze or integrate themes across the stories to construct a theory of commitment, but a reader will see many echoes of my findings in these collections. In particular, we see the role of relationships with people of color playing a prominent role along with moral concerns infused with strong emotion.[19]

One factor that I could not examine very closely was the impact of what is known as "prior activism" on the activists I studied. This factor has received much attention in research on social movements. Doug McAdam has stressed the importance of young people's activism prior to joining Freedom Summer in 1964 as a source of both values and personal connections to the movement. In contemporary research on racial justice activism, O'Brien has also found prior activism to be important to the activists she studied. The design and approach of my research, however, precludes much consideration of prior activism since I trace the development of commitment over time rather than the conditions that led to joining a movement at one point in time. A few activists do report participation in other types of activism in college, as I discuss in chapter two, but these accounts do not feature prominently in the study. In general, though, the whole idea of activists' being influenced by their experiences in activism over the course of their lives is entirely consistent with my findings.[20]

The power of relationships seems most consistent across the works discussed here and features in a couple of other relevant studies as well. Jennifer Eichstedt has interviewed sixteen gay antiracist activists and found that relationships with people of color were important to the development of their racial understanding. Her main focus, though, was on the dilemmas they faced negotiating a white identity within racial justice movements, a subject I discuss in chapter seven. In a historical review of racial justice efforts in the nation's first two hundred years, Herbert Aptheker has also observed that contact and relationships with African Americans seem to move whites toward antiracism.[21]

Perhaps surprisingly, moral frameworks and values do not feature prominently in any of these explanations of activism. Indeed, the violation of deeply held religious or democratic values and the construction of moral visions in which to embed notions of white interest in racial justice have received little attention. Studies of white activists in the civil rights movement, however, paid much more attention to these moral concerns. Young activists joined the movement in part because of moral outrage at a segregationist system's violation of their values. They often came to embrace Martin Luther King's vision of a Beloved Community. In the next section I discuss the importance of resurrecting moral leadership in the struggle for racial justice.[22]

Moral, Visionary Leadership

I turn now to some of the broader lessons of this study for moving white Americans from passivity to action for racial justice. This should be done with some caution, however. It may be that the processes and dynamics I have uncovered apply to activists more broadly but not to the average white

American. I offer two responses to that important concern. First, even if the findings of this study applied only to a minority of activist-inclined white Americans, its lessons would still be important. The activists in this study are highly engaged in trying to influence other white people and to make concrete changes in the operations of American institutional life. If the numbers of such activists were to increase significantly, even though they remained a minority, then we might see important progress in racial justice through the exercise of their leadership.

Second, I do not think that the activists in this study differ fundamentally from the average white person. The difference may be more of degree than kind. In other words, activists may care more than the average person about acting on their values, but average persons care about their values, too. Arguing that the social justice activists they studied in *Some Do Care* are not fundamentally different from the average person, Ann Colby and William Damon suggest that "Moral commitment, fortunately, is not a bizarre or even unusual part of human life. Almost everyone takes on moral commitments of some sort. These commitments become defining components of self in almost every case." At one time, scholars of social movements believed there was an activist personality type. However, the field has largely come to recognize that any individual has the potential to become an activist; whether and when the individual does so depends on a variety of structural and cultural factors.[23]

However, one important caveat remains. The activists in this study are not necessarily representative of white Americans across social class. I selected activists who worked for racial justice as a job—as educators, community organizers, and legal advocates. Consequently, the pool of subjects in the study was largely middle class. Many of them came from working-class backgrounds, but all had attended college and were currently middle class; a few were truly wealthy. At the same time, I can find nothing in the mechanisms I have identified to suggest that these processes would have less of an impact on working-class whites. Of course, more research will be necessary to determine whether they do. With these considerations in mind, however, let us discuss the broader lessons of the study.

One of the key implications of this study is the need to bring values to the fore and assert moral leadership in the struggle for racial justice. There are two ways of thinking about morality in this regard, however, captured in my distinction between the moral impulse and a moral vision. Whites can be exhorted to do the right thing, or they can be offered a chance to join in an effort to pursue the moral project of a better society for all with justice at its core. To some extent, as we have seen, probably both appeals are necessary.

Nevertheless, an appeal to conscience alone is insufficient. If whites feel only moral impulse, the result may be moralism rather than moral leadership. Perhaps that is the case for many well-meaning white people today. They believe racism is wrong, but they have not gone through the relationship-building and practice-based experiences that engage them in efforts to create and pursue values for a better society.

From this moralist point of view alone, the problem of racism is lodged in "bad" white people. Other whites are the problem, and moralists can easily denounce them. Even if they understand how racism functions in the institutional structure of American society, this still has nothing to do with them. Moralists have yet to discover two important and related lessons. First, as one activist in this study, Z. Holler, said, quoting Pogo, "The enemy is us."[24] In other words, all white people have been affected by racial indoctrination. Rather than dichotomizing the world into good and bad and simply blaming others, all white Americans have to take a close look at their own beliefs and behaviors.

Second, the perpetuation of racism is a complex problem. Whites need a serious, sustained effort to create institutional change and to deal with difficult challenges as they arise. Denouncing racism can make some whites feel good. Laboring in the trenches of the educational and criminal justice systems for sustained racial justice change, for example, is not all feel-good work even if it results in a rewarding life. The IAF organizers in this study, Perry Perkins and Christine Stephens, balked at my labeling them as activists because, in IAF thinking, activism represents short-term, unfocused action. I do not think the label "activism" necessarily means inconsistency or lack of commitment, but I do think their concerns help us appreciate that making serious advances in racial justice requires long-term engagement in public work to build power and new kinds of relationships that lead to real and positive change.[25]

Part of this serious work involves creating respectful, collaborative relationships with people of color. The moralists, the do-gooders working for people of color rather than with them, may continue to keep that separation. People of color are perhaps rightly suspicious of the white heroes who think they can solve problems for them. Rather, moral leadership involves building reciprocal relationships in common pursuit of justice goals. As John Heinemeier says in chapter seven, this kind of organic activism is about "sharing the life of a community, shoulder to shoulder, as opposed to coming in ideologically and as a flaming advocate."

In chapter five, we saw that moralism in relationship to other whites presents a constant challenge even for the most seasoned racial justice activists.

They struggle with honest confrontation with the racial beliefs and behaviors of other whites in a way that does not create defensiveness. They foster a sense of responsibility on the part of whites for action against racism. Responsibility is one thing, however; shaming and guilt trips are another. We have not seen much evidence in this study that shaming individual whites motivates a great deal of action. Indeed, the moral impulse arises not from shaming an individual as a bad person but from engaging positive values that people believe in and care about. Moral leadership lies in offering a moral vision, something to work for, a chance to become part of the racial justice family, as activist Christine Clark put it.

This study lends little support to the idea that confronting whites with their racial privilege constitutes an effective strategy to move them to action. Racial privilege may be a complex reality that white people need to grasp. Indeed, much important work to move whites toward racial justice understanding and action occurs under this banner.[26] However, stressing privilege as a strategy to engage whites seems to emphasize the wrong thing. It focuses on the narrow and short-term benefit whites receive from a racial hierarchy rather than their larger interest in a racially just future. Alone, it seems to engage shame and guilt rather than anger at injustice and hope for a better future. It is moralistic rather than visionary.

Moralism ignores interests in favor of altruism. By contrast, moral leadership takes interests seriously but reshapes white people's understanding of their interests and asks them to join a larger project that promises to create a better society for all. There is a material agenda here, one that offers better economic conditions and better social provision for people of color, as well as white families. However, this interest-based agenda is set and framed within a larger moral vision and political project.

There is evidence that suggests that this kind of moral leadership can be effective. Indeed, we are witnessing the rise of values-based activism in a variety of fields. For some, those values come from a religious faith that calls them to care for community and to act for social justice. Faith-based community organizing, for example, has emerged as a powerful force for engaging people in political action in their local communities. Indeed, several activists in this study are faith-based organizers and leaders. This kind of organizing engages value traditions while working for concrete, material improvements in the quality of people's lives in housing, jobs, and education.[27]

These values can also have secular roots like those based in the American democratic traditions of fairness, freedom, and justice. They can also be newer creations. Many activists in the environmental movement, for example, work not just to prevent ecological devastation but also to establish a new kind of society based upon the principles of working in balance and harmony with the world and caring about all forms of life. Environmentalists today try to live those values out in their relationships to each other and to the environment. In practice, both old and new values can be blended, as can religious and secular ones. More and more we are realizing that people care deeply about their values and can be engaged around them in progressive politics and other activist endeavors.[28]

In the end, moral leadership is about creating a vision that engages values to shape people's understanding of how their interests relate to racial justice. That, it seems to me, is precisely what Barack Obama achieved in the presidential election of 2008. Obama may not have placed racial justice explicitly at the center of that vision, but he offered people a chance to be part of a better, more just future, one whose policies will be more supportive of the needs of people of color, as well as of the average white person. Obama constantly referenced deeply held American values. He led with a vision and he stressed hope. Indeed, "Yes, we can" and the "audacity of hope" proved powerful themes that connected and moved many white Americans. Despite the struggles of the Obama administration to realize his vision in concrete legislation after the election, we can see the larger possibilities for whites to take steps toward racial justice that are inherent in that moment of visionary leadership.[29]

Building Multiracial Community

Another clear lesson of this study is the need to increase multiracial contact and collaboration in the United States. The activists in this study came to understand and care about racism through the people of color they knew personally. Certainly whites can teach other whites about racism. Indeed, the white activists in this study take that responsibility seriously. However, hearing stories directly from people of color engages the heart, as well as the head, and proves powerful. Through such relationships whites begin to care—and not just to know—about racism, and they begin to develop a sense of common identity and shared fate. Relationships, it appears, create the microfoundation for the broader visionary project of racial justice.

Studies of social capital, that is, social connections and ties between people, highlight the importance of these findings. Scholars of social capital like Robert Putnam have suggested that creating "bridging" ties across lines like race can create trust and cooperation and strengthen a sense of the common good. Yet we have far more "bonding" social capital, that is, ties among people who are like each other, than ties that bridge our differences. Nevertheless, despite persistent segregation, young people increasingly express a desire to be in a diverse setting. College, for the reasons discussed in chapter two, may in fact be a particularly important place for whites to begin to create bridging ties.[30]

Recent research by Robert Putnam highlights the importance of building these cross-racial ties. In studying racial diversity in localities across the United States, Putnam finds that areas with higher levels of racial diversity are lower in social trust. In other words, people appear to trust each other less when diversity is high. Whites trust blacks less and vice versa. Perhaps more surprisingly, however, people also trust other members of their own racial group less when diversity is high. In other words, diversity absent cross-racial relationships works against a sense of shared fate in the entire community. In this context, Putnam calls for investing in places where meaningful interactions across racial and ethnic lines occur, where people work, learn, and live together.[31]

As Putnam and others realize, however, contact across race in and of itself may not move whites toward racial justice. Years ago, Gordon Allport put forward the "contact thesis," which argued that contact with black people lessens prejudice in whites but does so only under certain conditions. Contact reduces prejudice in situations where whites and blacks hold relatively equal status, share common goals, and cooperate with each other in some way and where social norms support the contact.[32]

The findings of this study echo these themes. However, even more, they help us understand the processes that occur within these relationships to enhance support for racial justice. In other words, they open up the black box of bridging social capital to reveal what happens inside, which helps us understand how certain kinds of contact change minds.

Still, our interest goes beyond mere contact and the lessening of prejudice. We are concerned with the role of relationships in developing an understanding of racism and a commitment to racial justice. I find that many pressures work against racial equality within multiracial settings. Indeed, whites build relationships with people of color "under the weight of history," that is, in a context laden with unequal power relationships. Whites can unconsciously bring some of the prejudices they have learned from the larger society into multiracial settings, which leads people of color to mistrust their motives or commitments. In this context, positive action needs to be taken to construct institutional arrangements and policies that will promote truly collaborative relationships, as I discuss in chapter six. For example, explicit efforts to address racialized thinking or behavior prove important to lessening prejudice and moving whites toward racial justice. Moreover, I find that the more power that people of color hold in the situation, the more compelling the change in whites can be. More broadly, white activists emphasize the need for conversation based upon respect and honesty within these multiracial venues, as well as a genuine effort on their part to learn about the experience of people of color. To the extent that people can share stories across lines of race, mutuality and a sense of common cause develops.[33]

We are also interested in more than creating one-on-one relationships across lines of race. Although those individual connections serve as a foundation for building collectivities, it is through creating community that whites can form shared identities with people of color and other justice-oriented whites. These groups, networks, and communities become the crucible where white activists develop a vision for a future multiracial society and work to implement it today. In other words, we are interested in fostering deeply democratic practices within multiracial institutions and communities.[34]

Michelle Fine and her colleagues came to some similar conclusions in their study of interracial contact in desegregated schools. Because so many forces thwart racial justice, they found that simply desegregating schools proved insufficient even if they were constructed on the principles suggested by the contact thesis. Rather, intentional efforts were required to address issues of prejudice and power. Explicit action to build community and practice democracy proved necessary if desegregated schools were to be racially just. Such institutions, through their efforts to build community, forged a shared vision of justice and a sense of common identity across racial lines.[35]

None of this is to suggest that there is no role for separate spaces or organizations for people of color. Indeed, some of the activists in this study argue that, in the context of America's racialized past and current reality, people of color do need their own venues in which to support each other and achieve the power they need to make decisions for their communities. Some of these activists work in multiracial organizations that have formal caucuses by race within them, while others feature more informal networks. These strategies help create more equal status and power relationships when people then work together across racial lines within multiracial groups; they may help ensure that issues of race are not ignored. In the end, however, it is the building of multiracial relationships and community that works to deepen white commitment to racial justice.

Community means something more than coalition. In coalitions, different racial groups pursue a common agenda yet remain separate. People collaborate across racial lines in coalitions because they need each other. They
negotiate with each other over their separate interests. Building community
implies mutual necessity and sometimes negotiation and compromise. However, it also requires breaking down that separateness and achieving something that is more than the sum of the parts. In building community, people
forge meaningful relationships in which they come to know and care about
each other. Together they forge a shared vision and a shared practice to bring
about racial justice.[36]

Most white Americans live lives segregated from people of color or have
superficial contact with them. Even teachers who teach in urban schools
and social workers that provide services in the inner city relate to children
or adults who are relatively powerless; in that sense a certain distance pre-
vails. We need more venues where whites meet people of color as equals,
where they experience people of color as powerful actors, where people work
together for a common goal, and where they build meaningful relationships.
These venues may not automatically lead to the kind of open and honest
relationships that can produce change on the part of whites, but without
them, few white activists in this study would have had an opportunity to
strengthen their understanding of racism and deepen their commitment.

Barack Obama's presidential campaign also shows, to some extent, the
importance of personal relationships. During the campaign Obama worked
hard to have as much personal contact with white Americans as possible. All
politicians do this to some extent, but Obama had a special need to break
down suspicion and mistrust and to give white voters a chance to get to
know him personally. To do so, he emphasized his own personal story and his
family history as a way to connect with the values Americans broadly share.
Obama featured the pursuit of "a more perfect union," that is, the pursuit of
greater justice, as one of those values.

This relational and storytelling approach shaped the campaign's
vaunted field organization as well. Campaign volunteers sought out personal contact with voters and were trained to share their stories. Of course,
there were limits to Obama's community building. After all, community
cannot be built in a year or two, particularly in the heat of a presidential campaign. Yet many strong relationships appear to have been forged
within the campaign's field organization as a new, multiracial generation
of organizers worked together for a common vision of a better and more
just America.[37]

Beyond the White Ally

In the multiracial communities we have just discussed, white people develop an identity as racial justice activists by means of their work with others across racial lines. They become committed to working for a vision of a future society that has racial justice at its center. Yet we have also seen them struggle with their position—"stuck in the middle"—socially and racially identified as white but politically identified more with people of color. As we have seen, many of them struggle with their legitimacy as white leaders in the quest for racial justice. In the preface to this book I discuss the historic suspicion that has surrounded white racial justice activists. Perhaps because the racial divide has been so deep and sharp in the United States, as a society we cannot seem to accept the authenticity of a white person firmly committed to racial justice. As a result, the identity of the white racial justice activist remains a deeply problematic one.

We do not even have a good term for such a person. The most widely used one is probably *white ally*. Whites in the civil rights movement were often called allies. Even today, many activists use the term to describe themselves, including some of those in this study.[38]

Other liberation movements have also struggled with accepting a role for members of the dominant group. Men have faced particular challenges as participants in the feminist movement, and straight people have had to negotiate their position in the gay and lesbian movement. Given the centrality of racial division in this country's history, it is perhaps not surprising that whites face particularly great challenges when they try to cross over the color line.[39]

Yet the term ally and the concept underlying it remain limited. As an ally to the struggle for racial justice, white people find themselves supporting someone else's struggle, not their own. How can we ask white Americans to embrace racial justice as central to the future of the whole society and then sideline them to the role of supporters?

There are some good reasons that the term ally might be preferred. No matter how committed whites become to racial justice, they do not directly experience racial oppression. The term ally keeps the leadership of the struggle in the hands of people of color—those who are the most affected by racism and who cannot so easily walk away from it. Perhaps for many people of color, getting whites to become allies is all that they can hope for. It may even be for the best, as many people of color have felt betrayed by whites at times, even those ostensibly committed to the cause of fighting racism. Yet, ultimately, it represents a defeatist position. If whites remain simply allies, they will never fully embrace the struggle for racial justice as their own.

To overcome the ally concept, we have to break the association between social and political identity so that a person can be socially (racially) white and politically for racial justice. I think this is what Lani Guinier and Gerald Torres have in mind in their concept of "political race." In *The Miner's Canary,* Guinier and Torres argue that racism represents the key symptom of a broader disease undermining American life for all people. In their view, we can transform the social experience of people of color into a political project for racial justice that will benefit everyone because freeing African Americans will free all Americans. Whites can come to embrace the political project of racial justice as they see its centrality to their own values, transforming democracy toward the kind of society in which they want to live and raise their children.[40]

I am not suggesting we dissolve racial identities, as some have argued. We do not need to move to a postracial or color-blind society in that sense even if we could. I think Americans can come together around a values-based political project that includes racial justice while respecting many kinds of differences.[41]

Nevertheless, achieving a common political identity for racial justice across lines of race will depend to some extent on progress in creating new multiracial social identities, even as race-specific identities continue. The political project of racial justice cannot hang in the air without some form of social foundation. In other words, as we break the old race-specific connection between social and political identity, we also need to create new multiracial connections. Indeed, we have seen the importance of cross-race relationships to undergird white commitment to racial justice, and we have learned the importance of multiracial venues that build multiracial community. By working together, people forge social ties and create a sense that we are in this together. In these venues, activists can help to develop authentic ownership for whites in the struggle for racial justice while facilitating the leadership of those most affected by racism.

During his presidential campaign, Barack Obama called on Americans to cultivate a sense of the "we" while respecting racial and other differences. In his speech on race titled "A More Perfect Union," Obama spoke of different histories and the need to build a common future together:

> This was one of the tasks we set forth at the beginning of this campaign—to continue the long march of those who came before us, a march for a more just, more equal, more free, more caring, and more prosperous America. I chose to run for the presidency at this moment in history because I believe deeply that we cannot solve the

challenges of our time unless we solve them together—unless we perfect our union by understanding that we may have different stories, but we hold common hopes; that we may not look the same and we may not have come from the same place, but we all want to move in the same direction—toward a better future for all of our children and our grandchildren.[42]

In the Obama campaign, white fieldworkers were full participants. They were not allies to someone else's struggle.

Building toward a Movement

The election of Barack Obama represents a step forward to racial justice, but the road ahead is long and full of obstacles. We have seen many tensions and dilemmas in the work of the activists in this study. Efforts to raise the moral issue can descend into self-righteousness and do-gooder moralizing. Multiracial efforts work "under the weight" of history and can sink on the shoals of dominating white behavior or mistrust on the part of people of color. Racial identities remain so strong that many whites struggle to find an authentic place in racial justice efforts.

Perhaps the biggest challenge, however, lies in the isolated and fragmentary nature of racial justice efforts. The activists in this study work for racial justice and build community primarily in small settings, mostly at the local level and often around single issues. They are building the essential microfoundations for large-scale social change. However, such change will depend as well upon the development of a national movement. We know that years of patient local organizing established a basis for the emergence of the civil rights movement in the fifties, which in turn inspired stronger local organizing. Racial justice ctivists remain hopeful, yet feel little sense of a national movement.[43]

The struggle to change the deeply rooted operations of institutions presents specific challenges. There is no easy solution to achieving racial justice in our criminal justice system or to creating excellent schools in low-income communities of color. Significant progress in these domains will take the kind of hard work and persistence exhibited by the people in this study, as well as countless others. Many activists in fact say that one of their biggest accomplishments is simply that they have persisted in the face of so many obstacles.

Barack Obama's presidential campaign, meanwhile, represents the possibilities for the emergence of a national movement. I do not mean to suggest that his project features a full racial justice agenda. In fact, Obama's campaign typifies the difficulties involved in building broad white support for racial justice. At times, Obama spoke eloquently about the cause of racial justice and placed his campaign squarely in that tradition. At other times, he emphasized a broader vision of what Americans hold in common without much specific mention of racial justice. Nor do I think Obama's election to the presidency solves the problem of racism. Far from it. Nevertheless, it symbolizes an important step toward racial justice and was broadly recognized as such. It shows the potential of Americans to come together on a national level around values-based politics calling for change.

Barack Obama won over the minds and hearts of many white Americans. He offered tens of thousands of white volunteers an opportunity to lend their hand to advance the struggle for racial justice; millions more contributed their hard-earned dollars and their votes. In the end, he gave white Americans a chance to support a better future for themselves, for people of color, and for the entire country.

The Telling and the Told

Notes on Research Methods and Data

A LTHOUGH I HAVE explained the methods I employed in this study in some detail in chapter one, scholars and students might be interested in a further exploration of the methodological issues raised in my research. I discuss these issues here, but I do not repeat the points made in the first chapter. I also present further information about the data I collected and the procedures I employed to analyze the data.

In deciding to study white racial justice activists, I chose a phenomenon that has received little scholarly attention. As such, this is an exploratory work. Qualitative research of this sort is widely accepted as an appropriate way to investigate such phenomena and to generate knowledge and theory in a new area.[1]

My approach is interpretive in the Weberian tradition; that is, I am concerned with the meaning people ascribe to their social action. I selected fifty white people who are activists for racial justice and then asked them to talk with me about their lives in order to explore how they had developed a commitment to racial justice activism. I also asked them about their current experiences and views to reveal their understanding of what it means to live a life with such a commitment.[2]

In doing so, I have followed an established tradition of employing qualitative interviews as a way to explore meaning making in general and the development of social and political identities in particular. Recent influential studies of this sort include Michelle Lamont's study of the moral boundaries of white working-class men and Margaret Somers's study of English working-class formation. These kinds of interviews are particularly effective in examining the development of commitment to activism. Kathleen Blee used this method in her study of women in the Ku Klux Klan, Nathan Teske in his study of the identity development of political activists, Anne Colby and William Damon in their study of social and moral commitment, Molly Andrews in her study of the life commitments of British socialists, and Robert Wuthnow in his study of American volunteers, among others.[3]

The life history parts of the interviews allow us to explore development over time. Rather than assume that motivation leads to action at one point in time, we can examine the development of commitment as a more itera- tive or cyclical phenomenon. Although I do not directly investigate social contexts, the respondents can reveal the influence of social settings and social experiences, in other words, how they understood and responded to their environments. For example, in chapter two we learned about the effects on respondents of entering college as it was often the first place where they interacted with people of color in a meaningful way. In chapter three we then learned in great detail about the effects these kinds of relationships with people of color had on white activists.

Committing one's life to racial justice activism involves conscious choices. Opportunity structures of course shape the range of possible choices. At times, people can drift into situations by happenstance, as we saw. How- ever, in the end, the activists chose this kind of life and developed a con- sciousness about racism and a commitment to combat it. In-depth interviews allow us to understand how they came to make these choices, the purposes of their actions as they understand them, and the kinds of consciousness, moral visions, political views, and social identities they have developed. Indeed, as Richard Kearney, among others, has said, people can become purposive agents for change only when they transform the haphazard events of their lives into stories that have meaning for them.[4]

The Telling and the Told

I recognize that some analysts focus on the "telling" by analyzing the struc- ture of people's narrative accounts. However, I wanted to focus primarily on the "told," that is, the content of their stories. Nevertheless, I took some care to see whether there were patterned ways in which the subjects told me their stories. In particular, Kathleen Blee discovered that activist women in the Klan often tell conversion stories, that is, dramatic narrative accounts of their lives before and after joining an activist organization. Nathan Teske found this phenomenon, too, in his study of political activists, calling them involvement stories. I looked for but did not find these kinds of accounts. Perhaps this is because the activists in this study did not join a movement at one point in time; there was no clear before and after point. Rather they developed a commitment to racial justice activism over time and partly through activism itself. I did find people telling stories of experiences that I called seminal, but they did not always link them directly to activism. Many did not even volunteer these stories but presented them in answer to probing questions on my part about their earliest awareness of racism.[5]

Nevertheless, the question remains: Can these stories be believed? Did people tell me the truth? I leave aside the deep epistemological questions surrounding whether there is such a thing as an objective truth and, even if there is, whether we can ever fully know it. I take a more pragmatic approach. What are the threats to the trustworthiness or credibility of respondents' accounts of their lives?[6]

In part I asked people about the past, so I conducted what are sometimes called retrospective interviews. Problems with this type of interview are well known. People might misremember the past; they might selectively remember or embellish certain events; or they might attribute current understandings to past events. Similar questions can be raised about the trustworthiness of respondents' accounts of their contemporary views as well. People may not be fully aware of what they think or the influences on their lives. They may share their views selectively, emphasizing, for example, things that portray them in a positive light. Nonetheless, these problems are not confined to this study; they plague all qualitative interview research.[7]

In response to these concerns, I decided to take an active, probing approach to conducting the interview and a somewhat skeptical stance toward what I heard. I tried to listen for the story that seemed too rehearsed or one that did not seem to make sense given everything else the person had said.[8] I asked myself whether there was any reason not to believe the account I had been given. Was the person trying to tell me what they thought I wanted to hear? I took care to ask people about problems in their work and tensions in their lives in order to learn when they felt they had failed at something or only partially succeeded. To the extent that we might be concerned that respondents talk only about the positive aspects of their lives, I draw the reader's attention to chapter seven, which is full of tensions and dilemmas revealed to me by the activists in this study.

In this way I believe that I have achieved a reasonably balanced account of people's lives. I do not want to be naïve. However, neither do I take a cynical approach. In fact, I seek to maintain the more fundamental stance of respect. People are the experts on the meaning they make of their own lives.

This last point is critical. Although I asked people about their experiences, in the end what matters is the meaning people attribute to these experiences. For example, many white people might observe their neighbors participating in a racist hate march without being shaken up by the experience, as Jim Capraro was. The experience becomes seminal when it creates a moral shock—when whites respond to the event by coming to believe that their cherished values are being violated.[9]

Scholars will recognize that I have chosen my subjects by what is called selecting on the dependent variable, in other words, by selecting people who feature the phenomenon I want to explain. I selected people who were activists to ask them to describe how they had gotten there. How do we know that nonactivists did not experience some of the same things even though they did not become an activist as a result? The power of qualitative analysis does not rest in such a comparison, as would be the case in a quantitative study. Rather, as Joseph Maxwell has so carefully explained, the explanatory power of the qualitative analysis lies in showing *how* the process has the effect claimed. In the case of the seminal experience, for example, I explain how seminal experiences create moral shocks and lead to value conflict. I argue that because of the strength of society's dominant color-blind ideology, whites might need a direct experience to create such a moral shock. We again return to the idea that this kind of qualitative research is about the meaning people attach to their experiences, and we understand that meaning by listening to and analyzing people's stories about them.[10]

I am also careful about the claims I make about the processes I identify. I do not say, for example, that any white person who has a direct experience observing a racial injustice will develop value conflict and a moral impulse against racism. Such a claim would require an appropriate comparative analysis to demonstrate. Nor do I claim that there are no other routes to racial justice commitment and activism than those I have found. Because of the design of the study, I cannot tell you why these white people—and not others—respond to direct experiences with moral shock. Nevertheless, we can understand how a seminal experience or relationships with people of color—or any of the other processes I identify for that matter—can have the effect demonstrated. By comprehending the process or mechanism, we can understand why such an experience might be necessary (if not sufficient) to produce the result. I also relate the number of activists who had the experience reported to give a sense of how broadly the process might apply. Because the group of participants is rather small, we cannot generalize to all white people, but I think it matters whether the large majority or only a small proportion report the experience.[11]

Finally, I do not have any independent method of verifying the interviewees' accounts of their past or present lives. I did not directly observe them in their work for racial justice, nor did I interview other people who could be informants about their past or present or who could give me their own views about a particular subject. To have done so would have required a very different research design and, for practical purposes, would have meant narrowing the pool of activists I could study. I would have had to interview only a relatively few activists or those who work in only one or two settings. Instead, I wanted a broad and diverse pool of subjects. In the end, my priority was to learn about the activists' self-understanding, and the interviews proved appropriate and sufficient for that purpose.

It would be fascinating to find out the views of people of color with whom these activists work. In a different way, it would also be interesting to know how other white people see these activists. Being able to directly observe them building relationships with people of color and trying to influence other whites would also yield important insights. If someone could design a comparative study that included activists and nonactivists or could follow people's development over time and directly observe it, these methods would all help to test the propositions I put forward in this study and, more generally, deepen our understanding of white racial justice activism.

The Composition of the Activists

In the introductory chapter of this book I explain the procedures and criteria I used to select activists. Table 1 presents more details on the composition of the fifty respondents.[12]

My selection procedures yielded a group of activists that could reasonably be considered representative of contemporary white activists for racial justice, at least those who work at it full time, but we cannot know for sure. So, how generalizable are the findings in this study? The fact that I found the patterns I report across the large majority of a diverse group of fifty activists suggests that the processes I identified might well be broadly applicable to white activists. However, it's not their presence or absence that offers the strongest case. Rather, the credibility of my arguments lies mainly with the richness and power of the analysis. In other words, it lies in the explanations and arguments I provide for how these processes work and why they are necessary given how contemporary racism operates. In the conclusion, I also draw upon the findings of other studies of white racial justice activism to lend support to these claims. Finally, I employ understandings from a range

Gender

Male	26
Female	24

Annual Income

Less than $25,000	8
$25,000–50,000	15
$50,000–100,000	17
More than $100,000	10

Education

High school degree	2
Bachelor's degree	14
Graduate degree	34

Marital/Family Status

Married	36 (including 5 unmarried but living with long-term partner)
Single	14 (including 4 who are engaged)
Parents of children	30

Nine are in an interracial relationship; three more report a previous interracial relationship. I did not try to capture diversity in sexual preference. One respondent self-identifies as queer.

Age

Younger than 35	12
35–55 years old	19
Older than 55	19

Activist Generation

Civil-rights era	15
Seventies	12
Post-1980	23

This categorization refers to the time of first activism.

Faith-based/Secular Group

Secular	39
Faith-based	11

This refers to whether the activist group or organization in which they work is secular or faith based, not to the respondent's own spiritual beliefs. Respondents reported a wide variety of beliefs with Catholic, Protestant, Jewish, spiritual, and agnostic/atheist groups all well represented.

Field of Activism

Community	20
Education	16
Criminal justice	14 (including legal advocacy)

Some people's work overlapped different categories, but I assigned each to a primary domain.

of other literature, for example, research on the role of emotions in social movements, to suggest the broad applicability of the theory I develop. Nevertheless, I hope the propositions I have developed in this study will be tested on a broader sample of activists and with a variety of research methods.

An Iterative Approach to Data Analysis

I began analyzing the interview data by coding each transcript. I employed a small initial code list derived from the conceptual framework that guided the construction of the interview questions. However, most of the analysis was inductive; in other words, descriptive and analytic codes emerged from a line-by-line reading of each transcript. I used Atlas.ti, a qualitative data analysis software system, to aid in coding and analysis. Following advice by John Lofland and his associates, I conducted open coding of the interview transcripts, building a codebook over time. As the coding proceeded, I became more selective in my coding, following their focused coding procedure, but I still examined every transcript line by line.[13]

In the next stage of analysis I constructed a profile of each activist, following suggestions by Irving Seidman. This helped me conduct a holistic "within-case" analysis of each person to see how commitment developed over time and in specific contexts. I also tried to understand for each person how various processes interrelated and how current understandings might be connected to past ones.[14]

The third stage consisted of cross-case thematic analysis. In other words, I examined the codes across the activists to find themes and patterns. To assist in the thematic analysis, I produced data matrices, following procedures suggested by Matthew Miles and Michael Huberman.[15]

In the final stage, I worked with this detailed thematic analysis to construct the larger themes of the findings, that is, to build a theory. Part of that process required iterative consultation with extant theory and research that seemed relevant. As the larger themes of the project emerged and took the shape of the book's chapters, I tested them with a secondary analysis of the profiles I had constructed. In other words, I examined each profile for evidence to support or refute the themes and to deepen my understanding of them. I constructed some additional data matrices from this work to assist in comparing the secondary profile analyses across the cases. Finally, I considered the relationship between the themes. Their interconnection turned out to be central to the theory I constructed, that is, the head, heart, and hand relationship.

I made intentional efforts to consider what is called internal generalizability. In other words, I reported the number of activists to which each claim applied. Was it the large majority or only a smaller proportion? I give these counts in the footnotes to the chapters where the claims are made. It is also important to understand that these counts are the minimum number of activists to which the claim applies. I did try to ask the same basic set of questions to all subjects. However, because the interviews were semistructured and open ended, some of the activists may have occasionally failed to mention an experience or a view that is relevant to them.

Although I proceeded in the stages just discussed, in reality the process was quite iterative. In other words, I went back and forth between within-case and cross-case analysis, between profiles, data matrices, themes, broader literatures, and interview material. I found myself constantly returning to the interview transcripts. This was because, in the end, I was interested in understanding how a process worked, for example, how relationships with people of color had their impact. This understanding was ultimately revealed in the accounts of the individual activists.

The Researcher as Research Instrument

In qualitative research, we understand that the researcher is the research instrument, if you will. My hand appears throughout the project from beginning to end. I shaped the interviews as I asked questions and probed respondents. I analyzed the data and wrote up the findings. Yet, in the process of constructing the stories, I am working with people and their voices. For this reason, many scholars say that qualitative interviewing as a methodology features the coconstruction of knowledge between researcher and those researched. As I said earlier, I took an interpretive approach, and in the end I am reporting my interpretation. It is up to the reader to judge whether my account, my interpretation, appears reasonable given the evidence and the persuasiveness of the argument.[16]

In recent years, many scholars have emphasized the importance of researchers considering their own "positionality" in the research. I am a white person who has been a political activist in part for racial justice. I still consider myself something of an activist, although not in the fullest sense of the term. I am married to a black woman and father to our black/multiracial children. I conducted this project in part because of my own values and belief in the need for white Americans to take action for racial justice. I believe it was important for me to explain my motivations in the preface to this book.

In many ways, my own values and experiences as a white person committed to racial justice put me in a good position to conduct this study. They allowed me to create the kind of rapport in which white activists felt comfortable opening up to me. I was familiar with many of their references to historical events and to many of the issues they faced as activists. I believe it gave me greater insight into their experiences.

While I accept that my own values, understandings, and experiences affect my interpretation of the interviews, I wanted to make sure that I was not simply imposing my own preconceived understanding on the activists or on my analysis of what they told me. I took several steps to reduce the likelihood of this kind of imposition. First, I was careful not to share much of my own experiences and views with respondents prior to the interviews because I did not want them to be shaping their comments in response to these views. I often did this kind of sharing in lively discussions after the interviews. In the data-analysis phase, I wrote memos to myself where I tried to be explicit about my preconceived ideas or expectations. I then intentionally looked for data that would contradict these specific expectations. As I developed various themes, I also made sure to consider alternative explanations for the same phenomena. When the activists reported experiences or ideas that resonated strongly with my own personal experience, I made a special effort to stand back a bit and make sure to examine what they actually said, not what I already thought. In addition, I took particular care in these cases to examine how broadly the experiences or views were reported across the interviews.

As another check against my biases, I hired several research assistants to code the first twenty interview transcripts independently of me. I then compared my coding with theirs. These discussions helped deepen my analysis of the interviews even as they helped make the analysis more impartial. Over time I became more confident that I was coding the interviews in a consistent manner. The data matrices and the counts also helped keep my analysis evenhanded.

In the end, I feel confident that I made a fair-minded analysis of the data. I thought certain factors would be important, yet they did not play a very central role. I was careful not to force them onto the data. For example, I expected that developing a racial analysis would be particularly important. Yet, as discussed throughout the book, I found that developing such an analysis plays more of a supporting role in people's development. I also expected that people's own experiences with marginalization, perhaps as women or growing up working class, would play an important role; however, except for a few activists, this did not seem to be the case. Meanwhile, I believe I was open to unexpected findings. I was not prepared for the powerful role that emotions played for the respondents, for example, but found that theme emerging clearly from the interviews.[17]

Comparisons Lost and Found

One important expectation largely fell flat. I expected to find clearer comparisons across the activists than I did. In particular, I expected to see different patterns across generations. I was familiar with Nancy Whittier's research showing how the generation in which women entered the feminist movement mattered for their contemporary orientations. For my part, I thought that whites who became active in the movement era of the fifties and sixties might have gone through processes different from those of whites who came to activism later. America's dominant racial ideology shifted from overt to color-blind racism at the end of that movement, and I thought that might be significant. Yet, try as I might, I could not establish any clear differences in the central themes of the findings by generation or by any other dimension for that matter. The specifics varied across individuals, but there were no distinct patterns.[18]

This finding led me to reexamine my expectations. In doing so, I could find no clear rationale as to why, for the arguments I make in this book, there should be variation by generation. Take the impact of a seminal experience. Younger generations grew up largely in white communities with little understanding of the racial experiences of people of color, just as the older generation did. We look back and see that an older generation grew up under more overt forms of racism, while younger generations grew up under a more subtle form. Yet white people in the fifties and sixties did not necessarily see racism any more clearly than in later periods. In other words, even older generational activists seemed to require a direct experience of racism, a seminal event that could shock them into seeing the violation of community values in the treatment of people of color.

I also expected to find clearer differences between faith-based activists and those who were more secularly oriented. Instead, I found that both types of activists expressed a moral impulse against racism and that both fashioned a moral vision of a future community based upon truly human relationships. Perhaps because of the deep penetration of Judeo-Christian traditions into American culture, it turns out that many secular activists drew upon various faith beliefs and values. Similarly, even the faith-based activists embraced values from the American democratic tradition and sought to fulfill its promises through their work.[19]

I am not suggesting there were no differences among the group of activists I interviewed, just that those differences did not fall into clear patterns that proved important to the central claims of the book. They may be important in other ways, for different purposes, or in answer to different questions. Differences in region of country may matter for some things. Whether white people work against racism toward Latinos or African Americans may also matter, but the interviewees did not speak clearly to these differences.

I hope that this book will inspire more research on white racial justice activism. I would like to see scholars use a range of research designs both to test the propositions I suggest in this work and to discover new lines of analysis that can deepen our understanding of this important phenomenon. I imagine that research designed purposefully to explore differences between faith and secular activists, between activists from different generations, and between men and women for that matter could reveal some important findings that would provide a fuller account of white racial justice activism.

In the end, I follow the tradition of C. Wright Mills, who suggested that "neither the life of an individual nor the history of society can be understood without understanding both." We are not short of historical and structuralist accounts of racism. By studying the lives of these fifty individuals, I hope to have contributed to our understanding of racial justice activism and perhaps more broadly of human agency and social change.[20]

List of Activists and Their Organizational Affiliations

The following is a list of the activists featured in this book and their organizational affiliation at the time of the interview. Note: Organizations are listed for the purpose of affiliation only. Website addresses are current at time of publication.

JOHN AFFELDT, Public Advocates, San Francisco (www.publicadvocates.org)

DOUG ANDERSON, People's Institute for Survival and Beyond, New Orleans (www.pisab.org)

ROXANE AUER, UNITE-HERE Local 11, Los Angeles (www.herelocal11.org)

ROSE BRAZ, Critical Resistance, Oakland, CA (www.criticalresistance.org)

RACHEL BREUNLIN, Neighborhood Story Project, New Orleans (www .neighborhoodstoryproject.org); The Porch, New Orleans

CAROL BROOK, Federal Defender Program, Chicago

JIM CAPRARO, Greater Southwest Development Corporation, Chicago (www .greatersouthwest.org)

ALEX CAPUTO-PEARL, Crenshaw High School, Los Angeles (www .crenshawhs.org); Coalition for Educational Justice, Los Angeles

KATHERINE CARTER, Manzanita SEED Elementary School, Oakland, CA (www.smallschoolsfoundation.org/manzanitaseed)

INGRID CHAPMAN, Catalyst Project, San Francisco (www.collectiveliberation.org)

CHRISTINE CLARK, Office of Human Relations Programs, University of Maryland, College Park, MD (www.ohrp.umd.edu); National Association for Multicultural Education (www.nameorg.org)

ED CLOUTMAN, Law Offices of Edward Cloutman, Dallas

JOANNA DUBINSKY, New Orleans Worker Justice Coalition, New Orleans

KATHY DUDLEY, Dallas Leadership Foundation, Dallas (www.dlftx.org)

JOSEPH ELLWANGER, Milwaukee Inner-city Congregations Allied for Hope (www.micahempowers.org)

TONY FLEO, Dallas Area Interfaith, Plano, TX (www.dallasareainterfaith.org)

KATE FORAN, Word and World, Greensboro, NC (www.wordandworld.org)

PENDA HAIR, Advancement Project, Washington, DC (www .advancementproject.org)

PHYLLIS HART, Achievement Council, Los Angeles

CHESTER HARTMAN, Poverty and Race Research Action Council, Washington, DC (www.prrac.org)

ALEXA HAUSER, San Mateo County Office of Education, Redwood City, CA (www.smcoe.k12.ca.us); People's Institute West, Berkeley, CA

JOHN HEINEMEIER, Baltimoreans United in Leadership Development, Baltimore (www.buildiaf.org)

Z. HOLLER, Beloved Community Center, Greensboro, NC (www .belovedcommunitycenter.org)

RANDY JOHNSTON, Uplift, Inc., Greensboro, NC

JOSHUA KERN, Thurgood Marshall Academy, Washington, DC (www .thurgoodmarshallacademy.org)

SHARON MARTINAS, Challenging White Supremacy Workshop, San Francisco (www.cwsworkshop.org)

DEBORAH MENKART, Teaching for Change, Washington, DC (www .teachingforchange.org)

JANET MORRISON, Central Dallas Ministries, Dallas (www .centraldallasministries.org)

MOLLY MUNGER, Advancement Project, Los Angeles (www .advancementprojectca.org)

SETH NEWTON, AFSCME Local 3299, Oakland, CA (www.afscme3299.org)

LAURIE OLSEN, California Tomorrow, Oakland, CA (www.californiatomorrow.org)

PERRY PERKINS, Northern and Central Louisiana Interfaith (www .industrialareasfoundation.org)

BOB PETERSON, La Escuela Fratney, Milwaukee, WI; Rethinking Schools, Milwaukee, WI (www.rethinkingschools.org)

LEWIS PITTS, Legal Aid of North Carolina, Greensboro, NC (www.legalaidnc.org)

CATHY RION, Californians for Justice, Oakland, CA (www.caljustice.org); Heads Up Collective, Oakland, CA (www.headsupcollective.blogspot.com)

SUSAN SANDLER, Justice Matters, San Francisco (www.justicematters.org)

JIM SCHUTZE, Dallas Observer, Dallas (www.dallasobserver.com)

ED SHURNA, Chicago Coalition for the Homeless, Chicago (www
.chicagohomeless.org)

MICHAEL SIEGEL, Oakland Leaf, Oakland, CA (www.oaklandleaf.org)

MARK SOLER, Youth Law Center, Washington, DC (www.ylc.org); Current:
Center for Children's Law and Policy, Washington, DC (www.cclp.org)

CHRISTINE STEPHENS, Texas Industrial Areas Foundation (www
.industrialareasfoundation.org)

MADELINE TALBOTT, Action Now (formerly ACORN), Chicago (www
.actionnow.org)

DAVID UTTER, Juvenile Justice Project of Louisiana, New Orleans (www
.jjpl.org)

EMILY ZEANAH, Greensboro Truth and Reconciliation Commission,
Greensboro, NC (www.greensborotrc.org)

The following is a list of activists interviewed for the study but not featured
in the book.

JULIE BROWN, Business and Professional People for the Public Interest,
Chicago (www.bpichicago.org)

MIKE DANIEL, Daniel and Beshara, P.C., Dallas (www.danielbesharalawfirm.com)

GERHARD FISCHER, WISDOM, Milwaukee, WI (www.gamaliel.org);
Wisdom Antiracism team, Evangelical Lutheran Church of America

LANCE HILL, Southern Institute for Education and Research, New Orleans
(www.southerninstitute.info)

JOHN LUKEHEART, Leadership Council for Metropolitan Open
Communities, Chicago (www.luc.edu/curl/lcmoc)

LARRY MILLER, W.E.B. Du Bois High School, Milwaukee, WI; Rethinking
Schools, Milwaukee, WI (www.rethinkingschools.org)

FLINT TAYLOR, People's Law Office, Chicago (www.peopleslawoffice.com)

NOTES

Preface

1. Quoted from "A More Perfect Union," Barack Obama's (2008) speech on race.

2. On the shooting and protests in Oakland, see Jesse McKinley, "In California, Protests after Man Dies at Hands of Transit Police," January 9, 2008, *New York Times,* available online at http://www.nytimes.com.

3. One possible exception to the omission of studies of white antiracists is the relatively extensive treatment of white abolitionists by historians; see, for example, Paul Goodman (1998). A much smaller literature (e.g., McLeod 2001; Pinkney 1968) concerns white activists in the civil rights movement.

4. Herbert Aptheker, among others, has tried to resurrect the history of white antiracism; see his overview of antiracism in the first two hundred years of U.S. history (Aptheker 1992).

5. For a discussion of the scholarly treatment of John Brown, see Peterson (2002).

6. For his biography of Brown, see Du Bois (2001). For a recent treatment of white abolitionists, see Laurie (2005). For a discussion of the events in SNCC, see McAdam (1988).

7. See Becky Thompson (2001), O'Brien (2001), and Wise (2005); for another treatment, see Thompson, Schaefer, and Brod (2003).

8. For a sample of the literature on whiteness studies, see Roediger (2005) and Ignatiev (1996); on white identity development, see, for example, Helms (1990) and Clark and O'Donnell (1999).

Chapter One

1. For simplicity's sake, I use lowercase spellings for white and black even though I know that others prefer capitalizing these words as a way to recognize racial/ethnic identification. I also use black people alternatively for African Americans although I realize that there are now many other black people in the United States who do not share the historic African American experience.

2. In the evidence for his conclusion, Forman (2004, 55–58) analyzes changes in responses to a Gallup Survey question: "On the whole, do you think most white people want to see blacks get a better break, or do they want to keep blacks down, or don't you think they care either way?" The proportion of whites answering "don't care" increased from 33 percent in 1984 to 44 percent in 1998. For a related discussion of passivity, see Trepagnier (2006).

3. For the most comprehensive assessment of racial trends in well-being, see the two-volume report of the National Research Council (Smelser, Wilson, and Mitchell 2001), which contains most of the following data. For a detailed analysis of the growth of the black middle class, see Bowser (2007).

4. On black/white wealth disparities, see Oliver and Shapiro (1995). For an alternative view of the information in this section, one that emphasizes the extent of black progress, see Thernstrom and Thernstrom (1997).

5. William Julius Wilson (1996) has analyzed the consequences of growing up and living in neighborhoods of concentrated poverty. For an in-depth treatment of the geography of opportunity that shows how living in acute poverty and racially isolated neighborhoods limits a range of opportunities, see Squires and Kubrin (2006); for a close examination of housing opportunities that considers the workings both of explicit racial discrimination and apparently nonracial institutional processes, see Briggs (2005); moreover, Patrick Sharkey (2008) shows that black children who grow up in poor neighborhoods are likely to live in them as adults. On graduation rates, see Orfield et al. (2004). For a discussion of race and criminal justice, see Loury (2008).

6. Audit studies (Yinger 2001) do a good job of demonstrating racialized dynamics. William Julius Wilson (1978) first brought the relationship between race and economics to contemporary scholarly and public attention. For a more recent discussion on economic inequality in education, see Rothstein (2004). A large literature (e.g., Ferber et al. 2009; Rothenberg 2001) has explored the intersectionality of inequality and oppression, showing how a full understanding of any group's experience requires an examination of interacting patterns of race, class, gender, and sexual orientation. I focus on race in this study although I am aware that it presents a partial view.

7. The first set of data come from a 1997 Gallup poll as reported in Sears et al. (2000, 12). The Kaiser poll is reported in the *Washington Post*/Kaiser Family Foundation/Harvard University Survey Project (2001).

8. On residential segregation, see Massey and Denton (1992); on segregation in schools, see Orfield and Eaton (1997); on personal relationships, see Briggs (2007) and also Sigelman et al. (1996) and Korgen (2002).

9. See Hacker (1992). For a discussion of white identity, see McDermott and Samson (2005).

10. For a thorough treatment of contemporary racism that is developed around the concept of institutional racism, see the book *Whitewashing Race,* by Michael Brown and his associates (2003). My discussion in this section generally follows the approach taken by Brown and his colleagues. Other scholars have used the term *structural racism* to characterize the contemporary era. This approach is similar to the institutional one but stresses the dynamics between institutions, as well as within them; for an elaboration of the structural racism approach, see Bonilla-Silva (1997) and powell (2007). For a recent, useful overview of the causes of the persistence of

racial inequality, see the edited volume by Lin and Harris (2008). For further information on racial inequality in educational opportunity and its effects, see Darling-Hammond (1998). For a recent discussion of the exploitative practices that led to concentrated black poverty in Chicago, see Satter (2009).

11. See Brown et al. (2003, 227). For recent work on cumulative discrimination, see Blank (2005). For a broader discussion of the relationship between structure and culture in explaining black disadvantage, see Wilson (2009).

12. On real estate practices, see Turner and Ross (2005); on racial profiling, see Harris (2003); on job discrimination against inner-city African Americans, see Wilson (1996). For a more thorough discussion of the role of individual action and nonaction in relationship to institutional racism, see Trepagnier (2006).

13. For survey data, see Schuman, Steeh, and Bobo (1997); see also Blauner (1989). However, Picca and Feagin (2007) have found that many whites, including highly educated ones, harbor explicit racist notions and will express them in private settings even when they do not report such thinking in public attitudes. Meanwhile, even in survey data, some forms of old-fashioned racism appear to persist. A National Opinion Research Center survey in 1990 found that some 53 percent of whites still rated blacks as less intelligent than whites, 62 percent thought they were lazier, and 56 percent that they were more prone to violence; see Brown et al (2003, 40).

14. On the ambivalent and contradictory racial views of whites, see Bobo and Smith (1998) and also Quillian (2006). Bobo and Smith (1998, 200) conclude that "what were once viewed as categorical differences based in biology now appear to be seen as differences in degree or tendency," based upon culture. Dovidio and Gaertner (2004) have developed a theory of aversive racism, which emphasizes how the racial actions of white Americans depend on situationally specific contexts. In their view Americans profess egalitarian values but are influenced by unconscious, subtle racism that sometimes leads them to discriminate but other times does not. On prejudice and discrimination against middle-class African Americans, see Feagin and McKinney (2005).

15. Eduardo Bonilla-Silva has characterized modern racism as "color-blind" racism, analyzing its major tenets in the aptly titled *Racism without Racists* (Bonilla-Silva 2003). For a discussion of the relationship between the American dream and racial inequality, see Hochschild (1995).

16. For a discussion of racial imagery in the media, see Entman and Rojecki (2000).

17. On the resistance by whites when confronted with evidence of their racial privilege and their racist thinking, see Allan Johnson (2006) and Diane Goodman (2001).

18. For elaborations on this argument, see Bobo, Kluegel, and Smith (1997), Bonilla-Silva (2003), and Jackman (1994). Sidanius and Pratto (1999) elaborate a similar argument in the context of their social dominance theory.

19. For a multifaceted elaboration of white privilege, see Lipsitz (1997) and Rothenberg (2002). On the normalization of white culture, see Dyer (1997).

20. Indeed, African Americans are much more likely than whites to perceive the existence of racial discrimination. For example, blacks are twice as likely as whites to perceive socioeconomic inequality to be the result of racial discrimination (Schuman

et al. 1997). For a further discussion of the complexity of the issues surrounding white privilege, see the collection of articles by Kimmel and Ferber (2003) and also Kendall (2006).

21. See *The Souls of Black Folk* (Du Bois, 2007 [1903]) and the *Report of the National Advisory Commission on Civil Disorders* (Kerner Commission 1968). For the classic exposition of the Black Power critique of American society, see Ture and Hamilton (1992 [1967]). Brown et al. (2003) offer an elaboration of this argument concerning the failure of positive action.

22. For evidence of white opposition to racial discrimination, see Schuman, Steeh, and Bobo (1997). In her study of white high school students, Pamela Perry (2002) shows how white racial views are multiple, situation dependent, and fluid. In a broader treatment, Omi and Winant (1994) show that race relations are not fixed but contain multiple complexities and are subject to reformation through political action.

23. African Americans were more likely than whites to see racism at work in the Katrina events, but many whites were also outraged; for poll data on Katrina, see New America Media (2005).

24. See Wise (2005), Kivel (2002), and Hitchcock (2002). For information on the white privilege conference, see http://www.uccs.edu/~wpc/index.htm. For a prominent training program, see the People's Institute for Survival and Beyond at http://www.pisab.org/. Judith Katz (1978) first published her popular *White Awareness* training manual in the seventies, and it is now in its second edition. There has also been growing awareness in Europe of the need to combat racism; see, for example, Bonnett (1997) and Lentin (2004).

25. For a further discussion of the gap between the professed attitudes of whites on racial issues and their actions, see Brown et al. (2003, 41–42).

26. For a discussion of the importance of turning points, see Abbott (1997). I drew from a large number of treatments of qualitative interviewing to develop my approach, including Weiss (1994), Seidman (2006), and Clandinin and Connelly (2000). For the design of the study as a whole, I generally followed the approach taken by Maxwell (2005).

27. For a recent discussion of the centrality of the black/white divide, see Squires (2006). On white attitudes toward residential integration, see Emerson, Chai, and Yancey (2001); on white resistance to intimate relationships with African Americans, see Schuman, Steeh, and Bobo (1997); on employer preferences, see Moss and Tilly (2001).

28. For contrasting views on racism toward Latinos, see Bonilla-Silva and Dietrich (2008) and Yancey (2003). Telles and Ortiz (2008) examine issues of assimilation and race in their comprehensive treatment of the experiences of Mexican Americans across immigrant generations.

29. I present details of the composition of the activists along these lines in the appendix. It turns out that I did not find significant differences by age, gender, or faith/secular characteristics, an issue I discuss in the appendix.

30. Scholars now accept that racial categories, including "white," are socially constructed and are therefore malleable and subject to change. For a discussion, see McDermott and Samson (2005). There is no universally held definition of racial justice work. For a further discussion of various definitions of racial justice, see Pittz and Sen (2004); I follow their broad coverage.

31. For the foundation report, see Pittz and Sen (2004).

32. Since it is very unusual to be a white racial justice activist, and given that there is some history of tension between white activists and activists of color (see, e.g., McAdam 1988), I expected that the interviewees would have experienced tensions, problems, and a variety of troubling issues. I wanted to increase the odds that the people I interviewed would be forthright about their experiences. For these reasons I asked specifically for referrals to white activists who were considered honest and thoughtful, people who would be likely to offer a balanced assessment. I also tried to get a sense of openness from my initial contacts with potential subjects prior to the arrangement of the formal interviews.

33. Although I use the activists' real names, I employ pseudonyms for people to whom they refer unless these are public figures.

34. Scholars will recognize that I selected on the dependent variable. I discuss this issue in greater detail in the appendix. For a clear exposition of the explanatory power of qualitative studies like mine, see Maxwell (2004).

35. I would like to thank Julia Van Alt for suggesting this metaphor to me. Sara Lawrence-Lightfoot (1997, 85) employs a similar metaphor.

36. See Bonilla-Silva (2003, 9). For a further discussion of the defense of structural position, see Bonilla-Silva (1997). For a discussion of group conflict theory, see Bobo and Hutchings (1996). While interest-based accounts dominate the field, some scholars have stressed the political processes (Omi and Winant 1994) and moral boundaries (Lamont 2000) that shape race relations. In an important way, the race relations literature focuses on structure, whereas I focus on agency. For a broader discussion of the relationship between structure and agency, see Giddens (1984) and Sewell (1992); for an application to institutional racism, see Trepagnier (2006).

37. Social cleavages are often studied via electoral behavior; see, for example, Manza and Brooks (1999). For a thorough treatment of Marxist views on racism and the problems of coalition building, see Allen (1974). Wilson (1999) presents his argument in *The Bridge over the Racial Divide*.

38. For a discussion of the tendency for whites to abandon black interests within larger coalitions, see Jennings (1990) and J. Phillip Thompson (1998). Skocpol (1991) and others have argued that these universalistic projects may do more to benefit people of color than racially targeted social policies and that they are more politically viable. Saito (2009) offers a contrasting argument for the need to explicitly address issues of race in urban policy. Katznelson (2005) has shown that New Deal legislation itself favored whites over blacks in its policies and benefits.

39. On interest convergence, see Bell (2004) and also Cashin (2005). See J. Phillip Thompson (2005) and Wilson (1999). Much of this debate harkens back to the classic Black Power argument of the sixties, which suggested that whites and blacks should form coalitions based upon negotiations of their interests (Ture and Hamilton 1992 [1967]). Blacks had to come to these coalitions from a powerful position if they expected to reach some compromise with whites and to ensure the protection of their interests. Wilson (2009) has more recently altered his views to argue for the need to address race issues head-on.

40. In a representative work, Giugni and Passy (2001) call such solidarity politics, in which white allies work for racial justice, "political altruism." On white allies

in the civil rights movement, see, for example, McAdam (1988). For arguments about the failure of moral appeals to whites, see Klinkner and Smith (1999) and Mills (2004). For a critique of paternalism, see Jackman (1994). On the unreliability of the white ally, see Marx and Useem (1971).

41. *It Didn't Happen Here* is the title of a recent book that attempts to explain the failure of socialism in the United States; see Lipset and Marks (2000). On the construction of identities, see Somers (1992) and Polletta and Jasper (2001).

42. There is a large literature on activist recruitment. One of the key findings of this research is that people are more likely to join movements when they have social ties to other activists who can recruit them; see McAdam and Paulsen (1993).

43. On the development of oppositional consciousness, see Mansbridge and Morris (2001).

44. See Jasper (1997). On emotions and activism, see also Goodwin, Jasper, and Polletta (2004) and Haste (1990). I have not found the dominant theories of justice in moral and political philosophy to be of much relevance in understanding the foundation for racial justice. These theories focus on individual choices in abstract situations and pay little to no attention to the structural inequalities in society (Sandel 1998). For a useful discussion, see Shklar (1990); for a critique that emphasizes the lack of attention to how people live their lives and assess their society, see Taylor (1989).

45. See Nepstad (2004, 2007).

46. See O'Brien (2001). Other researchers (Eichstedt 2001; Frankenberg 1993; B. Thompson 2001) have also found that relationships are important to white activists. In the conclusion to this book, I discuss how my findings compare with other research on white activists.

47. See Teske (1997) and Colby and Damon (1992). For other discussions of defining the moral self in activism, see Andrews (1991) and Jasper (1997). Meanwhile, Becky Thompson (2001) has found that racial justice activism became a "way of life" for the white activists in her study.

48. On the Beloved Community, see Marsh (2005). On freedom dreams, see Kelley (2002).

49. Colby and Damon (1992), in their study of social justice activists, also found that these activists expressed powerful visions of a future society. As I discuss in chapter four, they found that the activists were not visionaries but rather built a vision of the future through their focus on day-to-day work.

50. On free spaces, see Evans and Boyte (1986); see also Whittier (1995) on micromobilization contexts. For further discussions of identity development in activist group settings, see Nepstad (2004) and Polletta and Jasper (2001).

51. Blee (2002), in fact, emphasizes that some people can simply drift into activism accidentally and then develop their commitment after participation has begun; see also Munson (2009).

Chapter Two

1. See Myrdal (1944). For a discussion of the critical commentary on Mydal's work, see Lyman (1998).

2. For a discussion of beliefs in American values, see Hochschild (1995). Another eight subjects indicate that their parents were clearly committed to racial justice; they will be discussed below.

3. See Gamson (1992, 32). As Gamson notes, and I also found in the interviewees' accounts, there must be a concrete target to blame for injustice—those who are the cause of the inequity. A vague sense of "the system" won't do.

4. In their study of the development of social justice commitment, Laurent Daloz and his associates (1996, 71) note that one event does not always change people's lives dramatically but that "the encounters we have described are best understood as crystallized moments of memory in a larger pattern of engagement with otherness."

5. For a thorough discussion of cognitive dissonance theory, see Cooper (2007).

6. See Teske (1997) and also Blee (2002). See the appendix for a further discussion of this issue.

7. For further discussion of conversion and compliance as routes to activism, see Linden and Klandermans (2007) and also Lofland et al. (2006), who include a discussion of the related phenomenon of religious conversion.

8. Rachel and her colleagues have written about this project in Breunlin, Himelstein, and Nelson (2008).

9. About half of the subjects, twenty-six, indicated that acquiring a frame had been important to their development, but only three identified a cognitive route to racial justice activism. I had initially expected more of them to report on the importance of reading about the experiences of people of color. Other scholars (e.g., O'Brien 2001) have suggested that such reading offers an important route to racial awareness, but I found direct experience to be far more important.

10. Thirty-three of the activists I interviewed identified college or graduate school as a critical time and place for the development of their commitment to racial justice; two more named the seminary. All but one of the fifty subjects attended college.

11. For a classical treatment, see Erikson (1968).

12. Brodkin (2007) also discusses the important role played by ethnic studies departments in the college experiences that led young people to become organizers in LA's labor movement in the nineties.

13. On young adulthood and student life as times of activism, see Feuer (1969). On the role of activist networks, see McAdam and Paulsen (1993).

14. In their research on white antiracists, O'Brien (2001) and George (2004) have also found that many activists became exposed to a racial analysis and to racial justice activism through prior activist experiences. Scholars of social movements (e.g., McAdam 1986) have long emphasized the importance of prior activism as a source of recruitment networks and favorable ideological orientations. I return to this issue further in the conclusion.

15. Seventeen of the fifty subjects spoke about the importance of foreign travel. However, fully eleven of the nineteen activists who came of age in the postseventies' generation mentioned its importance.

16. Seventeen of the fifty activists interviewed stated that they are carrying out faith values in their work, at least in part. Eleven of these found faith networks as routes into activism.

17. Other scholars of activism have discussed concepts similar to seminal experiences. Haste (1990) calls them "triggering events." O'Brien (2001) talks about seeds

planted early in activists' lives. Lofland et al. (2006) offer a broader discussion of the role of turning points in people's lives.

18. I take the term moral shock from Jasper and Poulsen (1995); see also Jasper (1997). Nepstad (2004, 2007) has also found that moral shocks played a role in the development of oppositional consciousness to U.S. foreign policy in Central America in the eighties.

19. For a classic treatment of frame alignment processes, see Snow et al. (1986). For an overview of social justice education, see Sleeter (1996). For a related discussion of frame-changing experiences in developing a commitment to community service, see Seider (2007).

20. See Jasper (1997, 16). For further discussion of the role of emotions among social movement scholars, see Flam and King (2005) and Goodwin, Jasper, and Polletta (2004, 2001).

21. See Haste (1990).

22. On cold anger, see Rogers (1990).

Chapter Three

1. James Douglas is a pseudonym.

2. Sam and Barbara are pseudonyms.

3. See Clinton Bolick, "Clinton's Quota Queens," *Wall Street Journal* (op-ed), April 30, 1993. For Lani Guinier's views on the nomination process, see Guinier (1994).

4. Thirty-nine of the interviewees said that these relationships were of significant importance, while seven said that they were somewhat important.

5. Tom Morrison is a pseudonym.

6. Thirty-two subjects in the study mentioned confronting their own stereotypes or racial practices because of relationships with people of color.

7. Sarah is a pseudonym.

8. At the time of the interview Madeline was actually director of Illinois ACORN (Association of Community Organizations for Reform Now). In 2008 Madeline and the large majority of ACORN members in Illinois left ACORN to form a new group called Action Now.

9. Thirty-three of the fifty subjects in the study spoke emphatically about the importance of building caring bonds with people of color, either with activists or nonactivists in communities of color. Another five subjects mentioned the importance of these bonds, but less emphatically.

10. Nine of the fifty subjects in the study are currently in interracial relationships. Three others have been in such relationships in the past.

11. Sixteen subjects spoke of finding warmth or caring in communities of color.

12. Fifteen of the activists in the study mentioned such limitations.

13. Dwayne is a pseudonym.

14. On cross-cutting cleavages and electoral behavior, see, for example, Manza and Brooks (1999).

15. Walker and Snarey (2004) are responding to a debate within moral and developmental psychology that has counterposed Lawrence Kohlberg's (1984) ethic of justice and the ethic of caring put forward by feminists like Carol Gilligan (1982) and Nell Noddings (1984).

16. O'Brien (2001) stresses the development of empathy through "approximating experiences" of racism gained through relationships. Goodwin, Jasper, and Polletta (2001, 9) discuss the role of emotions in creating a sense of shared identity. They argue that the strength of an identity, even one cognitively weak, comes from its emotional side. I return to these issues in the conclusion.

17. Becky Thompson (2001, 367–371) focuses on intimate interracial relationships, but I have found that white activists can make antiracism personal to them through less intimate connections as well.

Chapter Four

1. At the most, three of the activists stated that they had inherited a vision of a future society from their parents and that this vision was important to them early on in their activism.

2. Thirty-seven activists stated explicitly that this work creates meaning and purpose in their lives. Another eleven made comments that amount to an equivalent statement. These include remarks such as, "It allows me to live out my values." Only two activists failed to mention anything that could be considered meaning in life.

3. While virtually all of the interviewees mentioned the sense of purpose and fulfillment they find in racial justice activism, fifteen—nine of whom work in faith-based organizations—described this work specifically as a calling.

4. Twenty-eight of the activists in this study spoke about reclaiming humanity and/or stated that working for racial justice is constitutive of who they are.

5. These forty-six expressed visions of the future they stated were important to them. Only one activist claimed to have no vision. Three others offered elements of a future vision but did not describe them as of clear importance.

6. On social democratic values see Meyer (2007); on the Beloved Community see Marsh (2005); on the New Left see Miller (2004); on multiculturalism see Kymlicka (2009); and on the liberal project see Sandel (1998). Communism also inspired historic movements with a more radical vision of human emancipation and a society based upon human values, whatever its distortion in practice (Riemer 1987).

7. For a further discussion of the Beloved Community, see Marsh (2005). Lichterman (1996) argues that postsixties' activists have turned to a "personalized politics" in which individuals are the arbiters of moral choices that nevertheless allow them to act for social concerns.

8. Twelve of the interviewees mentioned only one aspect of a vision. I judged the thirty-four who mentioned multiple aspects to be leading with one aspect if they mentioned it multiple times or elaborated on it in a significantly deeper way compared to other aspects.

9. For an account of the Greensboro massacre from the point of view of the widow of one of the murdered protesters, see Waller (2002).

10. For a thorough discussion of the issues of segregation, real-estate block busting, and racial turnover, see Massey and Denton (1992). For a recent treatment that focuses on Chicago, see Satter (2009).

11. Seth refers to a quotation usually attributed to Lila Watson, an Australian Aboriginal woman, which reflects the sentiments of many activists in the study. The

exact quotation reads, "If you have come to help me, you are wasting your time. But if you recognize that your liberation and mine are bound up together, we can walk together."

12. Fourteen of the interviewees described themselves as radical or revolutionary in their politics.

13. On the San Francisco State strike, see Barlow and Shapiro (1971).

14. Ten activists mentioned a multicultural vision, and two of these emphasized it above other elements of a future society.

15. Twelve activists spoke directly to a liberal democratic vision, and nine of them emphasized it above other elements of a future society. Seven of the twelve are lawyers.

16. On meaning in activism, see, for example, Colby and Damon (1992), Daloz et al. (1996), and Teske (1997). The environmental movement is another realm of activism in which personal responsibility to act differently has high value. For a discussion of prefigurative politics in American social movements, see Polletta (2002).

17. See Teske (1997). In their study of individuals committed to social justice, Colby and Damon (1992, 300) argue that, "rather than denying the self, they define it with a moral center." For other treatments of this sort, see Daloz et al. (1996), Andrews (1991), and Wuthnow (1991). In her study of the rescuers of Jews during the Holocaust, Monroe (2004) also found that people said they had had no other choice but to act.

18. Tim Wise (2005), a white antiracist writer and speaker, stresses this point as well.

19. Philosopher Charles Taylor (1989) provides a helpful discussion of the link between an individual's moral vision and self-conception. Sociologist James Jasper (1997) offers a treatment as well. See Kelley (2002) for a discussion of the motivating visions of black radical activists.

20. I have analyzed the moral visions of activists concerning racial justice but have made no effort to closely examine their views on the full range of the features of a moral community, including, for example, its treatment of women or its relationship to world peace.

21. On moral principles in social movements, see Jasper (1997). On the related concept of moral vocabularies, see Lowe (2006). For a discussion of the construction of belief systems in activist groups, see Polletta (1999).

22. Only one activist out of the fifty did not express the view that white people's interests lie in racial justice.

23. For arguments in favor of universalism, see Skocpol (1991). On the need for race-specific policy, see J. Phillip Thompson (1998) and Saito (2009).

Chapter Five

1. For a further elaboration of Carmichael's views, see Ture and Hamilton (1992 [1967]).

2. The other ten may challenge whites in certain situations but do not focus on this work. The rest of this chapter draws mainly from the forty activists.

3. I discuss the nature of modern racism in more detail in chapter one. For a fuller discussion of color-blind racism see Bonilla-Silva (2003) and Brown et al.

(2003); on laissez-faire racism see Bobo, Kluegel, and Smith (1997); on unconscious bias see Dovidio and Gaertner (2004). People of color can also act in ways that perpetuate institutional racism, but this subject lies beyond the purposes of this chapter and of the research project.

4. See Bonilla-Silva (2003). On low expectations, see Ferguson (2007); on notions of black intellectual inferiority, see Theresa Perry (2003).

5. I discuss the concept of white privilege in greater detail in chapter one. For treatments of white privilege, see Lipsitz (1997) and McIntosh (1989).

6. Eileen O'Brien (2001, chapter 4) also offers a valuable discussion of strategies for influencing whites based upon her interviews with thirty-nine white antiracist activists.

7. Twenty-five of the forty activists mentioned the importance of addressing behavior. More activists would likely agree even if they did not specifically mention this issue in the open-ended question format of the interviews. A focus on behavior is emphasized in fields ranging from organizational processes to child rearing but may be particularly important where the accusation of being a racist carries great moral weight.

8. How to address the racism of avowed white supremacists requires a separate discussion and was not pursued in this research project. Meanwhile, people of color may also be influenced by racialized thinking, but this issue lies beyond the bounds of this research project as well.

9. Thirty-three of the forty activists stressed inclusiveness.

10. Twenty-seven of the forty activists stressed this point.

11. Twenty-seven of the forty activists spoke to the importance of relationships.

12. This theme was not as dominant as the others. Thirteen of the forty explicitly mentioned using themselves as an example. However, taking all of their comments into consideration, I feel confident that many others would agree with this point even if they did not volunteer that view in the interview.

13. A few of the activists in the study said they don't experience guilt at all, and a few said it's a good thing.

14. Nearly half of the forty activists mentioned this strategy specifically.

15. Twenty-six of the forty activists spoke about the importance of addressing racism through the work.

16. Of the twenty activists working in the community sector, eighteen placed an emphasis on influencing other whites. Seventeen of those eighteen stressed the importance of relationship and action.

17. For treatments of community organizing, see Warren (2001) and Wood (2002).

18. See, for example, Delgado (1997) and Jennings (1990).

19. For a discussion of this campaign see Warren (2001, chapter 5).

20. Fourteen of the sixteen educators in the study stressed the importance of working to influence other whites. This section is based upon the accounts of those fourteen. For a treatment of efforts to address racism in schooling, see Pollock (2008).

21. Emily is a pseudonym.

22. Enid Lee is a Canadian educator who works with school systems on issues of racial equity.

23. Jamal is a pseudonym.

24. See Olsen (1997).

25. Activists in this field were less likely to stress the importance to their work of influencing whites specifically. Eight of the fourteen activists stated that this task was important to them. The other six did not focus particularly on how to influence whites; rather, they focused on how to achieve their legal or policy goals more generally. For a treatment of advocacy group politics, see Strolovitch (2007).

26. See Menkart, Murray, and View (2004).

27. Chester discusses his personal and professional history in the introduction to a volume of his published articles; see Hartman (2002).

28. Six of the eight policy advocates who place importance on influencing other whites mentioned the importance of relationship building and of local work.

29. See the report *And Justice for Some* (Poe-Yamagata and Jones 2000).

Chapter Six

1. On segregation in residential life see Massey and Denton (1992); on public schools see Orfield and Eaton (1997); on congregations see Emerson and Woo (2006); on marriage see Childs (2005); on friendships see Briggs (2007); and on voluntary associations see Putnam (2000).

2. Forty of the fifty activists in this study placed a high priority on building multiracial venues. All of them stated that they do so in order to advance their work. Thirty-three of those forty also reported building them for prefigurative purposes.

3. Martin Luther King Jr. and other civil rights activists saw the same kind of twin purpose in building an interracial movement in the sixties. King worked to achieve an interracial Beloved Community not only in order to advance civil rights at the time but also to create a model for his vision of the future. For an extensive discussion of King's Beloved Community and its contemporary application, see Marsh (2005). For a discussion of prefigurative politics in the New Left, see Breines (1989); for a broader discussion of prefigurative politics in American social movements, see Polletta (2002).

4. On SNCC and CORE and the struggles over white participation in the civil rights movement generally, see Carson (1981), Marx and Useem (1971), Polletta (2002), and McAdam (1988). Becky Thompson (2001), however, complicates the notion that whites were simply "kicked out" of the movement, as she shows that many left voluntarily in appreciation of the need for black leadership and control. On the demand for black control of institutions, see Ture and Hamilton (1992 [1967]).

5. On how activists learned from the women's and various movements of the Left, see Becky Thompson (2001).

6. I realize that multiracial collaboration involves building relationships among many different racial groups. As elsewhere in this book, I focus on the association between whites on the one hand and people of color, mainly black and Latino, on the other. Building collaboration between blacks and Latinos, as well as between other racial/ethnic groups, represents an important challenge as well but lies beyond the purview of this study. For a discussion of racial dynamics among communities of color, see, for example, Joyce (2003) and Vaco (2004).

7. Thirty-two of the forty activists who develop such collaborations said that they are built on the basis of relationships. Thirty-eight of the forty reported mistrust as a problem.

8. Barbara is a pseudonym.

9. In the end, twenty-six of the forty activists who stated that they build collaborations discussed trust building over time by proving oneself in practice; eighteen of the forty talked about not taking mistrust personally; twenty-nine of the forty discussed relationship building through conversation and storytelling; and eighteen discussed the importance of multifaceted relationships that go beyond working together to include a deeper connection.

10. I quoted Gerald Britt to this effect in Warren (2001, 155).

11. One of the earliest writings about white privilege behavior is McIntosh (1989); for a more recent and extensive discussion see Kendall (2006). Thirty-two of the forty activists who stated that they strive to build multicultural collaborations mentioned white privilege behavior as a problem. Five of those called it "white behavior based upon prejudice" rather than naming it as privilege, but the content of the behavior is the same.

12. Thirty-one of the forty activists who said they build multiracial collaborations spoke to the importance of challenging white privilege behavior; twenty-nine of these forty mentioned the need to be self-reflective; twelve of the forty commented specifically on the need not to pander to people of color but to strive for personal authenticity and honesty in relationships.

13. For a discussion of SNCC and developments in the sixties see Carson (1981). For a broader discussion of Marxist movements that have often called for the right to self-determination for African Americans and other racial groups in the United States, see Dawson (2001). There was also a parallel development in some faith-based institutions that called for those who had been the most affected by injustice to play an important role in efforts to redress injustice; for the Catholic perspective see Palacios (2007).

14. See Bigelow and Peterson (1998).

15. Paula is a pseudonym.

16. Thirty-one of the forty activists who said they build collaborations highlighted the problem of white domination in leadership. Twenty-one of them articulated some version of the need for people of color to lead racial justice efforts. Thirty of the forty mentioned the need for whites to play leadership roles. Seventeen expressed both points of view. This means that only four of the forty activists expressed a "pure" view that whites should follow the leadership of people of color. On the other hand, thirteen of the forty stated that they support equal collaboration without too much concern for the special role of leadership by people of color. Moreover, eleven of the forty activists expressed support for self-determination for communities of color while twenty-three of the forty stressed the importance of building the leadership of people of color.

17. See Marx and Useem (1971).

18. O'Brien (2001) also found that white activists struggled to gain trust and respect from people of color. She called the obstacles to trust building false empathy, when whites try to dictate to people of color, and lack of humility, when whites failed to be open to criticism. For the literature on confronting white privilege, see Kendall (2006). For a discussion of differences between blacks and whites in cultural styles, see Kochman (1981).

19. See Amulya et al. (2004), Aspen Institute Roundtable on Community Change (2004), Delgado (1997), and Wiley (2003).

20. See Thompson (2001).

Chapter Seven

1. On the construction of racial categories in the United States see Haney López (1996) and Omi and Winant (1994). On political attitudes by race see Dawson (1994, 183–184).

2. Twenty-nine of the fifty activists reported tension of this sort.

3. Thirty-nine of the fifty activists in the study reported some degree of association with or membership in communities of color.

4. By NAME, Christine is referring to the National Association for Multicultural Education. See chapter six for a further discussion of her experiences in that organization.

5. Christine has coedited a volume on white identity and racial justice; see Clark and O'Donnell (1999).

6. Eight of the activists in the study came from families that were explicitly antiracist or strong proponents of racial justice.

7. Six of the seven activists who reported feeling the most self-conscious about their role as white activists are among the youngest in the group. Although theorists of racial identity development do not focus specifically on activists, they have argued that whites have to go through several stages of development before they can achieve self-acceptance; see Helms (1990). Twelve of the activists are or have been in intimate interracial relationships.

8. Forty-five of the fifty activists reported identifying closely with a multiracial activist community. Twenty-two stated that they continue to receive support from parents or extended family, although tension may also be there.

9. See W.E.B. Du Bois (2007 [1903]). For one example of the literature on blacks in white elite communities, see Zweigenhaft and Domhoff (2003). Sociology has a long tradition that goes back to the work of Robert Park (1928), which focuses on the "marginal man."

10. On oppositional consciousness, see Mansbridge and Morris (2001). On oppositional consciousness among the privileged, see Nepstad (2007).

11. Some white antiracist writers (e.g., Wise 2005) have suggested the same thing; see also Eichstedt (2001) among others.

12. Five of the fifty activists in this study reported little effort at building community with other racial justice activists, although even these few mentioned some effort.

13. Becky Thompson (2001), in her study of racial justice movements, found that white activists feel they live on the border between white and black; some see themselves as border crossers. Meanwhile, Thompson also stresses the importance of multiracial community to these activists. On building identities in small activist groups, see, for example, Taylor and Whittier (1992), Evans and Boyte (1986), and Polletta (1999).

Chapter Eight

1. See Du Bois (2001, xxv).

2. On high school drop-out rates, see Orfield et al. (2004). For a recent study of the consequences of dropping out, see Sum, Khatiwada, and McLaughlin (2009).

3. On the savage inequalities in education, see Kozol (1991). Barbara Trepagnier (2006) has also called passivity the main factor in perpetuating racism today; on the related concept of white apathy see Forman (2004).

4. One of the activists in the study, Tony Fleo, suggested the phrase "head, heart, and hand" in my interview with him. Although not typically found in the fields of race relations and social movements, this kind of metaphor has been used in other fields. Indigenous educator Gregory Cajete (1997), for example, talks about the face, heart, and feet (or foundation) in relation to self-knowledge, life's passion, and work/action.

5. On the morality of caring see Gilligan (1982), Noddings (1984), and Walker and Snarey (2004).

6. I would like to thank Marshall Ganz, who helped clarify the distinction between the "what" and the "why." This distinction also draws upon Max Weber's (1980) classic discussion of the rise of science and rationality in the world. In his view, science can tell people how to achieve their goals but does not provide the values that determine those goals in the first place.

7. Teske (1997) builds on the earlier efforts of Mansbridge (1990) to critique the limits of self-interest as the source of human motivation in political life. Other studies have also shown how activists acquire meaning in life as they develop an activist identity. In her study of people who rescued Jews during the Holocaust, for example, Kristin Monroe (2004, xi) concludes, "ethical acts emerge not from choice so much as through our sense of who we are, through our identities." A broader literature draws upon Charles Taylor's (1989) seminal work on modern identity to show how personal and collective identities affect activism. For a review see Polletta and Jasper (2001); for a recent treatment of identity in the activism of young organizers in the Los Angeles labor movement, see Brodkin (2007).

8. For a related discussion of the link between moral visions and personal identity, see Colby and Damon (1992). Sandra Morgen (2002) also stresses the personal meaning in life gained through women's activism in the women's health movement. Meanwhile, Wuthnow (1991) found that Americans inhabit a culture that encourages people to justify their social activism and volunteering in self-interested terms.

9. See Krause (2008, 125) and Marcus (2002); for other treatments see Neuman et al. (2007), Haste (1990), Westen (2007), and Nussbaum (2001). I discuss recent sociological work on emotions and social movements in chapter one. For one of these treatments of the link between cognition, emotions, and morality see Nepstad (2004, 119–120); for an overview see Goodwin, Jasper, and Polletta (2001). On recent work in neuroscience on the connection between emotions and cognition see Damasio (2005), Ledoux (1998), and Lane and Nadel (2000). Native scholars (e.g., Burkhart 2004) have sustained a critique of the Cartesian separation of mind and body as well, offering more integrated frameworks and epistemologies.

10. For a broader discussion of frame-changing experiences see Seider (2007).

11. For one important argument that cross-racial alliances would benefit whites see Wilson (1999).

12. See Thompson (2001).

13. See O'Brien (2001).

14. See Bonilla-Silva (2003). He classifies students as progressive if they support affirmative action and interracial marriage and recognize the significance of discrimination in the United States.

15. See O'Brien and Korgen (2007).

16. See O'Brien (1999).

17. Janet Helms (1990) first developed the racial identity development model as a sequence of stages. See Jones and Carter (1996) for an update that treats these stages more as statuses, not necessarily a linear developmental sequence. Wijeyesinghe and Jackson (2001) also offer a useful review.

18. See Frankenberg (1993).

19. See Thompson, Schaefer, and Brod (2003) and Clark and O'Donnell (1999). For another collection of autobiographical stories on race, see Thompson and Tyagi (1996).

20. See McAdam (1988) and O'Brien (1999). Jennifer Eichstedt (2001) also finds prior activism to be important, as does Mark Patrick George (2004) in an unpublished study of white activists.

21. See Aptheker (1992) and Eichstedt (2001). Eichstedt also finds that gay activists' own experiences with marginalization provided a link to the experience of people of color. Cynthia Brown (2002), in her portraits of four white racial justice activists, also discusses the impact of their relationships with people of color. See also Lauri Johnson (2002).

22. O'Brien's (2001) third type of approximating experience, "global approximation," identifies the influence of democratic principles and personal ethics, but these do not feature strongly in her account. In his unpublished work, George (2004) includes a more extensive treatment of the role of values in the white antiracist identity development of the activists he interviewed. For treatments of the moral commitments of white activists in the civil rights movement, see McAdam (1988) and Pinckney (1968).

23. See Colby and Damon (1992, 301). On social movement scholarship contrasted with personality type, see Friedman and McAdam (1993) and Jasper (1997).

24. Holler is quoted in chapter four. Pogo is the main character of a long-running comic strip of the same name by Walt Kelly. The exact quotation is "We have met the enemy and he is us."

25. Perry Perkins put it this way: "Activism for me usually connotes unfocused activity that does not take seriously the building of capacity and power in response to social conditions. I like the notion of being a public person who builds power over time in order to bring about concrete and constructive change."

26. Many educators teach white students about white privilege as a way to help them understand the reality of racism. An often-used text is "White Privilege: Unpacking the Invisible Knapsack" (McIntosh 1989). Meanwhile, many white activists gather annually to discuss their role in combating racism at the White Privilege conferences sponsored by the University of Colorado at Colorado Springs; see http://www.uccs.edu/~wpc/index.htm.

27. On faith-based community organizing, see Warren (2001) and Wood (2002). On the role of religious faith in social movement activism more broadly, see Smith (1996).

28. On the environmental movement see, for example, Kempton, Boster, and Hartley (1996) and Lichterman (1996). Many scholars (e.g., Williams 1999) have argued that American democratic values have been heavily shaped by Christian traditions, so the religious and the secular cannot perhaps be so easily dichotomized. On moral principles and values in activism more broadly, see Jasper (1997).

29. In his speech at the 2004 Democratic National Convention, Obama (2004) told his family's story in the context of American traditions and values. He addressed race directly in his speech "A More Perfect Union" (Obama 2008) delivered in March of 2008.

30. For Putnam's analysis of social capital, see *Bowling Alone* (Putnam 2000). For further discussions of the importance of bridging social capital, see Warren, Thompson, and Saegert (2001) and Briggs (1998). For information on public support for diversity in higher education, see the poll conducted for the Ford Foundation (*Diversity Digest* 1998).

31. See Putnam (2007).

32. See Allport (1954). In another classic treatment Sherif (1988) shows that previously hostile groups will cooperate when in pursuit of a common goal. In his review of contact research Yancey (2007) argues that, in the kinds of circumstances discussed here, interracial contact does change whites' racial attitudes. For other reviews of the extensive research on the contact thesis, see Pettigrew (1998) and Forbes (1997).

33. For another discussion of how sharing stories helps people learn to understand the experience of people across the racial divide, see Walsh (2007).

34. Phillip Thompson (2005) coins the term *deep democracy* to describe the open and critical processes that must occur within black civic associations and between whites, blacks, and other racial groups in forging progressive coalitions. See also Green (1999).

35. See Fine, Weis, and Powell (1997).

36. For the classic Black Power argument for coalitions, see Ture and Hamilton (1992 [1967]). Phillip Thompson (2005) offers a more recent treatment of the need for urban coalitions in which black civic groups play a central role.

37. The media have tended to focus on the Obama campaign's use of new technology. For treatments of the field organization see Exley (2007, 2008).

38. On the civil rights movement see, as just one example, Cynthia Brown (2002). Beverly Daniel Tatum (1994) is one of many who employ the term *white ally* today. For a defense of the concept of white ally, see Sleeter (1996).

39. On men in feminism see Digby (1998). On straight people as allies in the gay and lesbian movement see Myers (2008), who describes their participation as altruism. For a broader discussion of the differences between liberation movements against oppression and other types of new social movements, see Morris and Braine (2001).

40. See Guinier and Torres (2002).

41. Iris Marion Young (1990) has written extensively on the positive role of social group identities within a process of building inclusive democracy. For an example of an argument for the need to dissolve racial identities, see Kenneth Hoover (1997), who argues that we need to move away from racial categories as identities in order for us to move toward a more cooperative form of politics.

42. From "A More Perfect Union," Barack Obama's (2008) speech on race.

43. On local organizing and the civil rights movement see Payne (1995).

Appendix

1. See Ragin, Nagel, and White (2004).

2. For a discussion of interpretive social science see Rabinow and Sullivan (1987). Nathan Teske (1997, 143–148) also treats many of the issues discussed in this section.

3. See Lamont (2000), Somers (1992), Blee (2002), Teske (1997), Colby and Damon (1992), Andrews (1991), and Wuthnow (1991); for other studies that use this approach, see Nepstad (2004), Brodkin (2007), Linden and Klandermans (2007), and Luker (1984).

4. See Kearney (2002, 3). Margaret Somers (1994, 606) suggests, moreover, that "it is through narrativity that we come to know, understand, and make sense of the social world, and it is through narratives and narrativity that we constitute our social identities." James Jasper (1997) has called for more study of activist biography in order to shed light on the formation of activists' interpretive frameworks, to see the sources of protest that are not organized by formal groups and leaders, and to identify the cultural and biographical materials out of which new organizations arise.

5. See Blee (2002) and Teske (1997). I owe the language distinguishing the "telling and the told" to Riessman (2008), who attributes it to Mishler (1995). By focusing on the "told," I conduct what Riessman calls a "thematic analysis of narrative." For a broader discussion of conversion stories, see Lofland et al. (2006). For a discussion of the analysis of narrative structure and of issues surrounding narrative analysis, see Clandinin and Connelly (2000) and the readings in Clandinin's (2007) edited volume. Narrative analysis draws upon the work of Jerome Bruner (1990). Recently, social movement scholars (e.g., Polletta 2006) have focused on the kinds of stories activists tell. Perhaps because my respondents were not part of a single movement, however, I did not hear these kinds of movement stories.

6. Broadly, I follow the approach to knowledge taken by two closely related ontological positions, constructivist realism (e.g., Gorski 2004) and critical realism (e.g., Sayer 2000).

7. For a useful discussion of the conditional nature of knowledge gained from narrative interviews and of the use of personal narrative in the social sciences more generally, see Maynes, Pierce, and Laslett (2008). For a broader discussion of qualitative research as a methodology, see Lincoln and Guba (1985). For a recent treatment of the scientific standing of qualitative research, see Ragin, Nagel, and White (2004).

8. Of course, that doesn't mean there can be no contradictions in a story; people's lives can be complex, and they can hold opposing convictions at the same time.

9. For a discussion of narratives and lived experience see Clandinin and Rosiek (2007).

10. See Maxwell (2004); see also Rubin and Rubin (2005).

11. This approach is typical of the qualitative interview studies cited earlier. See, for example, Andrews (1991, 113), who says of her study of the life commitments of British socialists, "This chapter does not address why these individuals, and not others, became politically active; rather our focus is on why these particular people understood and subsequently responded to their environments in the way in which

they did." For further discussion of the causal and explanatory power of narrative analysis, see Abell (2004) and Heimer (2001).

12. I actually interviewed fifty-one activists but had to exclude one subject from the analysis, leaving a total of fifty.

13. On open and focused coding, see Lofland et al. (2006). I also followed many of the procedures outlined by Weiss (1994) and Miles and Huberman (1994).

14. See Seidman (2006).

15. See Miles and Huberman (1994).

16. For a discussion of the criteria of credibility in qualitative claims, see Maxwell (2004, 2005). On the coconstruction of knowledge see, for example, Holstein and Gubrium (1995).

17. Some of these expectations came from my own experience, as well as from other literature. Much attention among critical educators (e.g., Lawrence and Tatum 1997; Sleeter 1996), for example, is placed on developing a racial analysis among whites. Meanwhile, a number of scholars (e.g., Eichstedt 2001; Frankenberg 1993; O'Brien 2001) have suggested that white people's own experience with marginalization may help them understand the experience of racism.

18. See Whittier (1995). Eduardo Bonilla-Silva (2003) discusses the shift from overt racism to color-blind ideology.

19. Many scholars (e.g., Williams 1999) have noted the interpenetration of religious and political cultures in the United States.

20. The quotation comes from *The Sociological Imagination* (Mills 1959, 3). I am grateful to Sharon Nepstad (2004), who made the connection to Mills in her study of activists in the Central American solidarity movement. For a structuralist account of racism see Bonilsla-Silva (1997). For treatments of the relationship between structure and agency, see Giddens (1984) and Sewell (1992).

REFERENCES

Abbott, Andrew. 1997. On the concept of turning point. *Comparative Social Research* 16: 85–105.

Abell, Peter. 2004. Narrative explanation: An alternative to variable-centered explanation? *Annual Review of Sociology 30:* 287–310.

Allen, Robert L. 1974. *Reluctant reformers: Racism and social reform movements in the United States.* Washington, DC: Howard University Press.

Allport, Gordon W. 1954. *The nature of prejudice.* Cambridge, MA: Addison-Wesley.

Amulya, Joy, O'Campbell, Christie, Allen, Ryan, & McDowell, Ceasar. 2004. *Vital difference: The role of race in community building.* Cambridge, MA: Center for Reflective Practice, MIT.

Andrews, Molly. 1991. *Lifetimes of commitment: Aging, politics, psychology.* Cambridge, MA: Cambridge University Press.

Aptheker, Herbert. 1992. *Anti-racism in U.S. history: The first two hundred years.* New York: Greenwood.

Aspen Institute Roundtable on Community Change. 2004. *Structural racism and community building.* Washington, DC: Aspen Institute.

Barlow, William, & Shapiro, Peter. 1971. *An end to silence: The San Francisco State student movement in the '60s.* New York: Bobbs-Merrill.

Bell, Derrick. 2004. *Silent covenants:* Brown v. Board of Education *and the unfulfilled hopes for racial reform.* New York: Oxford University Press.

Bigelow, Bill, & Peterson, Bob. 1998. *Rethinking Columbus: The next 500 years.* Milwaukee: Rethinking Schools.

Blank, Rebecca M. 2005. Tracing the economic impact of cumulative discrimination. *American Economic Review* 95(2): 88–103.

Blauner, Robert. 1989. *Black lives, white lives: Three decades of race relations in America.* Berkeley: University of California Press.

Blee, Kathleen M. 2002. *Inside organized racism: Women in the hate movement.* Berkeley: University of California Press.

Bobo, Lawrence D., & Hutchings, Vincent L. 1996. Perceptions of racial group competition: Extending Blumer's theory of group position to a multiracial social context. *American Sociological Review* 61: 951–972.

Bobo, Lawrence D., Kluegel, James R., & Smith, Ryan A. 1997. Laissez-faire racism: The crystallization of a "kinder, gentler" anti-black ideology. In Steven A. Tuch & Jack K. Martin, Eds., *Racial attitudes in the 1990s: Continuity and change*, pp. 15–44. Westport, CT: Praeger.

Bobo, Lawrence D., & Smith, Ryan A. 1998. From Jim Crow racism to laissez-faire racism: The transformation of racial attitudes. In Wendy Katkin, Ned Landsman, & Andrea Tyree, Eds., *Beyond pluralism: The conception of groups and group identities in America*, pp. 182–220. Urbana: University of Illinois Press.

Bonilla-Silva, Eduardo. 1997. Rethinking racism: Toward a structural interpretation. *American Sociological Review* 62(3): 465–480.

Bonilla-Silva, Eduardo. 2003. *Racism without racists: Color-blind racism and the persistence of racial inequality in the United States*. Lanham, MD: Rowman & Littlefield.

Bonilla-Silva, Eduardo, & Dietrich, David R. 2008. The Latin Americanization of racial stratification in the U.S. In Ronald E. Hall, Ed., *Racism in the 21st century: An empirical analysis of skin color*, pp. 151–170. New York: Springer.

Bonnett, Alastair. 1997. Antiracism and the critique of "white" identities. *New Communities* 22(1): 97–110.

Bowser, Benjamin P. 2007. *The black middle class: Social mobility and vulnerability*. Boulder, CO: Rienner.

Breines, Wini. 1989. *Community and organization in the New Left, 1962–1968: The great refusal*. New Brunswick, NJ: Rutgers University Press.

Breunlin, Rachel, Himelstein, Abram, & Nelson, Ashley. 2008. "Our stories told by us": The Neighborhood Story Project in New Orleans. In Rickie Solinger, Madeline Fox, & Kayhan Irani, Eds., *Telling stories to change the world: Global voices on the power of narrative to build community and make social justice claims*, pp. 75–90. New York: Routledge.

Briggs, Xavier de Souza. 1998. Brown kids in white suburbs: Housing mobility and the many faces of social capital. *Housing Policy Debate* 9(1): 177–221.

Briggs, Xavier de Souza. 2007. "Some of my best friends are...": Interracial friendships, class, and segregation in America. *City & Community* 6(4): 263–290.

Briggs, Xavier de Souza, Ed. 2005. *The geography of opportunity: Race and housing choice in metropolitan America*. Washington, DC: Brookings Institution.

Brodkin, Karen. 2007. *Making democracy matter: Identity and activism in Los Angeles*. New Brunswick, NJ: Rutgers University Press.

Brown, Cynthia Stokes. 2002. *Refusing racism: White allies and the struggle for civil rights*. New York: Teachers College Press.

Brown, Michael K., Carnoy, Martin, Currie, Elliott, Duster, Troy, Oppenheimer, David B., Shultz, Marjorie M., & Wellman, David. 2003. *Whitewashing race: The myth of a color-blind society*. Berkeley: University of California Press.

Bruner, Jerome. 1990. *Acts of meaning*. Cambridge, MA: Harvard University Press.

Burkhart, Brian Yazzie. 2004. What Coyote and Thales can teach us: An outline of American Indian epistemology. In Anne Waters, Ed., *American Indian thought: Philosophical essays*, pp. 15–26. Malden, MA: Blackwell.

Cajete, Gregory. 1997. *Look to the mountain: An ecology of indigenous education.* Durango, CO: Kivaki.

Carson, Clayborne. 1981. *In struggle: SNCC and the black awakening of the 1960s.* Cambridge, MA: Harvard University Press.

Cashin, Sheryll D. 2005. Shall we overcome? Transcending race, class, and ideology through interest conversion. *St. John's Law Review* 79(2): 253–291.

Childs, Erica C. 2005. *Navigating interracial borders: Black-white couples and their social worlds.* New Brunswick, NJ: Rutgers University Press.

Clandinin, D. Jean, Ed. 2007. *Handbook of narrative inquiry: Mapping a methodology.* Thousand Oaks, CA: Sage.

Clandinin, D. Jean, & Connelly, F. Michael. 2000. *Narrative inquiry: Experience and story in qualitative research.* San Francisco: Jossey-Bass.

Clandinin, D. Jean, & Rosiek, Jerry. 2007. Mapping a landscape of narrative inquiry: Borderland spaces and tensions. In D. Jean Clandinin, Ed., *Handbook of narrative inquiry: Mapping a methodology,* pp. 35–76. Thousand Oaks, CA: Sage.

Clark, Christine, & O'Donnell, James, Eds. 1999. *Becoming and unbecoming white: Owning and disowning a racial identity.* Westport, CT: Bergin & Garvey.

Colby, Anne, & Damon, William. 1992. *Some do care: Contemporary lives of moral commitment.* New York: Free Press.

Cooper, Joel. 2007. *Cognitive dissonance: 50 years of a classic theory.* Thousand Oaks, CA: Sage.

Daloz, Laurent A. Parks, Keen, Cheryl H., Keen, James P., & Parks, Sharon Daloz. 1996. *Common fire: Leading lives of commitment in a complex world.* Boston: Beacon.

Damasio, Antonio. 2005. *Descartes' error: Emotion, reason, and the human brain.* New York: Penguin.

Darling-Hammond, Linda. 1998. Unequal opportunity: Race and education. *Brookings Review* 16(2): 28–32.

Dawson, Michael C. 1994. *Behind the mule: Race and class in African-American politics.* Princeton, NJ: Princeton University Press.

Dawson, Michael C. 2001. *Black visions: The roots of contemporary African-American political ideologies.* Chicago: University of Chicago Press.

Delgado, Gary. 1997. *Beyond the politics of place: New directions in community organizing in the 1990s.* Oakland, CA: Applied Research Center.

Digby, Tom. 1998. *Men doing feminism.* New York: Routledge.

Diversity Digest. 1998. National poll reveals strong public support for diversity in higher education. Association of American Colleges and Universities.

Dovidio, John F., & Gaertner, Samuel L. 2004. Aversive racism. In Mark P. Zanna, Ed., *Advances in experimental social psychology,* Vol. 36, pp. 1–51. San Diego: Academic Press.

Du Bois, W.E.B. 2001. *John Brown.* New York: Modern Library.

Du Bois, W.E.B. 2007 [1903]. *The souls of black folk.* New York: Oxford University Press.

Dyer, Richard. 1997. *White.* New York: Routledge.

Eichstedt, Jennifer L. 2001. Problematic white identities and a search for racial justice. *Sociological Forum* 16(3): 445–470.

Emerson, Michael O., Chai, Karen J., & Yancey, George. 2001. Does race matter in residential segregation? Exploring the preferences of white Americans. *American Sociological Review* 66(6): 922–935.

Emerson, Michael O., & Woo, Rodney M. 2006. *People of the dream: Multiracial congregations in the United States.* Princeton, NJ: Princeton University Press.

Entman, Robert M., & Rojecki, Andrew. 2000. *The black image in the white mind: Media and race in America.* Chicago: University of Chicago Press.

Erikson, Erik H. 1968. *Identity, youth and crisis.* New York: Norton.

Evans, Sara, & Boyte, Harry. 1986. *Free spaces: The sources of democratic change in America.* New York: Harper & Row.

Exley, Zack. 2007. Stories and numbers: A closer look at Camp Obama [Web log post]. Retrieved from http://www.huffingtonpost.com/zack-exley/stories-and-numbers-a-clo_b_62278.html.

Exley, Zack. 2008. The new organizers: What's really behind Obama's ground game [Web log post]. Retrieved from http://www.huffingtonpost.com/zack-exley/the-new-organizers-part-1_b_132782.html.

Feagin, Joe R., & and McKinney, Karyn D. 2005. *The many costs of racism.* Lanham, MD: Rowman & Littlefield.

Ferber, Abby L., Jimenez, Christina, Herrera, Andrea, & Samuels, Dena. 2009. *The matrix reader: Examining the dynamics of oppression and privilege.* Boston: McGraw-Hill.

Ferguson, Ronald F. 2007. *Toward excellence with equity: An emerging vision for closing the achievement gap.* Cambridge, MA: Harvard Education Press.

Feuer, Lewis. 1969. *The conflict of generations: The character and significance of student movements.* New York: Basic Books.

Fine, Michelle, Weis, Lois, & Powell, Linda C. 1997. Communities of difference: A critical look at desegregated spaces created for and by youth. *Harvard Educational Review* 67(2): 247–284.

Flam, Helena, & King, Debra, Eds. 2005. *Emotions and social movements.* New York: Routledge.

Forbes, Hugh Donald. 1997. *Ethnic conflict: Commerce, culture, and the contact hypothesis.* New Haven, CT: Yale University Press.

Forman, Tyrone A. 2004. Color-blind racism and racial indifference: The role of racial apathy in facilitating enduring inequalities. In Maria Krysan & Amanda E. Lewis, Eds., *The changing terrain of race and ethnicity,* pp. 43–66. New York: Russell Sage Foundation Press.

Frankenberg, Ruth. 1993. *White women, race matters: The social construction of whiteness.* Minneapolis: University of Minnesota Press.

Friedman, Debra, & McAdam, Doug. 1993. Collective identity and activism: Networks, choices, and the life of a social movement. In Aldon D. Morris & Carol McClurg Mueller, Eds., *Frontiers in social movement theory,* pp. 156–173. New Haven, CT: Yale University Press.

Gamson, William A. 1992. *Talking politics.* New York: Cambridge University Press.

George, Mark Patrick. 2004. *Race traitors: Exploring the motivation and action of white antiracists.* Unpublished doctoral dissertation, University of New Mexico, Albuquerque.

Giddens, Anthony. 1984. *The constitution of society: Outline of the theory of structuration.* Berkeley: University of California Press.

Gilligan, Carol. 1982. *In a different voice: Psychological theory and women's development.* Cambridge, MA: Harvard University Press.

Giugni, Marco, & Passy, Florence. 2001. *Political altruism? Solidarity movements in international perspective.* Lanham, MD: Rowman & Littlefield.

Goodman, Diane. 2001. *Promoting diversity and social justice: Educating people from privileged groups.* Thousand Oaks, CA: Sage.

Goodman, Paul. 1998. *Of one blood: Abolitionism and the origins of racial equality.* Berkeley: University of California Press.

Goodwin, Jeff, Jasper, James M., & Polletta, Francesca. 2004. Emotional dimensions of social movements. In David A. Snow, Sarah Soule, & Hanspeter Kriesi, Eds., *Blackwell companion to social movements,* pp. 413–432. Oxford: Blackwell.

Goodwin, Jeff, Jasper, James M., & Polletta, Francesca, Eds. 2001. *Passionate politics: Emotions and social movements.* Chicago: University of Chicago Press.

Gorski, Philip S. 2004. The poverty of deductivism: A constructivist realist model of sociological explanation. *Sociological Methodology 34:* 1–33.

Green, Judith M. 1999. *Deep democracy: Community, diversity, and transformation.* Lanham, MD: Rowman & Littlefield.

Guinier, Lani. 1994. *The tyranny of the majority: Fundamental fairness in representative democracy.* New York: Free Press.

Guinier, Lani, & Torres, Gerald. 2002. *The miner's canary: Enlisting race, resisting power, transforming democracy.* Cambridge, MA: Harvard University Press.

Hacker, Andrew. 1992. *Two nations: Black and white, separate, hostile, unequal.* New York: Scribner's.

Haney Lopez, Ian. 1996. *White by law: The legal construction of race.* New York: New York University Press.

Harris, David A. 2003. *Profiles in injustice: Why racial profiling cannot work.* New York: New Press.

Hartman, Chester. 2002. *Between eminence and notoriety: Four decades of radical urban planning.* New Brunswick, NJ: Center for Urban Policy Research.

Haste, Helen. 1990. Moral responsibility and moral commitment: The integration of affect and cognition. In Thomas E. Wren, Ed., *The moral domain: Essays in the ongoing discussion between philosophy and the social sciences,* pp. 315–359. Cambridge, MA: MIT Press.

Heimer, Carol A. 2001. Cases and biographies: An essay on routinization and the nature of comparison. *Annual Review of Sociology 27:* 47–76.

Helms, Janet E. 1990. *Black and white racial identity: Theory, research, and practice.* Westport, CT: Greenwood.

Hitchcock, Jeff. 2002. *Lifting the white veil: An exploration of white American culture in a multiracial context.* Roselle, NJ: Crandall, Dostie, & Douglass Books.

Hochschild, Jennifer L. 1995. *Facing up to the American dream: Race, class, and the soul of the nation.* Princeton, NJ: Princeton University Press.

Holstein, James A., & Gubrium, Jaber F. 1995. *The active interview.* Thousand Oaks, CA: Sage.

Hoover, Kenneth R. 1997. *The power of identity: Politics in a new key*. Chatham, NJ: Chatham House.

Ignatiev, Noel. 1996. *How the Irish became white*. New York: Routledge.

Jackman, Mary R. 1994. *The velvet glove: Paternalism and conflict in gender, class, and race relations*. Berkeley: University of California Press.

Jasper, James M. 1997. *The art of moral protest*. Chicago: University of Chicago Press.

Jasper, James M., & Poulsen, Jane. 1995. Recruiting strangers and friends: Moral shocks and social networks in animal rights and anti-nuclear protests. *Social Problems 42:* 493–512.

Jennings, James. 1990. The politics of black empowerment in urban America: Reflections on race, class, and community. In Joseph M. Kling & Prudence S. Posner, Eds., *Dilemmas of activism: Class, community, and the politics of local mobilization*, pp. 113–132. Philadelphia: Temple University Press.

Johnson, Allan G. 2006. *Privilege, power, and difference*. Boston: McGraw-Hill.

Johnson, Lauri. 2002. "My eyes have been opened": White teachers and racial awareness. *Journal of Teacher Education 3*(2): 153–167.

Jones, James M., & Carter, Robert T. 1996. Racism and white racial identity. In Benjamin P. Bowser & Raymond G. Hunt, Eds., *Impacts of racism on white Americans* (2nd ed.), pp. 1–23. Thousand Oaks, CA: Sage.

Joyce, Patrick D. 2003. *No fire next time: Black-Korean conflicts and the future of America's cities*. Ithaca, NY: Cornell University Press.

Katz, Judy H. 1978. *White awareness: Handbook for anti-racism training*. Norman: University of Oklahoma Press.

Katznelson, Ira. 2005. *When affirmative action was white: An untold history of racial inequality in twentieth-century America*. New York: Norton.

Kearney, Richard. 2002. *On stories*. London: Routledge.

Kelley, Robin D. G. 2002. *Freedom dreams: The black radical imagination*. Boston: Beacon.

Kempton, Willett M., Boster, James S., & Hartley, Jennifer A. 1996. *Environmental values in American culture*. Cambridge, MA: MIT Press.

Kendall, Frances E. 2006. *Understanding white privilege: Removing barriers to authentic relationships across race*. New York: Routledge.

Kerner Commission. 1968. *Report of the National Advisory Committee on Civil Disorders*. New York: Bantam.

Kimmel, Michael, & Ferber, Abby, Eds. 2003. *Privilege: A reader*. Boulder, CO: Westview.

Kivel, Paul. 2002. *Uprooting racism: How white people can work for racial justice* (2nd ed.). Gabriola Island, BC, Canada: New Society.

Klinkner, Philip A., & Smith, Rogers M. 1999. *The unsteady march: The rise and decline of racial equality in America*. Chicago: University of Chicago Press.

Kochman, Thomas. 1981. *Black and white styles in conflict*. Chicago: University of Chicago Press.

Kohlberg, Lawrence. 1984. *The psychology of moral development: The nature and validity of moral stages*. San Francisco: Harper & Row.

Korgen, Kathleen Odell. 2002. *Crossing the racial divide: Close friendships between black and white Americans*. Westport, CT: Praeger.

Kozol, Jonathan. 1991. *Savage inequalities: Children in America's schools.* New York: Crown.

Krause, Sharon R. 2008. *Civil passions: Moral sentiment and democratic deliberation.* Princeton, NJ: Princeton University Press.

Kymlicka, Will. 2009. *Multicultural odysseys: Navigating the new international politics of diversity.* New York: Oxford University Press.

Lamont, Michelle. 2000. *The dignity of working men: Morality and the boundaries of race, class, and immigration.* New York: Russell Sage Foundation Press; Cambridge, MA: Harvard University Press.

Lane, Richard D., & Nadel, Lynn, Eds. 2000. *Cognitive neuroscience of emotion.* New York: Oxford University Press.

Laurie, Bruce. 2005. *Beyond Garrison: Antislavery and social reform.* New York: Cambridge University Press.

Lawrence, Sandra M., & Tatum, Beverly Daniel. 1997. Teachers in transition: The impact of antiracist professional development on classroom practice. *Teachers College Record 1:* 162–178.

Lawrence-Lightfoot, Sara. 1997. Illumination: Expressing a point of view. In Sara Lawrence-Lightfoot & Jessica Hoffman Davis, Eds., *The art and science of portraiture,* pp. 85–105. San Francisco: Jossey-Bass.

Ledoux, Joseph. 1998. *The emotional brain: The mysterious underpinnings of emotional life.* New York: Simon & Schuster.

Lentin, Alana. 2004. *Racism and anti-racism in Europe.* London: Pluto.

Lichterman, Paul. 1996. *The search for political community: American activists reinventing commitment.* New York: Cambridge University Press.

Lin, Ann Chih, & Harris, David R. 2008. *The colors of poverty: Why racial and ethnic disparities persist.* New York: Russell Sage Foundation Press.

Lincoln, Yvonne S., & Guba, Egon G. 1985. *Naturalistic inquiry.* Beverly Hills, CA: Sage.

Linden, Annette, & Klandermans, Bert. 2007. Revolutionaries, wanderers, converts, and compliants: Life histories of extreme right activists. *Journal of Contemporary Ethnography 37*(2): 184–201.

Lipset, Seymour Martin, & Marks, Gary. 2000. *It didn't happen here: Why socialism failed in the United States.* New York: Norton.

Lipsitz, George. 1997. *The possessive investment in whiteness.* Philadelphia: Temple University Press.

Lofland, John, Snow, David A., Anderson, Leon, & Lofland, Lyn H. 2006. *Analyzing social settings: A guide to qualitative observation and analysis* (4th ed.). Belmont, CA: Wadsworth.

Loury, Glenn C. 2008. *Race, incarceration, and American values.* Cambridge, MA: MIT Press.

Lowe, Brian M. 2006. *Emerging moral vocabularies: The creation and establishment of new forms of moral and ethical meanings.* Lanham, MD: Lexington Books.

Luker, Kristen. 1984. *Abortion and the politics of motherhood.* Berkeley: University of California Press.

Lyman, Stanford M. 1998. Gunnar Myrdal's *An American dilemma* after a half century: Critics and anticritics. *International Journal of Politics, Culture, and Society 12*(2): 327–389.

Mansbridge, Jane J., Ed. 1990. *Beyond self-interest*. Chicago: University of Chicago Press.

Mansbridge, Jane J., & Morris, Aldon, Eds. 2001. *Oppositional consciousness: The subjective roots of social protest*. Chicago: University of Chicago Press.

Manza, Jeff, & Brooks, Clem. 1999. *Social cleavages and political change: Voter alignment and U.S. party coalitions*. New York: Oxford University Press.

Marcus, George E. 2002. *The sentimental citizen: Emotion in democratic politics*. University Park: Pennsylvania State University Press.

Marsh, Charles. 2005. *The beloved community: How faith shapes social justice, from the civil rights movement to today*. New York: Basic Books.

Marx, Gary T., & Useem, Michael. 1971. Majority involvement in minority movements: Civil rights, abolition, untouchability. *Journal of Social Issues* 27(1): 81–104.

Massey, Douglas, & Denton, Nancy. 1992. *American apartheid: Segregation and the making of the underclass*. Cambridge, MA: Harvard University Press.

Maxwell, Joseph A. 2004. Causal explanation, qualitative research, and scientific inquiry in education. *Educational Researcher 33*: 3–11.

Maxwell, Joseph A. 2005. *Qualitative research design: An interactive approach* (2nd ed.). Thousand Oaks, CA: Sage.

Maynes, Mary Jo, Pierce, Jennifer L., & Laslett, Barbara. 2008. *Telling stories: The use of personal narratives in the social sciences and history*. Ithaca, NY: Cornell University Press.

McAdam, Doug. 1986. Recruitment to high-risk activism: The case of Freedom Summer. *American Journal of Sociology 92*: 64–90.

McAdam, Doug. 1988. *Freedom summer*. New York: Oxford University Press.

McAdam, Doug, & Paulsen, Ronelle. 1993. Specifying the relationship between social ties and activism. *American Journal of Sociology 99:* 640–667.

McDermott, Monica, & Samson, Frank L. 2005. White racial and ethnic identity in the United States. *Annual Review of Sociology 31:* 245–261.

McIntosh, Peggy. 1989. White privilege: Unpacking the invisible knapsack. *Peace and Freedom* 49(4): 10–12.

McLeod, Bryan G. 2001. *Those few also paid a price: Southern whites who fought for civil rights*.

Menkart, Deborah, Murray, Alana D., & View, Jenice L., Eds. 2004. *Putting the movement back into civil rights teaching*. Washington, DC: Teaching for Change & the Poverty and Race Research Action Council.

Meyer, Thomas. 2007. *The theory of social democracy*. Cambridge, UK: Polity.

Miles, Matthew B., & Huberman, A. Michael. 1994. *Qualitative data analysis: An expanded sourcebook* (2nd ed.). Thousand Oaks, CA: Sage.

Miller, James. 2004. *Democracy is in the streets: From Port Huron to the siege of Chicago*. Cambridge, MA: Harvard University Press.

Mills, C. Wright. 1959. *The sociological imagination*. New York: Oxford University Press.

Mills, Charles W. 2004. Racial exploitation and the wages of whiteness. In Maria Krysan & Amanda E. Lewis, Eds., *The changing terrain of race and ethnicity*, pp. 235–262. New York: Russell Sage Foundation Press.

Mishler, Eliot G. 1995. Models of narrative analysis: A typology. *Journal of Narrative and Life History 5:* 87–123.

Monroe, Kristen R. 1996. *The heart of altruism: Perceptions of a common humanity*. Princeton, NJ: Princeton University Press.

Monroe, Kristen R. 2004. *The hand of compassion: Portraits of moral choice during the Holocaust*. Princeton, NJ: Princeton University Press.

Morgen, Sandra. 2002. *Into our own hands: The women's health movement in the United States, 1969–1990*. New Brunswick, NJ: Rutgers University Press.

Morris, Aldon, & Braine, Naomi. 2001. Social movements and oppositional consciousness. In Jane Mansbridge & Aldon Morris, Eds., *Oppositional consciousness: The subjective roots of social protest*, pp. 20–37. Chicago: University of Chicago Press.

Moss, Phillip I., & Tilly, Chris. 2001. *Stories employers tell: Race, skill, and hiring in America*. New York: Russell Sage Foundation Press.

Munson, Ziad W. 2009. *The making of pro-life activists: How social movement mobilization works*. Chicago: University of Chicago Press.

Myers, Daniel J. 2008. Ally identity: The politically gay. In Jo Reger, Daniel J. Myers, & Rachel L. Einwohner, Eds., *Identity work in social movements*, pp. 167–187. Minneapolis: University of Minnesota Press.

Myrdal, Gunnar. 1944. *An American dilemma: The Negro problem and modern democracy*. New York: Harper & Brothers.

Nepstad, Sharon Erickson. 2004. *Convictions of the soul: Religion, culture, and agency in the Central America solidarity movement*. New York: Oxford University Press.

Nepstad, Sharon Erickson. 2007. Oppositional consciousness among the privileged: Remaking religion in the Central American solidarity movement. *Critical Sociology 33:* 661–688.

Neuman, W. Russell, Marcus, George E., MacKuen, Michael, & Crigler, Ann N. 2007. *The affect effect: Dynamics of emotion in political thinking and behavior*. Chicago: University of Chicago Press.

New America Media. 2005. Lessons of Katrina: America's major racial and ethnic groups find common ground after the storm. Retrieved from http://www.newamericamedia.org.

Noddings, Nell. 1984. *Caring: A feminine approach to ethics and moral education*. Berkeley: University of California Press.

Nussbaum, Martha C. 2001. *Upheavals of thought: The intelligence of emotions*. New York: Cambridge University Press.

Obama, Barack. 2004. Keynote address at the Democratic National Convention. Retrieved from http://www.barackobama.com/2004/07/27/keynote_address_at_the_2004_de.php.

Obama, Barack. 2008. A more perfect union. Retrieved from http://www.barackobama.com/2008/03/18/remarks_of_senator_barack_obam_53.php.

O'Brien, Eileen. 1999. Mind, heart, and action: Understanding the dimensions of antiracism. *Research in Politics & Society 6:* 305–321.

O'Brien, Eileen. 2001. *Whites confront racism: Antiracists and their paths to action*. Lanham, MD: Rowman & Littlefield.

O'Brien, Eileen, & Korgen, Kathleen Odell. 2007. It's the message, not the messenger: The declining significance of black-white contact in a "colorblind" society. *Sociological Inquiry 77(3):* 356–382.

Oliver, Melvin L., & Shapiro, Thomas M. 1995. *Black wealth/white wealth: A new perspective on racial inequality*. New York: Routledge.

Olsen, Laurie. 1997. *Made in America: Immigrant students in our public schools.* New York: New Press.

Omi, Michael, & Winant, Howard. 1994. *Racial formation in the United States: From the 1960s to the 1980s* (2nd ed.). New York: Routledge.

Orfield, Gary, & Eaton, Susan E. 1997. *Dismantling desegregation: The quiet reversal of Brown v. Board of Education.* Boston: New Press.

Orfield, Gary, Losen, Daniel, Wald, Johanna, & Swanson, Christopher B. 2004. *Losing our future: How minority youth are being left behind by the graduation rate crisis.* Cambridge, MA: Civil Rights Project at Harvard University.

Palacios, Joseph M. 2007. *The Catholic social imagination: Activism and the just society in Mexico and the United States.* Chicago: University of Chicago Press.

Park, Robert E. 1928. Human migration and the marginal man. *American Journal of Sociology* 33(6): 881–893.

Payne, Charles M. 1995. *I've got the light of freedom: The organizing tradition and the Mississippi freedom struggle.* Berkeley: University of California Press.

Perry, Pamela. 2002. *Shades of white: White kids and racial identities in high school.* Durham, NC: Duke University Press.

Perry, Theresa. 2003. Freedom for literacy and literacy for freedom: The African-American philosophy of education. In Theresa Perry, Claude Steele, & Asa Hilliard III, Eds., *Young, gifted, and black: Promoting high achievement among African-American students,* pp. 11–51. Boston: Beacon.

Peterson, Merrill D. 2002. *John Brown: The legend revisited.* Charlottesville: University of Virginia Press.

Pettigrew, Thomas F. 1998. Intergroup contact theory. *Annual Review of Psychology* 49: 65–85.

Picca, Leslie Houts, & Feagin, Joe R. 2007. *Two-faced racism: Whites in the backstage and frontstage.* New York: Routledge.

Pinkney, Alphonso. 1968. *The committed: White activists in the civil rights movement.* New Haven, CT: College and University Press.

Pittz, Will, & Sen, Rinku. 2004. *Short changed: Foundation giving and communities of color.* Oakland, CA: Applied Research Center.

Poe-Yamagata, Eileen, & Jones, Michael. 2000. *And justice for some: Differential treatment of minority youth in the criminal justice system.* Oakland, CA: National Council on Crime and Delinquency.

Polletta, Francesca. 1999. "Free spaces" in collective action. *Theory and Society* 28: 1–38.

Polletta, Francesca. 2002. *Freedom is an endless meeting: Democracy in American social movements.* Chicago: University of Chicago Press.

Polletta, Francesca. 2006. *It was like a fever: Storytelling in protest and politics.* Chicago: University of Chicago Press.

Polletta, Francesca, & Jasper, James M. 2001. Collective identity and social movements. *Annual Review of Sociology* 27: 283–305.

Pollock, Mica. 2008. *Everyday antiracism: Getting real about race in school.* New York: New Press.

powell, john a. 2007. Structural racism and spatial Jim Crow. In Robert D. Bullard, Ed., *The black metropolis in the twenty-first century: Race, power, and the politics of place,* pp. 41–65. Lanham, MD: Rowman & Littlefield.

Putnam, Robert D. 2000. *Bowling alone: The collapse and revival of American community*. New York: Simon & Schuster.

Putnam, Robert D. 2007. *E pluribus unum:* Diversity and community in the twenty-first century. *Scandinavian Political Studies* 30(2): 137–174.

Quillian, Lincoln. 2006. New approaches to understanding prejudice and discrimination. *Annual Review of Sociology* 32: 299–328.

Rabinow, Paul, & Sullivan, William, Eds. 1987. *Interpretive social science: A second look*. Berkeley: University of California Press.

Ragin, Charles C., Nagel, Joane, & White, Patricia. 2004. *Report of the Workshop on Scientific Foundations of Qualitative Research*. Washington, DC: National Science Foundation.

Riemer, Neal. 1987. *Karl Marx and prophetic politics*. New York: Praeger.

Riessman, Catherine Kohler. 2008. *Narrative methods for the human sciences*. Thousand Oaks, CA: Sage.

Roediger, David R. 2005. *Working toward whiteness: How America's immigrants became white*. New York: Basic Books.

Rogers, Mary Beth. 1990. *Cold anger: A story of faith and power politics*. Denton: University of North Texas Press.

Rothenberg, Paula S. 2001. *Race, class, and gender in the United States: An integrated study* (5th ed.). New York: Freeman.

Rothenberg, Paula S., Ed. 2002. *White privilege: Essential readings on the other side of racism*. New York: Worth.

Rothstein, Richard. 2004. *Class and schools: Using social, economic, and educational reform to close the black-white achievement gap*. Washington, DC: Economic Policy Institute.

Rubin, Herbert J., & Rubin, Irene S. 2005. *Qualitative interviewing: The art of hearing data* (2nd ed.). Thousand Oaks, CA: Sage.

Saito, Leland T. 2009. *The politics of exclusion: The failure of race-neutral policies in urban America*. Stanford: Stanford University Press.

Sandel, Michael J. 1998. *Liberalism and the limits of justice* (2nd ed.). New York: Cambridge University Press.

Satter, Beryl. 2009. *Family properties: Race, real estate, and the exploitation of black urban America*. New York: Metropolitan.

Sayer, Andrew. 2000. *Realism and social science*. Thousand Oaks, CA: Sage.

Schuman, Howard, Steeh, Charlotte, & Bobo, Lawrence. 1997. *Racial attitudes in America: Trends and interpretations* (Rev. ed.). Cambridge, MA: Harvard University Press.

Sears, David O., Hetts, John J., Sidanius, Jim, & Bobo, Lawrence. 2000. Race in American politics: Framing the debates. In David O. Sears, Jim Sidanius, & Lawrence Bobo, Eds., *Racialized politics: The debate about racism in America*, pp. 1–43. Chicago: University of Chicago Press.

Seider, Scott. 2007. Frame-changing experiences and the freshman year: Catalyzing a commitment to service-work and social action. *Journal of College and Character* 8: 1–18.

Seidman, Irving. 2006. *Interviewing as qualitative research: A guide for researchers in education and the social sciences*. New York: Teachers College Press.

Sewell, William H. 1992. A theory of structure: Duality, agency, and transformation. *American Journal of Sociology* 98(1): 1–29.

Sharkey, Patrick. 2008. The intergenerational transmission of context. *American Journal of Sociology* 113(4): 931–969.

Sherif, Muzafer. 1988. *The Robbers Cave experiment: Intergroup conflict and cooperation.* Middletown, CT: Wesleyan University Press.

Shklar, Judith N. 1990. *The faces of injustice.* New Haven, CT: Yale University Press.

Sidanius, Jim, & Pratto, Felicia. 1999. *Social dominance: An intergroup theory of social hierarchy and oppression.* New York: Cambridge University Press.

Sigelman, Lee, Bledsoe, Timothy, Welch, Susan, & Combs, Michael W. 1996. Making contact? Black-white social interaction in an urban setting. *American Journal of Sociology* 101(5): 1306–1332.

Skocpol, Theda. 1991. Targeting within universalism: Politically viable policies to combat poverty in the United States. In Christopher Jencks & Paul E. Peterson, Eds., *The urban underclass,* pp. 411–436. Washington, DC: Brookings Institution.

Sleeter, Christine E. 1996. *Multicultural education as social activism.* Albany: State University of New York Press.

Smelser, Neil J., Wilson, William Julius, & Mitchell, Faith, Eds. 2001. *America becoming: Racial trends and their consequences.* Washington, DC: National Academy Press.

Smith, Christian, Ed. 1996. *Disruptive religion: The force of faith in social movement activism.* New York: Routledge.

Snow, David A., Rochford Jr., E. Burke, Worden, Steven K., & Benford, Robert D. 1986. Frame alignment processes, micromobilization, and movement participation. *American Sociological Review* 51: 464–481.

Somers, Margaret R. 1992. Narrativity, narrative identity, and social action: Rethinking English working-class formation. *Social Science History* 16: 591–629.

Somers, Margaret R. 1994. The narrative constitution of identity: A relational and network approach. *Theory and Society* 23(5): 605–649.

Squires, Gregory D. 2006. Reintroducing the black/white divide in racial discourse [Electronic Version]. *New Politics, X.* Retrieved October 31, 2008, from http://www.newpol.org.

Squires, Gregory D., & Kubrin, Charis E. 2006. *Privileged places: Race, residence, and the structure of opportunity.* Boulder, CO: Rienner.

Strolovitch, Dara Z. 2007. *Affirmative advocacy: Race, class, and gender in interest-group politics.* Chicago: University of Chicago Press.

Sum, Andrew, Khatiwada, Ishwar, & McLaughlin, Joseph. 2009. *The consequences of dropping out of high school.* Boston: Northeastern University Center for Labor Market Studies.

Tatum, Beverly Daniel. 1994. Teaching white students about racism: The search for white allies and the restoration of hope. *Teachers College Record* 95(4): 463–476.

Taylor, Charles. 1989. *Sources of the self: The making of the modern identity.* Cambridge, MA: Harvard University Press.

Taylor, Verta, & Whittier, Nancy. 1992. Collective identity in social movement communities: Lesbian feminist mobilization. In Aldon D. Morris & Carol McClurg Mueller, Eds., *Frontiers in social movement theory,* pp. 104–130. New Haven, CT: Yale University Press.

Telles, Edward Eric, & Ortiz, Vilma. 2008. *Generations of exclusion: Mexican Americans, assimilation, and race*. New York: Russell Sage Foundation Press.

Teske, Nathan. 1997. *Political activists in America: The identity construction model of political participation*. New York: Cambridge University Press.

Thernstrom, Stephen, & Thernstrom, Abigail. 1997. *America in black and white: One nation, indivisible*. New York: Simon & Schuster.

Thompson, Becky. 2001. *A promise and a way of life: White antiracist activism*. Minneapolis: University of Minnesota Press.

Thompson, Becky, & Tyagi, Sangeeta, Eds. 1996. *Names we call home: Autobiography on racial identity*. New York: Routledge.

Thompson, Cooper, Schaefer, Emmett, & Brod, Harry, Eds. 2003. *White men challenging racism: 35 personal stories*. Durham, NC: Duke University Press.

Thompson, J. Phillip. 1998. Universalism and deconcentration: Why race still matters in poverty and economic development. *Politics and Society* 26(2): 181–219.

Thompson, J. Phillip. 2005. *Double trouble: Black mayors, black communities, and the call for a deep democracy*. New York: Oxford University Press.

Trepagnier, Barbara. 2006. *Silent racism: How well-meaning white people perpetuate the racial divide*. Boulder, CO: Paradigm.

Ture, Kwame, & Hamilton, Charles V. 1992 [1967]. *Black power: The politics of liberation*. New York: Vintage.

Turner, Margery Austin, & Ross, Stephen L. 2005. How racial discrimination affects the search for housing. In Xavier de Souza Briggs, Ed., *The geography of opportunity: Race and housing choice in metropolitan America*, pp. 81–100. Washington, DC: Brookings Institution.

Vaco, Nick Corona. 2004. *The presumed alliance: The unspoken conflict between Latinos and blacks and what it means for America*. New York: Rayo.

Walker, Vanessa Siddle, & Snarey, John R. 2004. Race matters in moral formation. In Vanessa Siddle Walker & John R. Snarey, Eds., *Race-ing moral formation: African American perspectives on care and justice*, pp. 1–14. New York: Teachers College Press.

Waller, Signe. 2002. *Love and revolution: A political memoir: People's history of the Greensboro massacre, its setting and aftermath*. Lanham, MD: Rowman & Littlefield.

Walsh, Katherine Cramer. 2007. *Talking about race: Community dialogues and the politics of difference*. Chicago: University of Chicago Press.

Warren, Mark R. 2001. *Dry bones rattling: Community building to revitalize American democracy*. Princeton, NJ: Princeton University Press.

Warren, Mark R., Thompson, J. Phillip, & Saegert, Susan. 2001. The role of social capital in combating poverty. In Susan Saegert, J. Phillip Thompson, & Mark R. Warren, Eds., *Social capital and poor communities*, pp. 1–28. New York: Russell Sage Foundation Press.

Washington Post/Kaiser Family Foundation/Harvard University Survey Project. 2001. *Race and ethnicity in 2001: Attitudes, perceptions, and experiences*. Menlo Park, CA: Henry J. Kaiser Family Foundation.

Weber, Max. 1980. Science as a vocation. In Hans Heinrich Gerth & C. Wright Mills, Eds., *From Max Weber: Essays in sociology*, pp. 129–156. New York: Oxford University Press.

Weiss, Robert S. 1994. *Learning from strangers: The art and method of qualitative interview studies.* New York: Free Press.

Westen, Drew. 2007. *The political brain: The role of emotion in deciding the fate of the nation.* New York: Public Affairs.

Whittier, Nancy. 1995. *Feminist generations: The persistence of the radical women's movement.* Philadelphia: Temple University Press.

Wijeyesinghe, Charmaine L., & Jackson III, Bailey W. 2001. *New perspectives on racial identity development: A theoretical and practical anthology.* New York: New York University Press.

Wiley, Maya D. 2003. *Structural racism and multiracial coalition building.* Minneapolis: Institute on Race and Poverty.

Williams, Rhys H. 1999. Visions of the good society and the religious roots of American political culture. *Sociology of Religion* 60(1): 1–34.

Wilson, William Julius. 1978. *The declining significance of race: Blacks and changing American institutions.* Chicago: University of Chicago Press.

Wilson, William Julius. 1996. *When work disappears: The world of the new urban poor.* New York: Knopf.

Wilson, William Julius. 1999. *The bridge over the racial divide.* Berkeley: University of California Press.

Wilson, William Julius. 2009. *More than just race: Being black and poor in the inner city.* New York: Norton.

Wise, Tim. 2005. *White like me: Reflections on race from a privileged son.* Brooklyn: Soft Skull Press.

Wood, Richard L. 2002. *Faith in action: Religion, race, and democratic organizing in America.* Chicago: University of Chicago Press.

Wuthnow, Robert. 1991. *Acts of compassion: Caring for others and helping ourselves.* Princeton, NJ: Princeton University Press.

Yancey, George A. 2007. *Interracial contact and social change.* Boulder, CO: Rienner.

Yancey, George A. 2003. *Who is white? Latinos, Asians, and the new black/nonblack divide.* Boulder, CO: Rienner.

Yinger, John. 2001. Measuring racial discrimination with fair housing audits: Caught in the act. *American Economic Review* 76(5): 881–893.

Young, Iris Marion. 1990. *Justice and the politics of difference.* Princeton, NJ: Princeton University Press.

Zweigenhaft, Richard L., & Domhoff, G. William. 2003. *Blacks in the white elite: Will the progress continue?* Lanham, MD: Rowman & Littlefield.

INDEX

Page numbers in bold indicate figures or tables.

oppression, 19–20, 65–66, 84, 102, 154, 159, 180, 252n6
outrage, 39
overlapping approximations, 220

Paris, Peter, 153, 195
passion, 82, 217
passivity, racial, 1, 3–8, 37, 115–16, 139, 147, 212, 252n2
paternalism, xii, 17, 114, 130, 176, 187
patriarchy, 102
Payne, Charles, 84
People's History, 190
People's Institute for Survival and Beyond, xii, 182, 192, 219–20
Perkins, John, 85
Perkins, Perry, 82–84, 85, 87, 109, 112, 123–25, 148, 152–54, 175, 179, 194–96, 224, 266n25
personal development, 109–10
personal is political, 80
personalized politics, 259n7
Peterson, Bob, 72, 121, 170–73
Pitts, Lewis, 73, 115
Pogo, 93, 108, 224, 266n24
police, 4, 8, 24, 51, 60, 78, 101, 129, 145–47
political activism, 34, 46, 236–37
political identity, 184, 208, 230, 231
The Porch, 154–57
positionality, 242
postracial, x
poverty, 1–3, 47, 49, 52, 61, 115, 142–44, 177, 212
predatory lending, 25
prefigurative politics, 107–9
prejudice, 227
Presbyterian Church, 47, 92, 189, 191
prior activism, 221–22, 257n14
prison reform, 31–32, 61–62, 96, 137–39
progressives, 106, 141, 170, 187, 267n34
A Promise and a Way of Life, 218
promotion discrimination, 57
Proposition 209, 52
pseudonyms, 255n33
Public Advocates, 86, 105–6
purposeful life, 82–87, 110, 219
purposeful selection, 10
Putnam, Robert, 226–27
Putting the Movement Back into Civil Rights Teaching, 143

racial hierarchy, 6, 15–16, 115, 174, 225
racial indoctrination, 224
racial justice activist, 14, 79, 82
racial justice movement
    and coalitions, 16
    collaborative relationships, xii, 80
    confrontation, 118
    contemporary studies of, 218–22
    contradictions between values and reality, 52
    democracy, 85, 106, 148, 231
    and economic reform, 94–95
    inclusion, 118–20
    institutional racism and, 7
    interest convergence, 17
    moral leadership, 222–26
    and moral vision, 260n20
    multiracial collaborations, 150
    Obama election, 232–33
    organic approach, 200
    purposeful life, 82–87, 219
    radicals, 101–4
    and relationships, 79, 148
    seminal experiences and, 27
    shared identity, 80
    solidarity politics, 99–101
    University of Colorado conferences, 8
    values as key to activism, 106–7, 204, 225–26
racialized thinking, 117–18, 261n7
racism
    approximating experiences, 20
    aversive racism, 253n14
    college campuses, 43
    color-blind ideology, 5, 8, 114, 220
    contact thesis, 227
    and criminal justice, 141–42
    cultural deficits of blacks, 5–6
    as disruptor of progressivism, 103
    economic inequality, 2
    founding sin, 105
    and humanity, 111
    and inclusion, 118–19
    and inequality, 16
    institutional racism, 4, 6, 7, 12, 34–39, 161, 212, 252n10
    laissez-faire racism, 114
    Marquette Park, 26–27
    political race, 231
    private vs. public, 253n13

racism (*continued*)

and progressive policies, 141

structural racism, 41

Radcliffe College, 38

radicals, 101–4, 205–6

Reagan, Ronald, 20

reciprocity in relationships. *See* relationships

reconciliation, 91, 201–2. *See also* Truth and Reconciliation Commission

redlining, 25

rejection, by people of color, 196–97, 200

relationships. *See also* collaborative relationships; stories

and activism, 67–69, 110, 213, 236

and advocacy, 144–47

African American clients, 57

as antidote to stereotypes, 136

antiracist activism, 193–94, 220, 222

approximating experiences, 20

bonding, 72–75, 82, 258n9

borrowed approximations, 219

Central American solidarity movement, 99

college activism, 45

and commitment, 79, 221, 227–28, 231

and community organizing, 120, 122–30

Dallas Leadership Foundation (DLF), 198

defensiveness, 120–21

and dialog, 144

economic development and, 99

and empathy, 259n16, 263n18

enwrapment, 74–76

as key to understanding racism, 60–63, 224

limitations to, 77–79

Marquette Park, 27

and moral vision, 110, 112

multiracial collaborations, 150, 152, 177, 182, 262n6

multiracial communities, 100–101

as path to racial justice activism, 19–20

People's Institute for Survival and Beyond, 182

A Promise and a Way of Life, 218

and racial awareness, 40

and racial justice, 79, 148

racial justice movement, 79, 148

reciprocity in, 69–75, 79, 130, 155, 179, 224

right relationships, 179

romantic relationships, 74, 203, 218, 264n7

segregation in, 153

shared identity, 79

and stereotypes, 147

trusting relationships, 150–59, 262n6, 263n9, 263n18

welfare reform, 68

white activists and their families, 186

window on racism, 41

religion. See also *individual denominations*

and activism, 244

African American church, 80, 194–95

anti-Muslim discrimination, 11

Christian Community Development model, 85

Dallas Leadership Foundation (DLF), 85, 175–76, 178–79, 197–98

faith-based groups, 244

fundamentalism, 203–4

impact on activism, 26, 79, 225

Industrial Areas Foundation (IAF), 123–24

marginalization, 190

MICAH (Milwaukee Inner-city Congregations Allied for Hope), 95–97

moral vision, 214

multiracial collaborations, 152–53

multiracial communities, 149

as route to activism, 49–50

and segregation, 83–84

The Social Teaching of the Black Churches, 153, 195

values and activism, 53, 124

Voice of Hope Ministries, 85, 175–76

Witness for Peace, 47

Word and World, 50

worship styles, 191

reparations, 142, 206

research methodology

analysis, 15, 241–42

biases, 243

coding procedure, 14, 243

cross-case thematic analysis, 241–42

interest/altruist trap, 15–18

internal generalizability, 242

interviewees profiles, 11–12

interviews, 9–10

positionality, 242

pseudonyms, 255n33